The Cambridge Introduction to
Literary Posthumanism

At a time when scholars in both literary and scientific disciplines are advancing the term "posthumanism," this book offers a through-line. Beginning with Mary Shelley's *Frankenstein* and continuing into the postprint, born-digital excursions of Shelley Jackson's *Patchwork Girl*, this literary introduction defines posthumanism and provides a summary account of the key literary and cultural theorists in the field. It embraces humanist refusals from Melville's *Bartelby* to Thomas Pynchon's authorial surrogation, and more recent evasions and avoidances in the writing of William Gibson, Tom McCarthy, Colson Whitehead, Jeanette Winterson, and Claire-Louise Bennett. This book also provides close readings of key posthuman fiction, poetry, and conceptual approaches that help ground the discipline.

Joseph Tabbi is an American academic and literary theorist who relocated to the University of Bergen in 2019. He has made significant contributions to the field of experimental American fiction in both print and electronic media. He is the author of *Cognitive Fictions* (2002) and *Postmodern Sublime* (1995). He was the first scholar granted access to the William Gaddis archives and is the author of *Nobody Grew but the Business: On the Life and Work of William Gaddis* (2015).

The Cambridge Introduction to
Literary Posthumanism

JOSEPH TABBI

University of Bergen

CAMBRIDGE
UNIVERSITY PRESS

CAMBRIDGE
UNIVERSITY PRESS

Shaftesbury Road, Cambridge CB2 8EA, United Kingdom

One Liberty Plaza, 20th Floor, New York, NY 10006, USA

477 Williamstown Road, Port Melbourne, VIC 3207, Australia

314–321, 3rd Floor, Plot 3, Splendor Forum, Jasola District Centre,
New Delhi – 110025, India

103 Penang Road, #05–06/07, Visioncrest Commercial, Singapore 238467

Cambridge University Press is part of Cambridge University Press & Assessment,
a department of the University of Cambridge.

We share the University's mission to contribute to society through the pursuit of education,
learning and research at the highest international levels of excellence.

www.cambridge.org
Information on this title: www.cambridge.org/9781009256506

DOI: 10.1017/9781009256476

First published 2024

A catalogue record for this publication is available from the British Library

A Cataloging-in-Publication data record for this book is available from the Library of Congress

ISBN 978-1-009-25650-6 Hardback
ISBN 978-1-009-25645-2 Paperback

Contents

Illustrations

Acknowledgments

I should begin with a belated thanks to Stephen Weininger and Lance Schachterle at Worcester Polytechnic Institute, who founded the Society for Literature and Science (SLS) in 1985. I was then in my third year as an undergraduate at Cornell University, with a double major in engineering physics and literature. Like anything new, there was a speculative buzz in the air at the inaugural SLS meetings, which nicely complemented the courses I was taking at Cornell with Molly Hite, Jonathan Culler, and M. H. Abrams. By 2005, when I was cohosting meetings of "the SLSA" in Chicago, my colleagues and I had brought "the Arts" into the society, along with collaborators such as Bruce Clarke, N. Katherine Hayles, and Cary Wolfe, whose work in literary posthumanism has been foundational.

Aimed at early career scholars with an expanding set of cross-disciplinary and multimedial interests, the present volume addresses more recent shifts in undergraduate course structures and early career studies. While bringing literary works from multiple media into the current domain of "posthumanism," I've been mindful of the scholarly and creative assemblages that have emerged over the course of my career, and the communications they have sustained across literature, science, and the arts. The Electronic Literature Organization (ELO) is another actively cross-disciplinary institution, cofounded in 1999 by Robert Coover at Brown University, start-up entrepreneur Jeff Ballowe, and Scott Rettberg, who at the time was completing his dissertation at the University of Cincinnati under the supervision of literary systems scholar Tom LeClair. The unique combination of creative, critical, and organizational skill that Scott and Jill Walker Rettberg have brought to the e-Lit field enabled us to initiate a Center for Digital Narrative at the University of Bergen, Norway, where I relocated in 2019.

The prospect of a research and creative center reinforced my own collaboration with our principal investigators in Bergen and abroad: Nick Montfort at MIT; Lai-Tze Fan at the University of Waterloo, Canada; and Jason Nelson and Kristine Jörgensen in Bergen. In the lead-up to our digital center, my Bergen colleagues and I had already participated in a series of conferences with our literary and cultural colleagues at the University of Stuttgart: Gabriel Vichhauser and Sibylle Baumbach, with whom I am putting together a Living Glossary of Digital Narratives. Some of the prospective encyclopedic entries are sampled at the end of this volume.

Other topics in the present volume similarly emerged from active, intertextual, and interdisciplinary assemblages. Among these were a vast range of contemporary scholars contributing to *Pynchon Notes*, founded in 1979 by John Krafft and Khachig Tololyan in the USA, and advanced by Hanjo Berressem of the University of Cologne at several German conferences – one of which was keynoted by media theorist Friedrich Kittler (whom I introduced). The Kittler meeting was held in June 2002 at the University of Cologne conference "Site-Specific: Pynchon|Germany," while John Krafft was a Fulbright Senior Scholar in the University's English Department. This conference was later published as a special issue of *Pynchon Notes*. Another meeting in Mannheim was an international workshop on "Posthuman Perspectives," where Stefan Herbrechter presented a paper titled "Critical Posthumanism."

There is a long literary history, experienced differently in different scholarly communities, and many speculative narratives that are both shared and specific to the locations, groupings, and terminology that produce our present knowledge of the literary and posthuman fields. My thanks extend to the research assemblages and literary communities that are continuing to form and restructure our sense of what a literary career can be in these troubled but also transformative times.

This work was partially supported by the Research Council of Norway through its Centres of Excellence scheme, project number 33243, the Center for Digital Narrative.

Introduction
Not Just Another Period

The posthuman is a field of multiple and often conflicting definitions, timeframes, subject positions, bodily alterations, and rearrangements of knowledge. For some, the posthuman is an *extension* of human powers and lifetimes; a realization of new possibilities for human nature (Huxley, 1957), perhaps even its "perfectibility" (Bostrom, 2005a, 2). For others, more historically minded, it is a dramatic departure from humanist and Enlightenment traditions that have settled in over the past 500 years: after all, if a humanist disposition emerged along with the Gutenberg Press, we should not be surprised if humanism approaches its end during our present postdigital era. Indeed, some of the "fundamental premises of the Enlightenment" are being questioned, in particular "the progress of mankind through a self-regulatory and teleological ordained use of reason and of secular scientific rationality allegedly aimed at the perfectibility of 'Man'" (Braidotti, *The Posthuman*, 37; see also "A Theoretical Framework for the Critical Posthumanities," 18). The term "posthuman" takes on further resonances when we approach it from any one of the disciplines in the *humanities*: philosophy, the social sciences, and anthropology no less than the recently established departments of sociology, computer sciences, STEM, and other instrumentalist research emphases.

Any examination of the posthuman turn in recent scholarship and literary culture should bear in mind these competing strains, which have each swayed different authors and audiences, at least for a time. In his "Defense of Poetry," Romantic poet Percy Bysshe Shelley famously (and concisely) regarded the conflict as an inevitable clash between "two classes of mental action, which are called reason and imagination." The former, rational positioning (in Shelley's view) "may be considered as mind contemplating the relations borne by one thought to another, however produced, and the latter, as mind acting upon those thoughts so as to color them with its own light, and composing from them, as from

1

elements, other thoughts, each containing within itself the principle of its own integrity." Shelley continues:

> The one is the το ποιειν [*to poiein*, the poetry] or the principle of synthesis, and has for its objects those forms which are common to universal nature and existence itself; the other is the το λογιςειν [*to logisein*, the reason], or principle of analysis, and its action regards the relations of things simply as relations; considering thoughts, not in their integral unity, but as the algebraical representations which conduct to certain general results. Reason is the enumeration of qualities already known; imagination is the perception of the value of those qualities, both separately and as a whole. Reason respects the differences, and imagination the similitudes of things. Reason is to imagination as the instrument to the agent, as the body to the spirit, as the shadow to the substance. ("A Defense of Poetry," written 1821, published 1840; www.poetryfoundation.org/articles/69388/a-defence-of-poetry)

Posthumanist studies might also see these differing projects and discourses as multiple attempts to grapple with a complex and emerging set of realities that challenge the existing boundaries and procedures of academic knowledge. There are cogent arguments that posthumanism, in its attachment to material life-worlds and ecological transformations outside the academy, will be not so quickly superseded as our short-lived postmodernisms, our various linguistic, decon-structive, and postdigital turns. In that light, it is possible to view the posthuman as signaling not so much a break with our human nature (if that could ever have been settled) as a carrying forward and questioning of human*ism* into the current era. What we are looking at, then, is both a break and a continuity.

As Brian McHale has written of postmodernism, which comes after the modern but is nonetheless "continuous" with it, "no period is airtight or freestanding, and continuities can always be identified with periods that pre-cede and follow, and even with periods quite distant in time" (McHale 2015, 6). Nonetheless, in this *Introduction to Literary Posthumanism*, I wish to suggest that the posthuman is not just another period, let alone a kind of short-lived academic fashion. Instead, it offers a fundamental challenge to our existing understanding of periodicity – and, indeed, our understanding of our histor-icity, what we carry from our past (as recalled personally in memory and conveyed collectively in published works) into our present understanding and wish to communicate with future generations. Along these lines, Cary Wolfe notes how the posthuman "comes both before and after humanism":

> before in the sense that it names the embodiment and embeddedness of the human being in not just its biological but also its technological

world, the prosthetic coevolution of the human animal with the technicity of tools and external archival mechanisms (such as language and culture) ... But it comes after in the sense that posthumanism names a historical moment in which the decentering of the human by its imbrication in technical, medical, informatic, and economic networks is increasingly impossible to ignore, a historical development that points toward the necessity of new theoretical paradigms (but also thrusts them on us), a new mode of thought that comes after the cultural repressions and fantasies, the philosophical protocols and evasions, of humanism as a historically specific phenomenon. (*What is Posthumanism?* xv–xvi)

By the same token, we cannot understand posthuman works in literature and literary studies as simply the latest in the list of "miscellaneous" genres that Jonathan Culler observes in the field of literary theory, which extends to "works of anthropology, art history, film studies, gender studies, linguistics, philosophy, political theory, psychoanalysis, science studies, social and intellectual history, and sociology." For literary theory, and for Culler, the point of such inclusivity is not to extend our multidisciplinary activity as literary students and academic scholars so much as to "designate works that succeed in challenging and reorienting fields other than those to which they apparently belong" (Culler 4, cited by Herbrechter and Callus, "What's Wrong with Posthumanism?" 1). Cross-pollination takes precedence among fields of study and a reorienting away from binary Humanist defaults (literature/science, imaginative/rationalist). We might also regard such disciplinary reorientations as an opportunity to remove literary practice from the institutional confinements that put up walls between scientific knowledge and more general concerns of ethics and aesthetics. As N. Katherine Hayles remarks, in her own affirmation of "posthumanism's collective heterogeneous quality," any one person's "agency, desire, or will" cannot be clearly distinguished from the will of human, technological, or natural "others." By taking seriously the construction of our own subjectivity out of "a distributed cognition located in disparate parts that may be in only tenuous communication with one another," Hayles approaches the posthuman as neither a historical period nor yet another academic discipline, but rather a field of interactions, involving "continuities and discontinuities between a 'natural' self and a cybernetic posthuman" (*How We Became Posthuman*, 4).

What literary theory and posthumanism share, in their heterogeneity is a desire not to build a field or reinforce a discipline but rather to take apart, reconfigure or (in Jacques Derrida's term) deconstruct familiar works and concepts using "visions and arguments that have been suggestive or productive for people who are not studying these disciplines" (Culler, *Literary Theory*, 4).

Theory's goal, from Culler's perspective, is not so much to extend knowledge (and the range of human powers that knowledge facilitates), but rather to instead know the world differently, as something else: something *other* than what we thought was familiar and manageable. In this sense, both established literary theory and posthumanism are marked more by a *defamiliarizing* tendency than any extension or enhancement of human agency and cognition. Rather than extending "power relations and discourses that have historically situated the human *above* other life forms, and in control of them" (Nayar, *Posthumanism*, 3–4, italics in the original), a literary posthumanism studies and deflects such power relations. It seeks not so much to build a new discipline as to initiate a field of scholarly interactions (to again reference Hayles and Culler). By opening out to more objective, other-than-human beings, a posthumanist worldview does what literary arts and studies have always done: it seeks to make those parts of our lives and our worldly situation that we thought we knew – to make these taken-for-granted sensibilities strange, agential, and unfamiliar. Indeed, what Derrida has termed "*l'avenir*," a "future to come" that we cannot know in advance (or plan for), is in keeping with posthumanist tendencies to keep open the outcomes of our freewheeling, cross-disciplinary conversations and prospective agencies. (See the text box on Latour: "Posthuman Prospects and New Materialisms.")

Posthuman Prospects and New Materialisms

Bruno Latour, in his 2010 "Attempt at a 'Compositionist Manifesto,'" comes up with his own vision of a posthumanist future, which he (like Jacques Derrida and *l'avenir*) sees more as a future to come (not one scattered in the debris of modernization or the endless accumulation of inert facts). Latour writes:

> I don't wish to embrace [Walter] Benjamin's tired "Angel of History" trope, but there is something right in the position he attributed to the angel: it looks backward and not ahead. Where *we* see the appearance of a chain of events, *he* sees one single catastrophe, which unceasingly piles rubble on top of rubble and hurls it before his feet . . . . The French language, for once richer than English, differentiates "*le future*" from "*l'avenir.*" In French, I could say that the Moderns had "*un future*" but never "*un avenir.*" To define the present situation, I have to translate and say that the Moderns always had a future (the odd utopian future of someone fleeing His past in reverse!) but never a chance, until recently that is, to turn to what I could call their *prospect*: the shape of things to come. As it is now clear from the ecological crisis, one's future and one's prospect (if one takes on board these two words) bear almost no resemblance to one another. What makes the times we are living in so interesting (and why I still think it is useful to make this manifest through a manifesto) is that we are progressively discovering that, just at the time when people are despairing at realizing

that they might, in the end, have "no future," we suddenly have many *prospects*. Yet they are so utterly different from what we imagined *while fleeing ahead looking backwards* that we might cast them only as so many fragile illusions. Or find them ever more terrifying than what we were trying to escape from. (Latour, 2010, p. 486)

One further aspect of Latour's "Compositionist" approach that is worth mentioning here at the start is its participation in a *new materialism* that is more grounded in the natural and social sciences, and not so much in linguistic formulations. Or, rather, the act of literary composition may be regarded with a degree of objectivity similar to that of the sciences. We will see this orientation in the work of Karen Barad, N. Katherine Hayles, Jane Bennett, and others who do not outright reject the linguistic orientation of Derrida and other poststructuralist theorists so much as they bring the language of science into conversation with literary writing and the visual arts. We can engage, via Figure 0.1, a conversation begun by Walter Benjamin and continued a century later by Latour: in this respect, the compositionist approach resonates with *literary* practices whose meanings are kept open, revisited, and reconsidered through the generations.

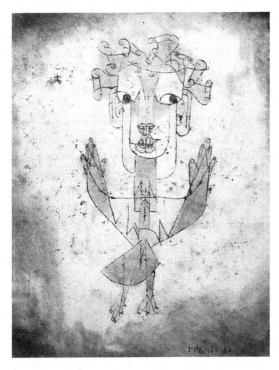

Figure 0.1 Paul Klee, *Angel Novus 1920*

The emphasis on defamiliarization and deconstruction that I have just described, and a more *aesthetic* composition that is at once intertextual and transmedial, brings Latour's analysis into conversation with literature and the arts, no less than science. And this transdisciplinary move, by a "philosopher, anthropologist, and social scientist" (to cite Latour's public credentials in Wikipedia), is very much in line with Jonathan Culler's characterization of literary theory as a challenge to established categorizations and a reorienting of fields other than those to which a scholar belongs. Note, for example (in the text box, again), the way that Latour apologizes for reviving a "tired" trope of Klee's *Angel of History* and Walter Benjamin's take on it. Latour recused himself similarly, in a chapter he contributed to a collection of essays on a younger contemporary, the novelist Richard Powers, whose work consistently references and aesthetically engages the science of his time, and ours (Latour 2008, 263–91). Latour, knowing that he is unprepared (and without the scholarly credentials) "to read Richard Powers as a literary critic would," treats Powers's fiction "as a tool box, to see how we could use even a hundredth of those skills to pursue our own science studies projects, instead of botching our own theories by our tragic inability to write in any realistic manner" (264). As the lives of literary characters find expression in a novel of ideas, like Powers', we also are presented with an imagined world of lived experience that escapes calculation. This is what litera-ture can bring to scientific discussions, a questioning and consistent attempt to observe science in action and to apply to prospective, lived lives a range of "visions and arguments" (Culler 4), along with ideas and facts drawn from science and technology.

Latour's 2010 "Compositionist Manifesto" is itself presented, again self-consciously, as an "Attempt." A composition, not a collection only (of scientific facts, or canonical fictions). Together, both literature and science engage not so much with already realized, agential knowledge but with *potentials*: present conundrums, prospective futures, and open-ended engagements between text-ual and material agencies. Science, for Latour, is no less imaginative than literature; and our common goal as interdisciplinary scholars is to trace *Intersections* (to cite the title of the collected *Essays on Richard Powers*, edited by Stephen Burn and Peter Dempsey) among contemporary fictions and a long line of cross-disciplinary and *intertextual* relations, both known to the authors of literary works and emerging accidentally. (The intertext, as we shall see, is a primary enactment of posthuman literary formations, compositions, and continuing articulations, in writing across disciplines and timeframes.)

Here is one literary passage, cited by Latour in Powers, that antici-pates the new materialist turn away from settled linguistic theories and toward the materiality of text itself, its cross-pollinations and intertextual engagements. As Latour notes, this is the moment when Powers's character Steve Spiegel, "a young engineering student at this point, first hears the heroine at a poetry reading party." The opening quotation is from William Butler Yeats, "Sailing to Byzantium" (1926):

> "Once out of nature I shall never take my bodily form out of any natural thing."
>
> The words, he supposed were beautiful. The girl, he decided, was almost. But the way she said them: that was the warrant, the arrest, and the lifetime sentencing. Out of her mouth came a stream of discrete, miraculous gadgets – tiny but mobile creatures so intricately small that generations marveled and would go on marveling at how the inventors got the motors into them.
>
> Once out of nature. The train of syllables struck the boy engineer as the most inconsolably bizarre thing that the universe had ever come up with. And this female mammal uttered the words as if they were so many fearsome, ornate Tinkertoys whose existence depended on their having no discernable purpose under heaven. The words would not feed the speaker, nor clothe her, nor shelter her from the elements. They couldn't win her a mate, get her with child, defeat her enemies, or in any measurable way advance the cause of her survival here on earth. And yet they were among the most elaborate artifacts ever made. What was the point? How did evolution justify this colossal expenditure of energy? Once upon a time, rhythmic words might have cast some protecting spell. But that spell had broken long ago. And still the words issued from her mouth, mechanical birds mimicking living things. Sounds with meaning, but meaning to no end . . . (Powers, *Plowing the Dark*, 199–200, cited in Latour, *Intersections*, 268.)

Words that convey "meaning to no end." They neither stop, nor do they reinforce an instrumentalist orientation within the academic milieu that brings the engineer and the heroine together at this moment in time. And nothing in this late 1990s gathering of humanities students and scholars from different disciplines – nothing is quite comparable to the "protecting spell" that we might assume was brought about by "rhythmic words" in prehumanist, epical performances "once upon a time." That said, when these words are heard at a modern gathering, read, and felt in their materiality, they can impart in Powers's characters, and in his readers, the prospective future, or *L'avenir* that Latour, citing Derrida, depicts in his Compositionist Manifesto. Here, in Powers's novel, the thought of the "boy engineer" is already infused with puns and other plays on language's materiality: the "sentencing," for example, that conflates a written format with a prison term; "The train of syllables" that both construct sentences and move the scene and setting forward, trainlike, in literary writing. And much else in the academic training and cross-disciplinary writing of Latour and subsequent theorists, scholars, and imaginative writers who regard literary composition as one way of situating human thought among nonhuman and ahuman *things*.

Among scholars trained in sociological and scientific fields, the tendency to maintain a disciplinary distance runs deep. But an emerging, compositionist tendency, enacted in this early, transdisciplinary excursion by Latour, seeks to *keep open* the possibilities for unexpected, alternative takes on objects that have been designated as "literary," "cultural," "scientific," or "technological." Latour's particular engagements with literature and the arts, framed as they are with hesitations, convey a willingness to explore the written text itself as one of many materialities on offer. After all, Latour, in his engagement with Walter Benjamin and Paul Klee, sets out (as we have seen) precisely with the intention of making "the times we are living in ... manifest through a manifesto" (2010, 486). The pun on composition (and similar manifestations) can be found in the various "new materialists" we will be citing in this book, as they bring forward the materiality of their text as much as any (equally detailed) advancements of knowledge from the sciences and other fields that they are not professionally engaged in.

We can start with a few examples. Here, for instance, is how Karen Barad, who made a career of resisting the "linguistic turn" in poststructural literary theory, nonetheless is capable of bringing a literary self-awareness into her own prose:

> Language has been granted too much power. The linguistic turn, the semiotic turn, the interpretative turn, the cultural turn: it seems that at every turn lately every "thing" – even materiality – is turned into a matter of language or some other form of cultural representation. The ubiquitous puns on "matter" do not, alas, mark a rethinking of key concepts (materiality and signification) and the relationship between them. Rather, it seems to be symptomatic of the extent to which matters of "fact" (so to speak) have been replaced with matters of signification (no scare quotes here). Language matters. Discourse matters. Culture matters. There is an important sense in which the only thing that does not seem to matter anymore is matter. (Barad 2003, 801)

Barad, clearly, sets out to bring into the field of "cultural representation" material objects that have for too long been set aside in mainstream, poststructuralist critical writing. Particularly, Barad found in Bohr's quantum mechanics an alternative to "Cartesian epistemology and its representationalist triadic structure of words, knowers, and things." Bruno Latour similarly seeks to bring together a semiotic triad of his own: a gathering (in the same breath) of "real, human, and semiotic entities" ("Actor–network theory," 1996, Abstract). What both scholars share is a desire to overcome (in Barad's words) "humanity's own captivity within language" (2003, 811–12). Latour, for his part, finds problematic the desire among the emergent actor–network community to "invent a vocabulary to deal with this new situation" ("Actor–network theory," 1996, 1). Yet neither Barad (with her propensity for neologisms such as "intra-active," "agential realism," and "matterrealities") nor Latour outright rejects attempts at collective, verbal invention. Such captivations, long a part of literary and philosophical practices, can now be considered cross-disciplinary, and even conversant with the sciences – those that advance knowledge rather than strengthen our human agency and individuality. (The field of posthumanism has in some ways distinguished itself with massive, community-built, encyclopedias; notably, Rosi Braidotti's and Maria Hlavajova's *Posthuman Glossary* [2018]; and again Braidotti, Emily Jones, and Goda Klumbyte's *More Glossary* [2022]; and Ivan Callus's and Stefan Herbrechter's ongoing *Geneology of the Posthuman* (https://criticalposthumanism.net/). A sampling of current entries focusing on literature is given at the end of this volume.)

At the same time as Barad engages science, her playful designations, like those of many other scholars writing in the wake of structuralism and deconstruction, are particularly aware of the uniquely *literary* context that can be effective in conveying and perpetuating conceptual expressions and creating imaginative engagement with bodies of knowledge no less than our entanglement with material beings and realities. The object-oriented ontology that replaces semiotic approaches, as it turns out, is neither objective nor is it knowable: no more than light is fully known to scientists as a wave or a particle. What new materialist approaches (by scholars such as Barad) bring to the discussion is a recognition that the objects and objectives of science, though measurable and nonverbal, are no less imaginary, representational, or fictive than literary subjects.

To cite another noteworthy and notably literary example: what we find in political scientist Jane Bennett's response to object-oriented theorists Graham Harman and Timothy Morton is an extension of new materialist tendencies to texts themselves, which are presented by Bennett as "special bodies" that enable us to feel the "liveliness" hidden in things:

> Texts are bodies that can light up, by rendering human perception more acute, those bodies whose favored vehicle of affectivity is less wordy: plants, animals, blades of grass, household objects, trash. One of the

stakes for me of the turn to things in contemporary theory is how it might help us live more sustainably, with less violence toward a variety of bodies. Poetry can help us feel more of the liveliness hidden in such things and reveal more of the threads of connection binding our fate to theirs. (Bennett, "Systems and Things," 232)

Like Latour, Bennett takes care to recognize the limits on how "qualified" she (or anyone) is "to say too much about the affectivity of a text as a material body." Different readers are affected differently, and a literary scholar (keyed to the long history of literary thingness) "can only gesture in the direction that Walt Whitman takes when he says that poetry, if enmeshed in a fortuitous assemblage of other (especially nontext) bodies, can have material effects as real as any." Bennett continues:

> If you read [Whitman's] *Leaves of Grass* in conjunction with "the open air every season of every year of your life," and also bound in affection to "the earth and sun and the animals," while also going "freely with powerful uneducated persons and with the young and with the mothers of families," then "your very flesh shall be a great poem and have the richest fluency not only in its words but in the silent lines of its lips and face and between the lashes of your eyes and in every motion of your body." (Whitman, "Preface 1855," cited in Bennett 2012, 232)

Literature, in such an account, is embraced by Bennett (and Latour, and Whitman) as a particularly suitable way to challenge and reorient fields other than those to which we, as scholars and literary makers, apparently belong. And the same holds, in Whitman's list of earth, sun, and animals *along with other*, "uneducated" and less than literate persons: but persons nonetheless who (with Bennett, Barad, and other feminist new materialists) are now entering the humanities in ever increasing numbers, with ever diversifying social and material interactions. Such an inclusive approach to a given author's work, recurring with the seasons, and not seeking or prognosing a determinate future, arguably is a better, more imaginative way of engaging the equally strange, "nonhuman vitalities" that condition our physical, biological, and cognitive being. As Bennett also points out, we are now "daily confronted with evidence of nonhuman vitalities actively at work around us and within us," and we need a wider literary framing of subject and object relations "if we are to respond intelligently to signs of the breakdown of the earth's carrying capacity for human life" (231).

We might welcome a posthuman perspective, then, as an extension not of our own individual agencies and cognitive capacity but a revitalization of our imaginative engagements, our renewal not through modernism's endless innovation but through rewritings, deconstructions, and (in Bruno Latour's more positive terminology) careful compositions out of elements that are only partially known, whose prospects are experienced in the present moment by those who are now living (not future generations, not past prognosticators). Any further, long-term effects (which may or may not include our human presence) cannot be predicted.

But should they be? Should the futures anticipated in speculative fictions be a reason for scientists to engage with literature? Or should our awareness of the unknowable, unpredictable, and often "destructing" futures initiate a more presential disposition? The here and now that has been suggested by Jane Bennett (citing Whitman) is also directly expressed by Australian Professor of Continental Philosophy Patricia MacCormack when she says,

> There are so many lives here and now that this obsession we have with the lives that don't exist seems to me to be a little bit peculiar, and destructing, ... "How are we caring for the lives now?" (MacCormack, 2013)

To be sure, neither the literary posthumanism of Derrida nor the ecological compositionist scenario brought forward by Latour and Jane Bennett advances an uncritical extension of human power, least of all the liberal humanist subject or enlightenment ideal of "Man" (cited by Tony Davies in the next text box: "Our Multiple Humanisms"). Neither should literature advance alongside our technological innovations with ever-renewing avant gardes and ever updating (but not always cognitively advancing) technologies. Instead of further upgrades in both the sciences and the arts, what is being reconceived are paradigms of *thought* within the framework of literary, cultural, and academic *humanities*: a pluralistic framework that is highly self-conscious about what is being carried over from humanist traditions and what is being left behind (not watched over and forever modernized in the manner of Paul Klee's and Walter Benjamin's *Angel Novus*).

Our Multiple Humanisms

Unlike the miscellaneous posthumanisms that are all with us now, in a jumble that resists periodization, our multiple humanisms can be given as a historical sequence, as this list by Tony Davies (1997, 130–31) illustrates, running from one period to the next over the five- or six-century course of the Enlightenment:

> The civic humanism of the *quattrocento* Italian city-states, the Protestant humanism of sixteenth-century northern Europe, the rationalistic humanism that attended at the revolutions of enlightened modernity, and

the romantic and positivistic humanisms through which the European bourgeoisies established their hegemony over it, the revolutionary humanism that shook the world and the liberal humanism that sought to tame it, the humanism of the Nazis and the humanism of their victims and opponents, the antihumanist humanism of Heidegger and the humanist antihumanism of Foucault and Althusser. *Humanism* (Routledge, 1997): pages 130–31.

Chapter 1

Beyond the Two Cultures?

Here, at the start, I introduce important emphases and divergences within a range of posthuman discourses. Particularly, the distinction between a transhuman empiricism and a reflective, critical posthumanism will be addressed (in this chapter) as a replay of the two-culture noncommunication that C. P. Snow observed (circa 1959) between poets who were deficient in science and scientists who were thought to be "shallowly optimistic, unaware of man's condition" (Snow, "Two Cultures," 5). This said, each of the posthumanist listings in the introduction by Latour, Hayles, Wolfe, Barad, Jane Bennett, and Patricia MacCormack offer encouraging signs that cross-disciplinary conversations and articulations are becoming the order of the day in twenty-first-century posthumanist discourse. Our "imbrication" (to again cite Wolfe 2010, xv) of human and nonhuman networking is thrust on us, not a matter of personal choice or subjective preference. We are now observing, in the literary arts no less than in scientific study, a reorientation of both fields away from entrenched formations and toward more *experimental* practices, each of which (in the words of Manuela Rossini and her coeditors in their book series description for Brill) "regularly borrows from any and all of the others in order to further its drive to experimentation, invention and innovation" (Rossini 2016). Rossini et al. have in mind the emergence – among creative writers, philosophers, and digital literary artists – of a new understanding of the "arts as research"; that is, "a particular form of knowledge production and practice among many others." By merging literature and science in "a practice-based as well as theory-driven poetics of knowledge," we may anticipate further opportunities to remove literary practice from the disciplinary confinements that put up walls between scientific knowledge and more general concerns of ethics and aesthetics.

No sooner is the critical (and questioning) approach named, however, than it is roundly criticized for bringing "humanities and technological-scientific approaches to a shared platform." In the words of Zoltán Boldizsár Simon:

> there is no shared understanding of what a posthuman future could possibly mean, and the tension between a technological-scientific

> prospect of posthumanity and the critical posthumanist scholarship of the humanities is growing palpable. Whereas the former harbors a novel sense of historicity signaled by the expectation of an evental change to bring about the technological posthuman as a previously nonexistent and other-than-human central subject, the latter theorizes a postanthropocentric subjectivity of beings still human. In doing so, it extends the already familiar emancipatory concerns of the human world over the nonhuman, with special attention paid to the ecological other. (Boldizsár Simon, "Two Cultures of the Posthuman Future," 171)

A "novel sense of historicity" and "evental change": we are here approaching neither the "odd utopian" futurity of modernist culture (criticized by Latour in our introductory chapter) nor the prospective, presential inclination of Latour's and Derrida's *avenir*. That inclination, and a renewed awareness of the materiality of words and sentences that we have read (and heard) in the voicings of Richard Powers's characters, reinforce a new materialist tendency in contemporary writing: a "novel sense of historicity" that is, arguably, best conveyed in the prospective formation of a literary poem, novel, or community-built, multimedial narrative. By contrast with these specifically literary materialisms, what Boldizsár Simon describes as "Two Cultures of the Posthuman Future" is instead a revival – and intensification – of a noncommunication between the respective "Two Cultures" (in C. P. Snow's words) of "literary intellectuals" and "physical scientists."

Boldizsár Simon, for his part, prefers the concrete (but never quite describable) expectation of an *event*; that is, a renewal or repurposing of human powers via technological means that would shift our bodily and mental formation, much as Darwinian shifts produced our present, human singularity among our fellow animal species. Such speculative formations, in Boldizsár Simon and many other *trans*humanist advocates that he supports and cites, are powerful precisely to the extent that the singularities they anticipate are, by definition, unforeseeable but grounded, somehow, in technological platforms. These are, for the most part, binary, nonverbal, nonsubjective (and unlettered) significations: characteristics that might insulate a discursive regime from critical enquiry and questioning. Indeed, for Boldizsár Simon and his transhumanist cohort, technological development takes on a peculiar, almost messianic status: "Instead of unfolding over the course of a historical process, the new epoch is signaled by the expectation of a singular event." The event, Boldizsár Simon goes on to say,

> is commonly referred to as "technological singularity," a notion that gained popularity following Vernor Vinge's presentation at a NASA conference in

1993. The singularity itself is the anticipated creation of greater-than-human intelligence, likely to give way to an "intelligence explosion" of such intelligence creating even greater intelligences at an increasing pace. In Vinge's words, the singularity "is a point where our models must be discarded and a new reality rules," representing a change "comparable to the rise of human life on Earth." (Boldizsár Simon, "Two Cultures," 8)

The "intelligence explosion" imagined by Vinge carries with it an implied Darwinian premise, but the speed at which the singularity unfolds is hardly (as Boldizsár Simon suggests) "comparable to the rise of human life on Earth." It is, rather, a displacement into the nonhuman, technological sphere of a form of vitalism humans themselves no longer possess. Indeed, it is precisely the augmentation and extension of our lived environment through technological means that now separates us from nature's own evolutionary agency: "a force that works slowly compared with human time scales." So write Jacob Wamberg and Mads Rosendahl Thomsen, who go on to note how "probably" this evolutionary force "has long since died out, since humans keep their anatomy constant by transferring the evolutionary pressures to their environments, rather than as earlier in evolution, by adapting their bodies to non-controlled environmental shifts. Instead of, for instance, growing fur or fins, humans fashion fur coats or build ships" ("The Posthuman in the Anthropocene," 2).

Wamberg and Rosendahl Thomsen reference Steve Jones's suggestion "that it is decreasing differences in survival and reproduction rates that eventually stopped 'the Darwin machine.'" Jones makes a case that human evolution could be over. And Cary Wolfe, for his part, sets aside the prospect that cognition and consciousness can be unique to humans. Rather than postulating human being as a singularity among our companion species, Wolfe supports a scholarly affirmation of cognitive processes "that are, strictly speaking, inhuman and ahuman. How do we know? Because we now know that the very same processes produce similar products in nonhuman beings, as well-known experiments with great apes (such as those conducted by scientist Sue Savage-Rumbaugh with the bonobo, Kanzi) have shown." (See the text box, and Wolfe's entry on "posthumanism" in Braidotti's and Hlavajova's *Posthuman Glossary*, 356–60 [Wolfe 2018].)

Sue, Liz, William, and Three Bonobo Apes

When the back door swung open, out climbed Sue Savage-Rumbaugh, her sister and collaborator Liz Pugh, a man named William Fields, and three bonobo apes, who were joining a group of five bonobos who had recently arrived at the facility. The $10 million, 18-room compound, known then as the Great Ape Trust, bore little resemblance to a traditional research center. Instead of in conventional cages, the apes, who ranged in age from 4 to 35, lived in rooms, linked by elevated walkways and hydraulic doors they could open themselves. There was a music room with drums and a keyboard, chalk for drawing, an indoor waterfall, and a sun-washed greenhouse stocked with bananas and sugar cane. Every feature of the facility was designed to encourage the apes' agency: They could help prepare food in a specialized kitchen, press the buttons of a vending machine for snacks, and select DVDs to watch on a television. A monitor connected to a camera outside allowed the bonobos to screen human visitors who rang the doorbell; pressing a button, they granted or denied visitors access to a viewing area secured by laminated glass. But the center's signature feature was the keyboard of pictorial symbols accessible on computerized touchscreens and packets placed in every room and even printed on researchers' T-shirts. It consisted of more than 300 "lexigrams" corresponding to English words – a lingua franca that Savage-Rumbaugh had developed over many years to enable the bonobos to communicate with human beings.

> Lindsay Stern, What Can Bonobos Teach Us About the Nature of Language? *Smithsonian Magazine* (July 2020). www.smithsonianmag .com/science-nature/bonobos-teach-humans-about-nature-language-180975191/.

Unlike the behavioral extensions cited by Wolfe, which give us a particular and realizable future for the emergence of consciousness in other-than-human animals, the entirely speculative singularities in Bostrom, Boldizsár Simon, Vinge, and many other *trans*humanist advocates are less concerned with consciousness and trans-species communicability. The transhumanist concerns, as Wolfe points out, have more to do with developing an ability to overcome "diseases and infirmities" and eventually to achieve "radically extended lifespans, and even immortality" (Wolfe, *Posthuman Glossary*, 2018, 357).

Donna Haraway, for her part, calls such disembodied and "singular" dispositions a "god trick": a unified vision and purported objectivity that sidelines more individual and subjective ways of knowing. Part of Haraway's concern with god-trick objectivity is the uncertain state of culpability. She argues "against various forms of unlocatable, and so irresponsible, knowledge claims. Irresponsible means unable to be called into account" ("Situated," 583). The critical, new materialist approach that Haraway anticipates in the mid-1980s is less doctrinaire, more situated than the notional, human-centered singularities, and, thus, open to disciplinary transactions. As she remarks:

> I would like a doctrine of embodied objectivity that accommodates paradoxical and critical feminist science projects: Feminist objectivity means quite simply situated knowledges. (1988: 581)

Situated, and also answerable – if we are to take seriously the transhumanist claims to historical accountability. The "Situated Knowledges" that Haraway points to in her so-titled 1988 essay would be realized through a concerted gathering of *new materialist* scholars around the turn of the twenty-first century. Appropriately, this "theoretical turn away from the persistent dualisms in modernist and humanist traditions," not least the two-cultures dualism, more openly seeks "a repositioning of the human among nonhuman actants." So argues Kameron Sanzo in his glossary entry for the *Geneologies of Critical Posthumanism* (see https://criticalposthumanism.net/new-materialisms/). "The discourses catalogued under new materialism(s)," Sanzo argues, "share an agenda with posthumanism in that they seek a repositioning of the human among nonhuman actants, they question the stability of an individuated, liberal subject, and they advocate a critical materialist attention to the global, distributed influences of late capitalism and climate change."

Snow and Plato

[C. P.] Snow was hardly original in his thesis about two cultures. It takes little reflection to realize that the idea originated in Plato. Of course, Plato did not content himself with wittily chastising poets for their deficiency in science, as Snow did. Plato wanted to ban them from the ideal Republic for their failure to know reality. After Plato, and in spite of Aristotle, the relevant history of competing epistemologies in our culture endows Snow's themes in *The Two Cultures* with a certain plausibility.

(Alan Thiher, *Fiction Refracts Science*, 5)

What for Jonathan Culler (cited in our introductory chapter) and other descendants of Snow's "literary intellectuals" is a taking apart and reconceptualizing of the academic disciplines in the context of a long literary history is for Snow's (and Boldizsár Simon's) "physical scientists" a denial of our present material being: "There might be," Boldizsár Simon proposes, "much more to technology-oriented approaches to the posthuman than a reductionist understanding of them as simply defenders of 'humanist values' and 'the liberal subject'" (2019, 177). In calling for a cultural recuperation of scientific practice, new possibilities are put forth by Boldizsár Simon and philosopher Nick Bostrom, among many others, for regeneration and improvement within our expanding knowledge base. And, so, there is understandably less interest in deconstructing the human centeredness of past narratives, less concern with an ungrounded, perpetually signifying tendency of literary analyses and more interest in science and technology studies, whose outcome is imagined as nothing less than the *replacement* of humans by the technology we have created.

Indeed, the sciences themselves offer some of the most cogent redefinitions (or *defamiliarizations*) of our nonhuman environments. Take, for example, the quantum theory of light, notable for the intermixing of three elements: the human observer, this person's subjective awareness, and a natural, measurable materiality:

> [Neils] Bohr's break with Newton, Descartes, and Democritus is not based in "mere idle philosophical reflection" but on new empirical findings in the domain of atomic physics that came to light during the first quarter of the twentieth century. Bohr's struggle to provide a theoretical understanding of these findings resulted in his radical proposal that an entirely new epistemological framework is required. (Barad 2003, 813–4; citing Heidegger on "idle talk")

That "entirely new epistemological framework" helped to situate the Heisenberg uncertainty principle, which brought into question whether one might describe light as a wavelike phenomenon (because of observable diffraction patterns, when light is sent through a grating) or a set of particles (known as photons, which can be observed when the grating is modified). The light that we observe passing in wavelike formations shows no signs of its particulate composition, yet these same diffraction patterns are unobservable in gratings that are designed to detect particles.

"Classically," Karen Barad remarks, "these two results together seem contradictory – frustrating efforts to specify the true ontological nature of light" ("Posthuman Performativity," 815):

> The notions of "wave" and "particle" do not refer to inherent characteristics of an object. There are no such independently existing objects with inherent characteristics, as there are in more large scale, gravitational interactions among planets or moving objects in Newtonian physics; no clear separation of mind and body, subjective and objective entities, as are found in Descartes's humanist philosophy (with its grounding in *cogito ergo sum*). Neither is such Heisenbergian indeterminacy an issue in the atomic theories of Democritus (born circa 460 BC), who proposed that all objects are composed of *individual* units that are "uncuttable" or "inseparable." (Barad, "Posthuman Performativity," 813)

The medium through which we observe light, then, determines what we see, and this experimental binary brings into question our ability to describe light's materiality as consisting of either particles or waves. One measuring apparatus gives meaning to the notion of "wave," while another provides determinate meaning to the notion of "particle." What we know for sure is that our agency as observers is limited, and any awareness we might have of our most universal and present environmental object (sunlight), is destined to remain forever estranged and defamiliarized, in science no less than in literature. From this perspective, the "constructivist" inclinations of social and cultural theory find resonances in the sciences, whose "objectivity" (particulate? wavelike?) is less grounded than we might have thought.

With the knowing subject so "enmeshed in a thick web of representations," the human mind "cannot see its way through to objects that are now forever out of reach and all that is visible is the sticky problem of humanity's own captivity within language" (Barad 2003, 811–2). Unlike many new materialists, Barad does not entirely abandon the "linguistic turn." Such captivations, long a part of "humanity's" literary and philosophical practices, can now be considered cross-disciplinary, and even conversant with the sciences – those that advance knowledge rather than (exclusively) strengthening our human agency and individuality. At the same time as we can observe an "object oriented" embrace of scientific materiality in literary and cultural discourse, we find strains of speculation in the sciences, as transhumanist scientists embrace indefinable, largely imagined (and likely impossible) technology-driven futures.

Haraway's God-Trick and Jill Walker Rettberg's Machine Vision

Visual technologies from satellite surveillance to medical imaging seem to promise the impossible: "the god trick of seeing everything from nowhere," as Haraway writes ("Situated Knowledge," 581). In contrast to this "god trick," Haraway argues that knowledge is embodied. Therefore "objectivity turns out to be about particular and specific embodiment" (582). When I write that vision is situated I mean that we always see from our own situation in the world, from a particular standpoint and within the limitations of the physical constraints of our bodies. When I look out of my window, I see a view of my neighborhood that is slightly different from what a neighbor would see from their window, and quite different from what a satellite image of the neighborhood would capture. What I see is also situated by how sharp my vision is, by my personal experiences (do I know who lives in each building or what it means that my neighbour hasn't put the trash out as they usually do), by the time and season (is it dark or light) and many other things.

Machine vision technologies often present dazzling overviews that appear to escape this situatedness: Satellite images showing the globe in amazing detail, images of distant galaxies or of the microscopic worlds inside the cells of our bodies. These kinds of image appear to be able to

> show the world as though we are outside of it. They appear to be objective and to show the world as it really is. Haraway argues, and I agree with her, that this objective outside view is impossible.
>
> > Jill Walker Rettberg, *Machine Vision: How Algorithms are Changing the Way we See the World* (Politi Press, 2023)
>
> "The trust in technology as an almost divine power," Rettberg states, is a "recurring theme" in her book. The present volume, similarly, observes a transfer of messianic beliefs away from religion and toward an anticipated, greater-than-human "intelligence explosion," creating "even greater intelligences at an increasing pace."
>
> > Vinge, cited in Boldizsár Simon, "Two Cultures," 8

The End of the World as We Know It

Probably the most important difference between transhumanism and post-humanism is that the former is best understood as an intensification of humanism – that is, as a form of hyper-humanism embracing the classic ideals of Enlightenment (reason, science, individualism, progress, and self-perfection) yet intensified and "updated" with both a strong belief in and a clear affirmation of the use of advanced technoscientific means to realize these ideals, whereas the latter explicitly considers itself to represent a break with humanism, therefore being emphatically a posthumanism (Ranisch and Lorenz Sorgner, 2014, 8). Transhumanists in general share the opinion "that humans should take evolution in their own hands and undertake broad-scale attempts to incorporate technologies into their lives" (Ranisch and Lorenz Sorgner, 2014, 13). Posthumanists, on the other hand, are more in the business of questioning traditional concepts of the human and criticizing the idea that "man is the measure of all things."

It is not unexpected that we might favor, in a literary and academic introduction to posthumanism, tendencies that are *critical* and, at times, contentious. That said, we should not overlook a certain apocalyptic strain in the physical sciences: namely, the idea of a human perfectibility whereby we (humans) might take into our "own hands" the scientific and technological means to evolutionary and transformative events (Ranisch and Lorenz Sorgner, 2014, 13). Even so, such *transhumanist* futures are also, at times taken on faith: the "god trick" advanced by Donna Haraway and the unbounded measurements of transhumanists who wish to take evolution into their own hands. It is a situation that puts into question all the trust in

Enlightenment ideals (of "reason, science, individualism, progress and self-perfection," to cite Lemmens, 2015, reviewing Ranisch and Lorenz Sorgner).

We might consider, for example, the persistence of "subjectivity" (albeit a subject that asserts itself as "postanthropocentric" [Boldizsár Simon, 2019, 172 *et seq*]). Such a conceptual, subjective reformation is not just another philosophical criticism; nor is it only an extension, as Boldizsár Simon goes on to say, of our "emancipatory concerns" (171) to the larger ecological world. If our goal, to put it bluntly, is to save the planet through our own subjective and communal impulses, that "remains an overtly anthropocentric agenda: *it matters to humans that humans matter less*" (Boldizsár Simon, 2019, 180 [emphasis original]).

Some "Critical Posthumanists"

In his essay, "Two Cultures of the Posthuman Future," Boldizsár Simon lists a number of notable scholars with whom he is disagreeing (regardless of whether they explicitly affiliate with critical posthumanism):

> in Braidotti's quasi-panpsychism with *zoe* (life) as a "cosmic energy" that forms the immanent bound [*The Posthuman*, esp. 130–8]; in Domanska's effort to theorize a new ecological humanities [186–210]; in Haraway's "web of entangled companion species" [*When Species Meet*]; or in Joyce Chaplin's paraphrase of the subaltern question ["Can the Nonhuman Speak?" 509–29]. (2019, 180)

For the most part, the present introduction to literary posthumanism sides with the critical posthumanism and new materialism initiated by Braidotti, Haraway, and others.

Fair enough, and there will be, inevitably, all too many, all too human attitudes that find their way into some, though not all branches of critical posthumanism and postanthropocentric subjectivity. But there can also be other ways of *imagining ourselves* into a world that is relational and never wholly subject to our own (admittedly advanced) powers of rational control, with all the uncontrolled destruction that has entailed – not least the accelerated extinction of animal and plant species with whom we humans coevolved (see the next text box: "Facts"). It will not be possible, given the speculative nature of both positions – that of the humanities and of more technology-oriented STEM scholarship – to resolve this decades-long dispute, and no attempt need be made in these pages to work our way through the "multifarious scholarship on the posthuman" that Boldizsár Simon references, and classifies into "discordant social imaginaries" ("Two Cultures," 176). It will be enough, at the start, to note a few, particularly *literary* elements shared by each of the two – posthumanist and transhuman – cultures.

Facts

- 16,928 plant and animal species are known to be threatened with extinction. This may be a gross underestimate because less than 3% of the world's 1.9 million described species have been assessed for the IUCN Red List of Threatened Species.
- Only 1.9 million species have been described out of an estimated 13–14 million species that exist.
- In the last 500 years, human activity is known to have forced 869 species to extinction (or extinction in the wild).
- One in four mammals and one in eight birds face a high risk of extinction in the near future.
- One in three amphibians and almost half of all tortoises and freshwater turtles are threatened.
- The current species extinction rate is estimated to be between 1,000 and 10,000 times higher than the natural or "background" rate.
- The total number of known threatened animal species has increased from 5,205 to 8,462 since 1996.

  International Union for Conservation of Nature (IUCN). https://springbrooknaturecenter.org/DocumentCenter/View/749/Species-Extinction-05-2007-PDF?bidId=#:~:text=16%2C928%20plant%20and%20animal%20species,Red%20List%20of%20Threatened%20Species

The same can be said of the "evental" change that has still not happened, not since Snow's lecture of 1959 (see Snow, 1961) nor Vinge's 1993 presentation at NASA. But the idea (or aesthetic imaginary) of a "singularity" remains very much with us. And this singularity cannot situate itself in scientific discourse because it is not falsifiable (or questionable in a meaningful way) as scientific theories need to be (see Popper, 1935). Boldizsár Simon and others in the technocentric camp complain that humanities scholars pay insufficient attention to the technological platforms from which alternative powers (and not necessarily human extensions) might be forming. Yet any such event, or "singularity," by definition is impossible for humans to visualize or abstract from our present technological lifeworld. For this reason, the singularity remains firmly in the realm of imagination. And we would do well to consult (with Herbrechter and Callus) "the apocalyptic narratives from *Revelations* through H. G. Wells's *The Time Machine* to *The Matrix*," and this latter film's inspiration in the cyberpunk fiction *Neuromancer* by

William Gibson (1984) if we wish to sharpen our sense of the oncoming, albeit ever imaginary, singularity.

And not only contemporary fictions or literature in print should be consulted: As we will now see, one of the clearest and continuing embodiments of singularity is Mary Shelley's early-nineteenth-century novel, *Frankenstein*. Shelley herself could well be taken to task by Zoltán Boldizsár Simon and many other technocentric transhumanists. She, too, could be accused (in Boldizsár Simon's words) of not having a particularly "technologically oriented approach" to her topic. Her narrative offers hardly any details, other than the use of electricity and some vague references to "Galvanism" when describing the overachieving, and socially isolated Victor Frankenstein's construction of a monstrous posthuman out of lifeless body parts. Mary Shelley's literary anticipations, which arguably are the first in this particular aesthetic imaginary, do not in themselves "refer to anything like a shared vision of scientists working in laboratories that aim at a posthuman future" (Boldizsár Simon, ibid.). What Mary Shelley's work does engage, along with her namesake Shelley Jackson's digital reconfiguration and Jeanette Winterson's twenty-first-century remake of the *Frankenstein* narrative, is the location of scientific knowledge, and our *ways of knowing* within a continuing, transformative realm of both the literary and scientific *humanities*.

When Did We Become Fully Human?

Fossils and DNA suggest people looking like us, anatomically modern *Homo sapiens*, evolved around 300,000 years ago. Surprisingly, archaeology – tools, artefacts, cave art – suggest that complex technology and cultures, "behavioural modernity," evolved more recently: 50,000–65,000 years ago.

Some scientists interpret this as suggesting the earliest *Homo sapiens* weren't entirely modern. Yet the different data tracks different things. Skulls and genes tell us about brains, artefacts about culture. Our brains probably became modern before our cultures.

. . . Starting about 65,000 to 50,000 years ago, more advanced technology started appearing: complex projectile weapons such as bows and spear-throwers, fishhooks, ceramics, sewing needles. People made representational art – cave paintings of horses, ivory goddesses (such as the Venus of Brassempouy; Figure 1.1), lion-headed idols showing artistic flair and imagination. A bird-bone flute hints at music. Meanwhile, arrival of humans in Australia 65,000 years ago shows we'd mastered seafaring.

The Conversation, Nicholas R. Longrich, Senior Lecturer in Evolutionary Biology and Paleontology, University of Bath: "When did we become fully human?" https://theconversation.com/when-did-we-become-fully-human-what-fossils-and-dna-tell-us-about-the-evolution-of-modern-intelligence-143717.

Figure 1.1 The Venus of Brassempouy, 25,000 years old: "The oldest known realistic depiction of a human face . . . carved from mammoth ivory during the Ice Age."
AtlasObscura.

Thinking Literary Posthumanism: A Future to Come

An introduction to literary posthumanism need not engage directly with the many ongoing scientific debates, nor will we be explicating in detail or listing all our many emerging media and technological platforms, our multiple posthumanist positionings, disciplinary distinctions, deviations, radical departures, and romantic, modernist, and postmodern avant-gardes. Rather, we will here observe the ways that any posthuman formulation, "far from surpassing or rejecting the human – actually enables us to describe the human and its characteristic modes of communication, interaction, meaning, social significations, and affective investments" (Wolfe 2010, xxv). Which is to say, a literary posthumanism will specify manifold ways of *thinking* and *communicating* within and among distinct systems, human and nonhuman organisms, places, and cognitive frameworks that can take us beyond "the ontologically closed domain of consciousness, reason, reflection and so on" (ibid.). For this, a partial, imaginative opening of perceptions, subjectivities, and systems once thought to be closed will be shown to be essential. And this focus on the supreme value of the *imagination*, a position already advanced by Percy Bysshe Shelley in the early 1800s (and cited at the start of this book), will take precedence over predictions or speculations on transhuman singularities or technologically empowered embodiments.

Such deeply relational descriptions, by forcing us to "rethink our taken-for-granted modes of human experience" (Wolfe, ibid.) are particularly well enacted in literature, which traditionally (but also in ever-renewing experimental modes) seeks to *defamiliarize* our normative, everyday lives and interactions. It is no accident that Wolfe, in *What Is Posthumanism?*, engages Ralph Waldo Emerson's nineteenth-century romanticism alongside philosopher Stanley Cavell's twentieth-century skepticism, while finding an enactment of Niklas Luhmann's systems theory in Wallace Stevens's "Idea of Order at Key West" – which is also an idea of second-order *observation* of one's own consciousness; a self-conscious awareness of our larger than human subjectivity. It is here, in explorations that move beyond the "ontologically closed domain of consciousness, reason, reflection, and so on" (ibid.), that we will encounter unfamiliar *ways of thinking* that come after the cultural repressions and fantasies, the philosophical protocols and evasions. The exploration of context and connection, which are the soul of historical understanding, will be foremost in the present reconsideration of long-running literary encounters as they engage, repurpose, and often resist the norms of scientific knowledge at any given moment in history. And for this reason, literature, unlike the sciences, can preserve and sustain perspectives and cognitive dispositions that connect not just different disciplines, but eras.

Poetry As Paradox

> She sang beyond the genius of the sea.
> The water never formed to mind or voice,
> Like a body wholly body, fluttering
> Its empty sleeves; and yet its mimic motion
> Made constant cry, caused constantly a cry,
> That was not ours although we understood,
> Inhuman, of the veritable ocean.
> Wallace Stevens, "The Idea of Order at Key West"

"Not ours," but nonetheless "understood": the paradoxical situation of a woman's felt affinity with the ocean is at once rationally "veritable," but more affectively understood. Cary Wolfe articulates how in Stevens's poem, the woman's observation of the natural world makes "the sky acutest at its vanishing," thus disclosing a "spirit" (Stevens) and "not a substance: not the binaries of mind/nature, subject/object, imagination/reality and so on, among which we must chose as either philosophical idealists or realists, but rather a *form*, a *movement* of observation . . . with no resting place" (Wolfe 2010, 280). The paradox is not resolved, not by Stevens nor by his readers. Wolfe instead finds in this paradox a "constitutive structure" arguably for poetry generally. And this is done not by holding fast to qualities we already know, via rational thought. As we have seen, for example, in Percy Bysshe Shelley's "Defense of Poetry" (1840), empirical observations – and the world they bring to us – are transformed into multiple, meaningful modes of understanding via the literary imagination.

Neither can we explore every classic work of literature that intersects, sometimes in synch but more often in tension, with the science and technology of its historical moment, and ours. While our posthuman emphasis will be best observed in percipient fictions and poetries of the present, connections with past genres and practices will be no less important as we further explore the long-running, highly relational aesthetic that joins our human consciousness with other, nonconscious and often discomforting perspectives. We might start with Samuel Taylor Coleridge, for example, whose Ancient Mariner walks in fear, because he knows "that some frightful fiend / Doth close behind him tread." Or with William Wordsworth's inhuman, "sounding cataract," which haunted him "like a passion" in the poem *Tintern Abbey* (1798). Wordsworth's thoughts, anticipating Stevens, "connect . . . the landscape with the quiet of the sky." We could go further back to Dante Alighieri's *Divine Comedy* (circa 1320) or to Milton in *Paradise Lost* (1667):

> Did I request thee, Maker, from my clay
> To mold me man? Did I solicit thee
> From darkness to promote me?

Posthumanist themes were present long before human science and literary humanism emerged as pre-eminent post-Enlightenment discourses. We could explore the past no less than current successors who have put our own humanity (and humanities) into question. But it happens that our explorations, citations, and repurposing of literary precursors have been already performed, by Mary Wollstonecraft Shelley in *Frankenstein; or, The Modern Prometheus*. As early as 1818, Shelley's novel already captured, and dramatized, some of the strains on humanist discourse. And with this proto-modernist work – and postmodern fictions that repurpose and remediate the novel for circulation in today's digital reading environment – we can begin to outline formative strains, and transformations, within human nature and our various literary creations and self-conceptions.

Mary Shelley's *Frankenstein*

> There never was a wilder story imagined, yet, like most of the fictions of this age, it has an air of reality attached to it.
>
> *The Edinburgh Magazine*, 1818. (Cited by Jeanette Winterson in *Frankissstein: A Love Story*, 2019, 53)

Chapter 2

Mary Shelley's Modern and Shelley Jackson's Postmodern Prometheus

> We need first to understand that the human form – including human desire and all its external representations – may be changing radically, and thus must be revisioned. We need to understand that five hundred years of humanism may be coming to an end, as humanism transforms itself into something that we must helplessly call posthumanism.

So writes Ihab Hassan, who is widely agreed to have coined the term "posthumanism." The occasion of his remarks was a symposium on postmodern performance, in a 1977 talk titled "Prometheus as Performer: Towards a Posthumanist Culture." And, like Mary Wollstonecraft Shelley in her presentation of *Frankenstein; or, The Modern Prometheus*, Hassan is highly conflicted about the promethean promise of the posthuman, which he presents as a "dubious neologism." At the same time, he recognizes that "five hundred years of humanism may be coming to an end," and with it we can no longer accept without question the narrative of man as an autonomous rational agent – one that relies on universal and anthropocentric orientations cofounded on human reason.

In the minds of many, the novel *Frankenstein* (1818) is the first and still foremost literary imagining of a posthuman being. Yet it is seldom noted that the creation by Victor Frankenstein of an artificial human that is more powerful, more eloquent than his maker could not have happened without this adventurous scientist's education as a humanist and his collegial welcome into a community of working scientists. Indeed, much as Dr. Frankenstein's monster has entered mainstream imagination, particularly in its twentieth-century film and serial television depictions, it is easy to overlook the distinctively *humanistic* character of this inventor's background, along with that of Mary Shelley herself. Often overlooked is the context of Victor Frankenstein's education as more than a mere inventor. His tutelege as a "disciple" of one Dr. Waldman at the university he attended at Ingolstadt, in Bavaria, for example, and the respect that Frankenstein himself receives from his colleagues at the university, all suggests a self-regard and involvement with others that is linked explicitly to the humanistic context for the scientific study he undertakes:

> "I am happy," said M. Waldman, "to have gained a disciple; and if your application equals your ability, I have no doubt of your success. Chemistry is that branch of natural philosophy in which the greatest improvements have been and may be made; it is on that account that I have made it my peculiar study; but at the same time I have not neglected the other branches of science. A man would make but a very sorry chemist, if he attended to that department of human knowledge alone. If your wish is to become really a man of science, and not merely a petty experimentalist, I should advise you to apply to every branch of natural philosophy, including mathematics." (32 [page references to *Frankenstein* are to the Third Norton critical edition])

For Waldman, science is not so much a specialization as it is a branch of knowledge placed *in relation to* other branches, all of which contribute to an education in what would then (early in the 1800s) have been called "natural philosophy" (32). Frankenstein receives from Waldman a list of books in this field, and thus "ended a day memorable to me: it decided my future destiny" (32). A bibliography of assigned readings from past ages, no less than any one specific experimental technique, is what determines young Frankenstein's future.

A similar multidisciplinarity (and a conflation of high and popular literary genres) is observable in Mary Shelley's own lifeworld. She recalls the origin of the Frankenstein story, as a challenge undertaken during a summer visit to Lake Geneva with her spouse, Percy Bysshe Shelley, and their friend Lord Byron, who brought to the gathering "some volumes of ghost stories, translated from the German into French" (218). "'We will each write a ghost story,' said Lord Byron, and his proposition was acceded to" (219). As it happened, Mary was the only one of the three who wrote the story, but that was achieved in no small degree by her *including in the work* conversations that resemble the ones that took place during that fortnight visit. Indeed, Mary Shelley's recollection of the Geneva gathering in the 1831 Preface to *Frankenstein* recalls all the characteristics of a graduate seminar:

> Many and long were the conversations between Lord Byron and Shelley, to which I was a devout but nearly silent listener. During one of these, various philosophical doctrines were discussed, and among others the nature and principle of life, and whether there was any probability of its ever being discovered and communicated. They talked of the experiments of Dr. Darwin, (I speak not of what the Doctor really did, or

said that he did, but, as more to my purpose, of what was then spoken of
as having been done by him) who preserved a piece of vermicelli in
a glass case, till by some extraordinary means it began to move with
voluntary motion. Not thus, after all, would life be given. Perhaps
a corpse would be re-animated; galvanism had given token of such
things: perhaps the component parts of a creature might be
manufactured, brought together, and endued with vital warmth.

Mary Shelley, "Introduction to *Frankenstein*," Third Edition (1818: 220)

Electrical current – galvanism – is what imparts lifelike powers and a feeling
of futurity to otherwise inanimate matter; still more, electricity can *enhance*
"voluntary" human agency and possibly replace a body's animating force. In
her novel, Shelley does not describe the science in detail, nor does she identify
where the body parts come from or how they are assembled.

Karloff, Clive, and the 1931 Horror Film

In the 1931 flawed film adaptation (which acknowledges in its credits the novel
written by "Mrs P. B. Shelley"), every detail is given of the monster's reconstruction
from body parts of several exhumed corpses: the "normal brain" that is on display
in a jar during a lecture by one of Frankenstein's university colleagues is replaced by
another, clearly labeled "abnormal brain" that was on display in the same lecture.
Later, Dr. Frankenstein (played by Colin Clive) will observe the moving hand and
undead scowl of his creation (Boris Karloff): the living corpse is perceived not with
the horror experienced by Mary Shelley's failed "Victor," but with a transhumanist
glorification: "It's alive! It's alive! A live . . . " utters Colin (C)live. The spoken words
that follow are censored in many editions of the movie: "In the name of God! Now
I know what it feels like to *be* God!"

Indeed, Mary Shelley's dismissive reference to what Erasmus Darwin (1731–
1802) "said that he did" and what others have merely "spoken of" is given far
less attention in the novel than the academic environment that enables such
extended conversations and critiques. We observe, in some detail, the (fictional) figure of Professor Waldman entering the "lecturing room" (30) and
there recapitulating "the history of chemistry and the various improvements
made by different men of learning, pronouncing with fervour the names of the
most distinguished discoverers" (31). When Victor Frankenstein, as what we
would now call an early career researcher, begins to make discoveries of his
own, he is recognized by "the several professors of the university" (46): "D –
n the fellow," says one of them, "he has outstripped us all" (46). When
Frankenstein and his more language-oriented colleague, Henry Clerval,
head out to Bavaria to take a walking tour in "the environs of Ingolstadt"

(47), the conversation that elevates the minds of both young men fits Mary Shelley's description of the "Many and long" conversations between her husband and Lord Byron ("Introduction," 220). In the novel, Clerval's conversation is described similarly as being, like Byron's, "full of imagination; and very often, in imitation of the Persian and Arabic writers, he invented tales of wonderful fancy and passion" (48). Such multilingual tales are not unlike Mary Shelley's personal recollection of the ghost stories that found their way to the Swiss retreat of Lord Byron, Percy Bysshe Shelley, and herself.

Feminist Wollstonecraft, Philosopher Godwin, Poet Shelley

Frankenstein; or, the Modem Prometheus is the full title of Mary Wollstonecraft Godwin Shelley's inaugural science fiction novel, which she began before she was nineteen and finished less than a year later. Mary Shelley's full name is as important in understanding Frankenstein as is the book's full title. The novel intends us to see its protagonist, Dr. Victor Frankenstein, as the modern Prometheus, stealing creative fire from heaven in order to make a creature, a New Adam, whom most of us now call "the monster," because we have seen so many motion picture versions of Frankenstein. Despite his crimes, the creature is as much angel as monster, and we do best by following the book in calling him "the daemon." This ill-starred daemon is, in certain respects, a critique of all three illustrious figures who meet in Mary Shelley's full name: her mother, the radical feminist Mary Wollstonecraft; her father, the radical philosopher William Godwin; and her husband, the revolutionary lyrical poet Percy Bysshe Shelley.

Thus Harold Bloom, in his *Modern Introduction to Frankenstein* (2007), identifies shared aspirations in the lives of Mary Shelley, her invented characters, and the "three great idealists" in Mary's family who had each "envisioned a new humanity in a newly structured society, and all had hoped that human nature could be redesigned, so as to eliminate exploitation, timidity, remorse, and conventional morality." Mary Shelley's own anarchist parents, William Godwin and Mary Wollstonecraft, provided one model of generational care, and Mary received encouragement from her spouse, Percy Bysshe Shelley, explicitly (in her own words) to "prove myself worthy of my parentage, and enrol myself on the page of fame" ("Introduction to *Frankenstein*," Third Edition (1818), *Norton*, 218). We will find a similar authorial self-awareness (and self-reliance) in the transcendentalist movement in the United States, a generation or two after the romanticism of Percy Bysshe Shelley, William Wordsworth, and Samuel Taylor Coleridge (to name only those poets explicitly cited in the course of Mary Shelley's novel).

What is being depicted in Mary Shelley's narrative is as much a literary enactment of an early-nineteenth-century emerging *humanities* as a tale of artificial life and intelligence. And the encounters between Frankenstein (the aspiring natural philosopher) and Clerval (the more language-oriented colleague) offer a clear antecedent to the trans- and posthumanist dispositions of today. Indeed, the horror of young Frankenstein's creation is closely related to the inventor's own withdrawal from precisely the *social*, collaborative, conversational, and interactive practices that the "human sciences" cultivate. Dr. Frankenstein notes how his two-year course of study, before its enactment in bringing an assemblage of bodily parts to life, had secluded him "from the intercourse of my fellow-creatures, and rendered me unsocial" (48). He promises himself "exercise and amusement" once he's completed his creation, but the nightly "slow fever" and diminishment of his own health is a cost of his ambition to create beauty from undead body parts (37). Having carefully made sure that the creature's "limbs were in proportion" and his "features . . . beautiful," Frankenstein abandons his invention the moment he observes the creature's coming to life: his "yellow skin" barely covering "the work of muscles and arteries beneath; his hair was of a lustrous black, and flowing; his teeth of a pearly whiteness; but these luxuriances only formed a more horrid contrast with his watery eyes, that seemed almost of the same colour as the dun white sockets in which they were set, his shrivelled complexion, and straight black lips" (38).

The passive, suggestively feminine "luxuriance," lustrousness, and beauty have been marked and scarred by material appearances and dull, grayish-brown colorings. This is the "dull, yellow eye" that opens, as the Frankenstein monster comes to life (Figure 2.1). His features are not only unattractive (and, arguably, racially tinged for a designer who valued white masculinity): the unanticipated admixture of skin coloring set a monstrous limit to Dr. Frankenstein's illusion of instrumental mastery and threatens his control of the materially mixed creature he has brought into being. In passing, Frankenstein mentions "the feelings of human nature" that are more change-able than the everyday, "different accidents of life" (38). But these feelings were never thought through by him; they were never a part of his "purpose," which was a wholly instrumental, prosthetic infusion of "life into an inani-mate body" (38). Frankenstein's immediate and unthinking abandonment of his creature the moment its eyes open, its limbs move, and its first breath is taken reveal the limitations of a technological worldview and electrical enab-ling of earthly life. Its horrendous and uncontrollable nature, which Dr Frankenstein sensed at the start, are no more likely to be overcome by transhumanist hopes regarding our own "different accidents of life" in the present.

At this point in Mary Shelley's narrative, on the "dreary night of November" (37) when Frankenstein beholds what he has done, the daemon's monstrous appearance is pretty much all that we know. Only later will we be told, in the

"By the glimmer of the half-extinguished light, I saw the dull, yellow eye of the creature open; it breathed hard, and a convulsive motion agitated its limbs, . . . I rushed out of the room."

Figure 2.1 *Frankenstein*, 1831 edition, reproduced from The Project Gutenberg

voice of the daemon himself, of his own accidental education when he overhears the conversations of cottagers alongside the hidden hovel that he occupies for some months. In some ways, these scenes (which are presented from the daemon's outsider viewpoint) have the feeling of being observed by a lonely child at the back of a classroom (or a modern child watching TV, Zoom schooling, or doomscrolling during pandemic times). Indeed, as the daemon's self-education proceeds and he observes the cottagers' friendships, courtships, and socioeconomic situation, the undead daemon comes to an awareness of his own identity (and displacement) in the human scheme:

> And what was I? Of my creation and creator I was absolutely ignorant; but I knew that I possessed no money, no friends, no kind of property. I was, besides, endowed with a figure hideously deformed and loathsome; I was not even of the same nature as man. I was more agile than they, and could subsist upon coarser diet; I bore the extremes of heat and cold with less injury to my frame; my stature far exceeded their's. When I looked around, I saw and heard none like me. Was I then a monster, a blot upon the earth, from which all men fled, and whom all men disowned? (87)

The daemon was, in essence, an enhanced human: a prototype of the *transhuman* being that overcomes human limitations and extends familiar powers. Transhumanism can be seen as a stance, already observable in Mary Shelley's *Frankenstein* and developing in both modern culture and its literary figurations, that affirms the radical transformation of a human being's biological capacities and social conditions by means of technologies. According to the World Transhumanist Association (WTA), the term "transhumanism" – an abbreviation for a "transitional human" – embraces neither the determined "destiny" of a single creator, such as Frankenstein, nor that of the monstrous, transhuman creation (whose future remains unknown: a singularity that cannot be foretold). Where Mary Shelley focuses her narrative on the personal, unrealized futures of Victor Frankenstein and his displaced, daemon offspring, since the 1990s there have emerged a number of organizations, such as the WTA, that speak for a larger transhumanist future, an "intellectual and cultural movement that affirms the possibility and desirability of fundamentally improving the human condition through applied reason, especially by developing and making widely available technologies to eliminate aging and to greatly enhance human intellectual, physical, and psychological capacities" (Humanity+, cited in Ranisch and Lorenz Sorgner, 2014). What was still imaginable, in Mary Shelley's time, as a personal exploit (supported by the young Frankenstein's scientific education), is now seen as a destiny for humankind more generally. "In this regard," write Robert Ranisch and Stefan Lorenz Sorgner, transhumanism can be understood as "a contemporary renewal of humanism. It embraces and eventually amplifies central aspects of secular and Enlightenment humanist thought, such as belief in reason, individualism, science, progress, as well as self-perfection or cultivation" (8).

For such a movement to take hold, not just for an individual genius inventor such as Victor Frankenstein but for an extended social network, a new, electrified *medium* needed to be in place: one that is itself connected to the life-giving powers and monstrous agency of the material world. The media that we now consult continually are less individualized than the printed, codex book: not so clearly separated from the living embodiments, communicative linkages, and interactions that are now forming, and continually reforming all around us. As we can see (in the text box: "Huxley's Transhumanism and Teilard's *Phenomenon of Man*"), the transhumanist movement was already named in the early 1950s; but only when the internet established a broader worldwide connectivity could transhumanism as a movement gain momentum.

Huxley's Transhumanism and Teilard's *Phenomenon of Man*

> The human species can, if it wishes, transcend itself – not just sporadically, an individual here in one way, an individual there in another way, but in its entirety, as humanity. We need a name for this new belief. Perhaps transhumanism will serve: man remaining man, but transcending himself, by realizing new possibilities of and for his human nature. "I believe in transhumanism": once there are enough people who can truly say that, the human species will be on the threshold of a new kind of existence, as different from ours as ours is from that of Peking man. It will at last be consciously fulfilling its real destiny. (Julian Huxley 1957, 17)

Huxley, grandson of Charles Darwin's "bulldog," Thomas Henry Huxley (1825–95), is well positioned to assert a transhuman lineage of empowerment across generations. We can be less confident, however that our present embrace of a technologically enhanced "human nature" will enact an evolutionary jump in our own time. It is one thing to explore the transition over two or three million years from ape to humankind, with "Peking man" as an (assumed) intermediary. It is quite another to showcase our own "consciously" devised technologies, with their ongoing destruction of thousands of the world's animal and plant species, as the "real destiny" of *Homo Erectus*. Huxley's reductive analogy typifies transhumanist thought at the start of its naming and development.

Another near contemporary of Julian Huxley is worth further investigation regarding the history of transhumanism: the Jesuit priest and paleontologist Pierre Teilhard de Chardin (1881–1955). Huxley, who contributed a forward to Teilhard's posthumously published *The Phenomenon of Man* (1955), is not the first to consider "trans-human" conditions. Teilhard referred to similar concepts before Huxley. In an unpublished essay from February 1949 entitled "The Essence of the Democratic Idea," Teilhard suggests some biological definitions of central democratic concepts. As for "liberty," he states that this is "the chance offered to every man ... of 'transhumanising' himself by developing his potentialities to the fullest extent" (Teilhard de Chardin 1964 [1949], 241).

With this material, mediated framework in mind, we will now consider Shelley Jackson's digital hypertext rewriting of *Frankenstein*, published by Eastgate in 1995. More than a retelling or updating of Mary Shelley's text, the *relocation* of Shelley Jackson's narrative in an electronic network can be regarded as a rewriting of our individual humanity and of the institutional *humanities* that have facilitated the long-standing literary careers of both Shelley Jackson and Mary Shelley.

Rewriting Humanity; Or: Who Is Who?

A Shaggy Man in the Land of Oz

In "*The Wizard of Oz*: A Parable on Populism" (1964), Henry Littlefield, a high-school teacher, interpreted L. Frank Baum's novel as an extended metaphor for American politics in the 1890s. He argued that Baum, who in 1888 moved to the territory that became South Dakota, sympathised with the plight of the region's farmers and was influenced by the views of a man with whom he sang in a barbershop quartet, who later became a senator for the Populist Party. Littlefield saw *The Wizard of Oz* as an allegory of the populist movement of the late nineteenth century, which wanted to use silver as well as gold to back the dollar, thus increasing the money supply. The resulting inflation would put "free silver" in the hands of the "common man," like the Dakota farmer. In this reading, Dorothy represents the Kansas agronomists, while her silver shoes (they aren't red in the book) and the yellow brick road signify America's bimetal destiny.

Niela Orr, "Brand New Day," *The London Review of Books*, March 18, 2021.

Baum himself, "the Historian" in the Prologue to *The Patchwork Girl of Oz*, indicates the story's origin in a request, from Dorothy herself, for access to the wizard's medium of wireless telegraphy: "Dorothy heard that the Historian wanted to speak with her, and there was a Shaggy Man in the Land of Oz who knew how to telegraph a wireless reply. The result was that the Historian begged so hard to be told the latest news of Oz, so that he could write it down for the children to read, that Dorothy asked permission of Ozma and Ozma graciously consented." (Frank Baum, Prologue to *The Patchwork Girl of Oz*. Project Gutenberg)

We have heard, quite often in the above explications, references to the Frankenstein monster "himself," to the author Mary Shelley herself, and (in the text box) to the fiction and film character Dorothy herself, a dreamy young girl from the back woods of Middle America who wishes to speak with the popular author, Baum himself, who made her. Amidst all the miscellaneous and

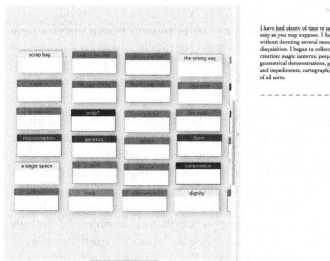

scrap bag

I have had plenty of time to make the girl. Yet the task was not so easy as you may suppose. I found that I could not compose a female without devoting several months to profound study and laborious disquisition. I began to collect the materials necessary for my new creation: magic lanterns, peep show boxes, waking dreams, geometrical demonstrations, philosophical doctrines, fortifications and impediments, cartographic surveys, and engineering machines of all sorts.

Figure 2.2 Screenshot from *Patchwork Girl*, showing links to various lexia and the text for the one titled "scrap bag."

patchwork, real and imagined but always other-than-human self-creations, there appears a continuing modernist anxiety about authorship; about self-presentation in narrative forms and imaginary characters; about outlines and limitations of an extended, repurposed human agency. Even as Dr. Frankenstein runs away from his creation the moment the daemon shows signs of life (see Figure 2.1), we are immersed in patterns of disappearance, a repression or relocation of the creative, authorial self in imaginative literature, film, and arts. I will close this chapter with a discussion of a digital rewriting of both *Frankenstein* and the Oz narrative; namely: *Patchwork Girl; or A Modern Monster by Mary/Shelley and Herself* (published by Eastgate, 1995).

Shelley Jackson's "irreverent rewriting of Mary Shelley's *Frankenstein*" is well described by Laura Shackelford in her study *Tactics of the Human: Experimental Technics in American Fiction* (2014). The experiment undertaken by Jackson with digital hypertext "features the female monster destroyed by Victor Frankenstein as its protagonist," a creative extension of "Mary Shelley's literary print classic to this digital context":

> Using Storyspace, the early digital hypertext authoring program
> designed by Mark Bernstein, Jay Bolter, and Michael Joyce, to create this
> stand-alone digital hypertext, *Patchwork Girl* reassembles the female
> monster (last seen in pieces at the bottom of a lake in Mary Shelley's

> novel) in five different sections. Each section is composed of *lexia*, boxes of text connected by multiple links. As the patchwork girl explains, "My birth takes place more than once. In the plea of a bygone monster; from a muddy hole by corpse light; under the needle; and under the pen; or it took place not at all." The five sections of the work – "story," "graveyard," "crazy quilt," "journal," and "body of text" – correspond to these separate births. (Shackelford, *Tactics*, 80)

Jackson's patchwork girl is "literally an assemblage, her multiple and multi-plicit subjectivities, as illustrated in each section, are inextricable from the technics that motivate and materialize specific kinds of legibility, illegibility, intersubjectivity, and desire" (*Tactics* 81). The carrying over of Mary Shelley's theme (and her person) into a literary medium that has itself been electrified enables readers to enter both the author's text and person imaginatively, and actively – by selecting pathways and sequences that will be ordered differently on each reading. In this sense, as author Shelley Jackson (herself) notes in her keynote presentation for the *Transformations of the Book* conference held in November 1997 at MIT, the identity of a literary author, reader, and work are each, in their separate ways, patchworks:

> The body is a patchwork, though the stitches might not show. It's run by committee, a loose aggregate of entities we can't really call human, but which have what look like lives of a sort; though they lack the brains to nominate themselves part of the animal kingdom, yet they are certainly not what we think of as objects, nor are they simple appendages, directly responsible to the conscious brain. (*Stitch Bitch: the patchwork girl*, https://web.mit.edu/m-i-t/articles/jackson.html)

With this move, from authorial work to material text and then on to the body's (and brain's) equally patchwork (self) constructions, Shelley Jackson carries her literary experiment beyond the "rudimentary" technological reconstructions of human consciousness. These are not dismissed by Jackson, nor are they subordinated to an all-controlling, higher conscious-ness. Rather, the objective, transhumanist experiments are extended into a larger, nonconscious, and ever-changing cognitive sphere. Jackson asks us, for example, to consider the human body's own operations that might not count as "thinking exactly," but which act as "more than objects":

> Watch white blood cells surround an invader, watch a cell divide. What we see is not thinking exactly, but it is "intelligent," or at least ordered, responsive, purposeful. We can feel a sort of camaraderie with those rudimentary machæinic minds, but not identity. Nor, if we could watch a spark dart across a synaptic gap in a brain, would we cry out "Mom!" or

"Uncle Toby!", for thinking is conducted by entities we don't know, wouldn't recognize on the street. Call them yours if you want, but puff and blow all you like, you cannot make them stop their work one second to salute you.

The body is not even experienced as whole. We never see it all, we can't feel our liver working or messages shuttling through our spine. We patch a phantom body together out of a cacophony of sense impressions, bright and partial views. (*Stitch Bitch: the patchwork girl*, https://web .mit.edu/m-i-t/articles/jackson.html)

Thinking for Jackson, as for feminist theorists of posthumanism such as Jane Bennett, Francesca Ferrando, and Rosi Braidotti, has never been (in Braidotti's words) "the exclusive prerogative of Man/Anthropos, but is rather distributed across a wide spectrum of human and nonhuman entities" ("Preface" to Ferrando, *Philosophical Posthumanism*, 2019, xi). Indeed, one finds in current literary scholarship not just a new set of topics and themes but instead an emerging, multimedial, and expansive *cognitive* framework for literary expression. To write literature, in such an unprecedented and never fully knowable (or controllable) material environment, is no longer so much a task taken on by an isolated author. It is rather, to cite Braidotti again, a "collective task of constructing new subjects of knowledge, through immanent assemblages or transversal alliances between multiple actors" ("A Theoretical Framework for the Critical Posthumanities," 6). A posthumanist literature is likely to be as much "cartographic" as language based (ibid., 6), mapped as much as narrated, symbolized as much as imagined. Rather than focusing too much on one's own – or a fictional character's – personal experience that a swath of readers can identify with, we are brought into a more stringent appraisal of "power relations operational and immanent to the production and circulation of knowledge" (ibid., 2).

What Is an Assemblage?

Assemblages are ad hoc groupings of diverse elements, of vibrant materials of all sorts. Assemblages are living, throbbing confederations that are able to function despite the persistent presence of energies that confound them from within . . . Assemblages are not governed by any central head: no one materiality or type of material has sufficient competence to determine consistently the trajectory or impact of the group. The effects generated by an assemblage are, rather, emergent properties, emergent in that their ability to make something happen (a newly inflected materialism, a blackout, a hurricane, a war on terror) is distinct from the sum of the vital force of each materiality considered alone. Each member and proto-member of the

> assemblage has a certain vital force, but there is also an effectivity proper to the grouping as such: an agency *of* the assemblage ... an assemblage is never a stolid block but an open-ended collective, a "non-totalizable sum." (Jane Bennett, *Vibrant Matter: A Political Ecology of Things*, 23–4)
>
> The term, "non-totalizable sum," Bennett notes, is taken from Patrick Hayden's essay "Gilles Deleuze and Naturalism" (1997). For Deleuze, and for the vitalist philosopher Henri Bergson, too, Bennett writes: "the universe is a non-totalizable sum," a "whole that is not given" because its evolution produces *new* members and thus an ever-changing array of effects. The world is "an indivisible process" of movement and creation, where there is "radical contingency in process, incommensurability between what goes before and what follows – in short, duration." (See Bergson, 1998, 29n1 and chapter 4 of *Vibrant Matter*.)

Not least among such embodied and relational entities is the stitching together of *literary texts* that, as we have seen, was no less important to Mary Shelley's *Frankenstein* than it would be to this novel's recrafting by Shelley Jackson, and its later recasting in 2019 by Jeanette Winterson in the novel *Frankissstein*: a work that will be addressed in Chapter 6, along with a selection of other *intertexts* that have emerged in the centuries after Mary Shelley's work. And by thus thinking creatively about the work of our predecessors, we stand a better chance of knowing what we ourselves might become. Literary authorship, in Jackson's rewriting, is no longer a modest effort to enter a tradition so much as it is a way for an aspiring author to "leapfrog out of the muddle of my several births to the day I parted for the last time with the author of my being, and set out to write my own destiny." For Jackson's patchwork girl, no less than Mary Shelley or her fictional protagonist Victor Frankenstein, that destiny was shaped in no small part, by a modest bibliography whose texts are available for citation, and (cognitive) suture.

We see this happening in hypertextual, electronic literature such as *Patchwork Girl*. There, we find a "phantom body," not a horrendous being like the Frankenstein daemon assembled out of revitalized body parts. The hypertext is literally a patchwork, as much a one as the imagined, phantom body: "In this same way she was beautiful," to cite the lexia, *she stood* (reproduced in this chapter, Figure 2.3). The predominance of unknown, never fully conscious activities in a human mind and body is consistent with the work's own electronic formatting. The denatured colorings and unpredictable shades in the Frankenstein daemon are embraced by Jackson as an exuberant mode of being that might take us into the realm of the "not yet." The "destiny" that is discoverable in past literatures can arise only after they are recast in present

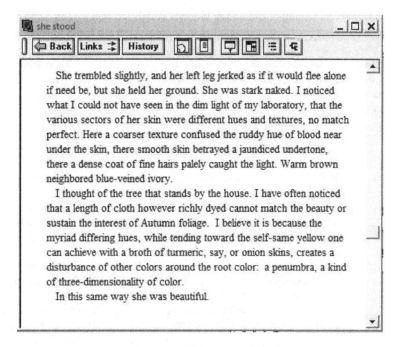

Figure 2.3 Screenshot "she stood" from *Patchwork Girl.*

patchworks. The particular patchwork girl that Jackson describes in her MIT lecture is not so much a character as a collection of "scraps floating loose, bits we can't control or don't want to perceive," "clusters of intensities," and "composites" (*Stitch Bitch: the patchwork girl*). These terms apply equally in Jackson's digital writing to her own textual fragments as to the human bodies and subjectivities that are enacted in the text.

Posthuman Identity in the Gaps Between

It is, of course, a fortunate coincidence that Jackson's first name is Shelley, the last name of the author of *Frankenstein* (1818), one of the novels Jackson rewrites in her text; the other being L. F. Baum's *The Patchwork Girl of Oz* (1913). Along with excerpts from the fictitious diary of Mary Shelley and a number of other literary texts, images, and voices, Jackson sews a quilt that becomes the textual body of the monster.

But the monster's body is also produced in the reading act and this is why Patchwork Girl can say "My birth takes place more than once." On the material level, the plural intercorporeality of the monster is reflected in being composed of body parts pertaining once to other women, yet also to two men as well as to animals. I read her hybrid existence as an alternative to the humanist idea of the unitary and autonomous subject. Patchwork Girl herself postulates that identity is to be found between socially fixed, diametrically opposed poles like man/woman, human/animal, black/white, normal/abnormal, and so forth: "I am most myself in the gaps between my parts." In the space between, we encounter the scars of the stitches, the dotted line (——), which connects yet also severs bodies from each other. It is the "best line" for Jackson:

> It indicates a difference without cleaving apart for good what it distinguishes.
>   It is a permeable membrane: some substance necessary to both can pass from one side to the other.
>   It is a potential line, an indication of the way out of two dimensions (fold along dotted line): In three dimensions what is separate can be brought together without ripping apart what is already joined, the two sides of a page flow moebiusly into one another. ...
>   Because it is a potential line, it folds/unfolds the imagination in one move. It suggests action (fold here), a chance at change, yet it acknowledges the viewer's freedom to do nothing but imagine.
>   The reference to the Moebius strip is significant here: like the ants on M. C. Escher's picture *Möbius-Band II*, human beings walk through life by crossing boundaries between inside and outside, self and other. In the process, the identity of neither remains the same. Most important of all, the dotted line incites the imagination. The reader or literary critic is reminded that we have the freedom to imagineer posthumanity in our own terms – nothing less is at stake.
>   Manuela Rossini, "Figurations of Posthumanity in Contemporary Science/Fiction – all too Human(ist)?" Published in "Literature and Science," *Revista canaria de estudios ingleses* (No.50 April 2005).

The stories by Mary Shelley and L. Frank Baum that inspired Jackson are not only rewritten. They are meant to be reassembled *by the reader* of Jackson's hypertext. Each narrative thread will be read differently by each one, at each reading. *Patchwork Girl* is itself stable and available for rereading (with uncounted variations) within its original Storyspace medium. The original disk version has also been preserved, in audio and visual recordings of readers (including Jackson herself) as they work their way through the text in Dene Grigar's and John Barber's Electronic Literature Lab in Vancouver, Oregon – thus turning reading into a performance in its own right, and an extension of the technical affordances (and limitations) that the digital medium and Storyspace platform facilitate. Yearly Electronic Literature Lab (ELL) gatherings of

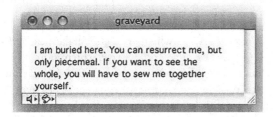

Figure 2.4 Screenshot "graveyard" from *Patchwork Girl*

the Digital Humanities Study Initiative generate new readings by invited participants, from advanced undergrads to established scholars. The publication history of Jackson's work thus itself enacts a still-in-progress reconfiguration of the academic humanities in our own digital era.

All Coming from Female Imagination

Perhaps the true paradigmatic work of the era, Shelley Jackson's elegantly designed, beautifully composed Patchwork Girl offers the patient reader, if there are any left in the world, just such an experience of losing oneself to a text, for as one plunges deeper and deeper into one's own personal exploration of the relations here of creator to created and of body to text, one never fails to be rewarded and so is drawn ever deeper, until clicking the mouse is as unconscious an act as turning a page, and much less constraining, more compelling.

Robert Coover
Eastgate: Patchwork Girl

Like the cognitive assemblages Jackson identifies in bodies, brains, and other interacting elements, her hypertext is also self-contained, multiplicitous in its operations, recurrent in its thematics, and reproduceable. But every reading, by each reader, will be assembled differently. The reading of *Patchwork Girl*, in this sense is arguably a continual act of *recrafting*, even as Mary Shelley's own work (as we remarked in the lead-up to this chapter) is a rewriting of earlier works by Coleridge, Wordsworth, Milton, Dante, and many others. Alexandra Glavanakova-Yaneva, in her essay for the *Journal of American Studies of Turkey*, points out how *Patchwork Girl*, like other strains in postmodern literature, doesn't just include "numerous intertextual references," but also revises "whole classical texts." Shelley Jackson follows this tradition, and among her more recent and familiar precursors are women rewriting men:

> Jane Smiley's *A Thousand Acres*, which "revisits" Shakespeare's *King Lear*; Joyce Carol Oates' *The Turn of the Screw*, which indirectly comments on Henry James' work; Kathy Acker's *Don Quixote* and her *Great Expectations* "revising" in significant ways some passages from Charles Dickens' novel. Shelley Jackson's cyberfiction is inspired by a male text, L. Frank Baum's *Patchwork Girl of Oz*, and a female text, Mary Shelley's *Frankenstein*. (Glavanakova-Yaneva, 2003, 66)

In the course of her analysis, Glavanakova-Yaneva mentions how "the monster in Jackson's 'recrafting' of the story becomes Mary Shelley's lover and then travels to America, where it goes through numerous adventures and acquires the name Patchwork Girl" (67). Generally, the narrative reflects issues of female creativity and sexuality – precisely what went missing in Victor Frankenstein's masculinist replacement of female procreativity with a sequence of technological enhancements. In much the same way as Mary Shelley describes Frankenstein's daemon, Jackson describes the patchwork

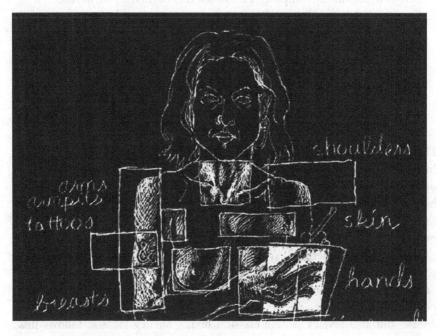

Figure 2.5 Screenshot from *Patchwork Girl*.

girl: "the various sectors of her skin were different hues and textures, no match perfect ... arm brown neighbored blue veined ivory." And we have noted, with Laura Shackelford, how "the patchwork girl's failed aspirations to an implicitly white femininity, modeled on Mary Shelley, foreground, once again, the multiplicity of the feminine" (*Tactics*, 86). It is precisely this acceptance, and celebration, of female imagination that distinguishes a literary posthumanism; which is to say: an aesthetic that patiently explores rather than transcends powers that inhere in nature – powers, and unforeseen assemblages that we humans would do well to let be.

The conversations engendered by the monster's recrafting in Jackson's hypertext are at once intergenerational – within the strictures of living traditions – and transdisciplinary. We've seen something similar in the *Frankenstein* backstory, which started with Mary listening in on the mansplaining of Percy Bysshe Shelley and Lord Byron, and then going on to write the novel. The resulting posthumanist explorations not only transport us to distant and unfamiliar landscapes (such as the early-nineteenth-century arctic regions never before visited by humans, where Frankenstein's daemon absconds, after his creator's death at the end of Mary Shelley's novel). Nor will these later digital works (from the 1990s on) limit themselves to individual human characters, and actors. Shelley Jackson often uses the word "composite" to describe her hypertextual practice. The word also resides in "composition," a more authorial activity that Jackson hands over (in part) to her reader. This dispersal of authorship, and the creation of an active, and activated audience also carries a compositional context into the machinery of her argument. (An argument that conforms to the Compositionist Manifesto that Bruno Latour advanced two decades later: see the text boxes on "Posthuman Prospects and New Materialisms" in the Introduction and "Frankissstein" in Chapter 6.)

Traditionally, readers of print fictions are not given a choice in ordering the narrative elements. By contrast, readers of born-digital, hypertext fictions become coauthors and compositionists, in a way that Jackson describes as "problematic" (but whose "problems" are the lifeblood of a literary composition):

> In a text like this [*Patchwork Girl*], gaps are problematic. The mind becomes self-conscious, falters, forgets its way, might choose another way, might opt out of this text into another, might "lose the thread of the argument," might be unconvinced. Transitional phrases smooth over gaps, even huge logical gaps, suppress contradiction, whisk you past options. I noticed in school that I could argue anything. I might find myself delivering conclusions I disagreed with because I had built such an irresistible machine for persuasion. The trick was to allow the reader only one way to read it, and to make the going smooth. To seal the

machine, keep out grit. Such a machine can only do two things: convince or break down. Thought is made of leaps, but rhetoric conducts you across the gaps by a cute cobbled path, full of grey phrases like "therefore," "extrapolating from," "as we have seen," giving you something to look at so you don't look at the nothing on the side of the path. Hypertext leaves you naked with yourself in every leap, it shows you the gamble thought is, and it invites criticism, refusal even. Books are designed to keep you reading the next thing until the end, but hypertext invites choice. Writing hypertext, you've got to accept the possibility your reader will just stop reading. Why not? The choice to go do something else might be the best outcome of a text. Who wants a numb reader/reader-by-numbers anyway? Go write your own text. Go paint a mural. You must change your life. I want piratical readers, plagiarists and opportunists, who take what they want from my ideas and knot it into their own arguments. Or even their own novels. From which, possibly, I'll steal it back.

The "choice" invited at every turn in Jackson's hypertext; the "gaps" it leaves the reader to fill in – these are all ways of defamiliarizing the bookish habits we may have learned in school (those of us who are Jackson's age and older). For

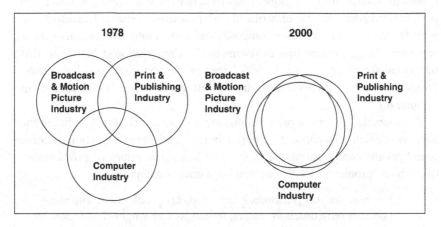

Figure 2.6 Possibly the best-known affirmation, by Nicholas Negroponte, of the sidelining of books and films by the computer industry. Creative Commons – Attribution 4.0 International. Stewart Brand's book "The Media Lab: Inventing the Future at MIT" includes this graphic and a caption: "With these diagrams, Negroponte made the case for the creation of a Media Laboratory at MIT."
Credit: MIT Media Lab. Nicholas Negroponte.

such discrepancies to work, individualized conceptions of both authorship and readerly engagement need to be rethought. We can see here, in the Negroponte Screenshot (Figure 2.6), how much of our communication via print and publishing, radio broadcast and filmic industry, has been taken over by digital media. In the next chapter, the very notion of what constitutes a literary *audience* will be explored, with particular attention being given to the ways that our media are not just conveying texts (and contexts), but are also acting on what we are thinking, saying, and writing. More than anything, media themselves are changing our lives. As our reading and writing is now done nearly exclusively online (even when we are reading and writing print texts like this one), our citations, our circulation of texts and documents, and our literary communities have undergone a deep reformation. And just as the mass availability of newspapers and magazines (for example) enabled the emergence of both a mass audience and a shared sense of what counts as *realism*, the digital reconstruction of our present collectivities (not least those in the academic humanities) need to be taken into consideration.

Chapter 3

Postperiodization

The term and concept "posthumanism," emerging as it did in the late twentieth century, differs from earlier literary and historical periodizations. In part, that's because our media of communication, which expanded exponentially around this time, are themselves operating at scales that exceed human understanding. Like photography, film, and video before them, but on a different scale, digital media situate what we think and say within communicative networks that are larger than consciousness. Conveying messages and accessing information over distances and at speeds that are imperceptible to our senses, our media are also *acting on* what we are thinking, saying, and writing; scouring our words for patterns and preferences in ways few of us notice when we are posting on Facebook, Twitter, and Instagram or sending emails and writing blog posts. They are also collecting lists and recommendations for things we might listen to, view, or read based on what we (or those who share our profile) have opened and skimmed. As twenty-first-century British novelist Tom McCarthy has noted, platforms are being used "to help companies achieve deeper penetration of their markets, to advise cities how to brand and rebrand themselves, and governments how better to narrate their policy agendas." And note that twist at the end: "to narrate." McCarthy is here relocating narration away from his own anthropological or literary practices. Indeed, the acceleration of corporate capitalism via technological means and its impact on everything we say or do is now forcing writers "to rethink their whole role and function, to remap their entire universe" (*The Guardian*, March 7, 2015, "The death of writing – if James Joyce was alive today he'd be working for Google").

Re-imagining Community: From Big Brother to Big Data

This chapter aims to identify, in the first instance, some of the undesirable effects of living, in McCarthy's words, "in the shadow of omnipresent and omniscient data that makes a mockery of any notion that the writer may have something to inform us" (*Guardian*, ibid.). The repurposing of human thought and sensual affect by "a technologically underwritten capitalism that both writes and reads itself" – this describes one universalizing impulse, and a drastic reduction of subjective interchange, that is better placed under the heading "transhumanism." A furthering of programable devices that are more controlling than they are communicative or interactive, the transhuman relies on narratives that are already in place, extending, strengthening, and repurposing human (and humanist) concepts that are well established; but not opening themselves to ways that our posthuman communities might be reimagined and made better.

By contrast with such transhuman repurposing, *posthumanist* scholarship and literature understands that big data, for its part, really isn't that big: As Nick Montfort, an experimental author of many born-digital literary works, has noted in a tweet of his own (dated 2014–09–16 14:16:16 +0000):

> "Big data." It's like calling the Model T not a "horseless carriage," but a "fast car."

What might seem massive and "omniscient" to the average internet user, or what did in 2014 when Montfort's tweet was sent, is in fact quite modest in comparison with the remapping that is going on behind closed doors and moving paywalls. And few of us in the academic humanities have open access to the stores of textual, transactional, and sensory data that corporations have amassed: these – the Gettys, Alamys, and Associated Presses – are the truly immense reservoirs, controlling about 90 percent of image licensing at the time of this writing. But we are still awaiting the appearance of our age's George Orwell, who will project the social and cultural impact not of an already automatized Big Brother, but instead an assemblage of Big Data that cannot be so easily humanized or parodied. Even if our literature, and our scholarship, offer a realistic glimpse or visualization of what is being stored up, the millions, the billions, and the trillions remain abstract and weirdly disembodied. Once they are designated and accounted for as data, they are knowable at best in some other, mappable, and more easily visualizable schema. That is to say, these assemblages will never have the cognitive capacity and felt presence of the hundred or so billions of neurons in an embodied human brain, for example, that respond continually, each time an electric current touches any one of them.

Musil's *Man Without Qualities*

He was standing behind a window gazing through the fine green filter of the garden air to the brownish street beyond, and for the last ten minutes he had been ticking off on his stopwatch the passing cars, trucks, trolleys, and pedestrians, whose faces were washed out by the distance, timing everything whirling past that he could catch in the net of his eye. He was gauging their speeds, their angles, all the living forces of mass hurtling past that drew the eye to follow them like lightning, holding on, letting go, forcing the attention for a split second to resist, to snap, to leap in pursuit of the next term... then, after doing the arithmetic in his head for a while, he slipped the watch back into his pocket with a laugh and decided to stop all this nonsense.

If all those leaps of attention, flexings of eye muscles, fluctuations of the psyche, if all the effort it takes for a man just to hold himself upright within the flow of traffic on a busy street could be measured, he thought – as he toyed with calculating the incalculable – the grand total would surely dwarf the energy needed by Atlas to hold up the world, and one could then estimate the enormous undertaking it is nowadays merely to be a person who does nothing at all. At the moment the man without qualities was just such a person. (Robert Musil, *The Man Without Qualities*, 6–7)

In this passage from Part I, "A Sort of Introduction" to the unfinished, two-volume novel published from his posthumous papers in 1951, Musil was well in advance of the handheld apps for counting steps and calories. But he nonetheless fully understood the decline in human agential powers that such interests inaugurate. Turning thoughtless everyday objects and activities into big data is a primary occupation of Musil's fiction without narrative: much as his man without qualities might have preferred "a solid middle-class life," Musil recognizes that the modernist future was taking him – and society at large – "in another direction." Musil asks whether it is not "precisely the philistine who is alive with intimations of a colossally new, collective, ant-like heroism? It will be called a rationalized heroism, and greatly admired." Few works have so successfully displaced the humanist "Man" with a new, nonagential (and collective) being. In place of narrative with a promise of shared destiny such as we find in Percy and Mary Shelley's romanticism, in Musil's modernity we are given a distinctly modernist, technocentered interest in "the sum total of everybody's little everyday efforts," which "when added together, doubtless releases far more energy into the world than do rare heroic feats. This total makes even the single act of heroic feat look positively minuscule, like a grain of sand on a mountaintop with a megalomaniacal sense of its own importance" (*The Man Without Qualities*, 7).

Musil, who was trained as an engineer but wrote his doctoral dissertation on the Austrian physicist and philosopher Earnest Mach, features in Alan Thiher's book, *Fiction Rivals Science* (2001). There, Musil's critique of Mach's positivism is clearly carried into the concern with writing a fiction about a man who aspires to do "nothing at all": a Bartleby-like rejection that extends to *narration*. (See Chapter 5: "Ah Bartelby, Ah Humanities! From Transcendentalism to Posthumanism.") To toy with the thought of "calculating the incalculable" is consistent with a commitment, from the Romantic era to Musil's Modernism, to bring "qualities already known" about the external world into the realm of the "imagination" that transforms these empirical observations – and the world with it – into meaningful expressions of human spirit, abandonments, and counternarratives unlike those found in realist fiction.

The way that materials and masses are embedded, in us and in nature, will be explored in a selection of posthumanist narratives (and theoretical explications) that are not nearly so prevalent but are more far-ranging than conventional, so-called realist fictions. The reductive outcomes of our digital culture are in many ways consistent with our "imagined communities" (Benedict Anderson 1983) that turn vast geographic regions, whose people and landscapes could never be known *in toto* by any one citizen, into a mappable, graspable entity; one that can then generate systems of commitment and belief. While the present, digitized versions of everyday interaction tend to ignore national boundaries, they too require narratives – other ones, different from the conventional fallbacks and, to again cite Tom McCarthy: "naive escapist fantasy (of individual self-expression, or the transcendent human spirit, or art-as-redemption and so forth – in other words, the very fantasies to which a conservative view of fiction still clings)" (*The Guardian*, 2015).

Object-Oriented Ontologies (Musil to Vermeulen)

Friedrich's wanderer (Figure 3.1) is both humbled by the expansive indifference of nature and empowered by his ability to conceptualize and represent it. It is this romantic, transcendental orientation that is replaced, in Musil's modernist *Man Without Qualities*, by grains of sand and data. To stand over, literally, and transcend the natural world becomes, in Musil, "megalomaniacal" (7). We are instead being brought toward something closer to the flattened, "object-oriented" ontology that would emerge in the twenty-first-century writings of Bruno Latour, Graham Harmon, Ian Bogost, and Timothy Morton, among others: a posthumanist subjectivity more attuned to bodily extensions through new media technologies and other "non-human agencies."

Shifting away from the fog of human emotion to a more object-oriented collection of "posthuman affects," Pieter Vermeulen deflects the traditional structure of the sublime, which now

> describes a feeling of terror incited by the spectacle of something that appears to overwhelm human capacities; in a compensatory move, this negative sensation is supplemented by the pleasurable realization that the apparent threat to human sovereignty has not managed to overwhelm it and has therefore strengthened the subject's sense of dignity. While seeming to touch on the limits of the human, the sublime is in fact a tremendous ego booster. Read less generously, it appears as a strategy that only cultivates liminal experiences in order to triumphantly reaffirm the human. (Vermeulen, 2014, "Posthuman Affect," 123–4)

Figure 3.1 Caspar David Friedrich, 1818, *Wanderer Above the Sea of Fog*
(Photo by Deagostini/Getty Images. Hamburger Kunsthalle)

What it might take for researchers and creative writers to recognize and
reinforce alternative, posthuman strains in contemporary literature is an
acceptance of the idea that periodization itself has run its course. Terms
such as "twentieth-century modernism" or "nineteenth-century romanticism" can now be seen to have been part of an ongoing, *humanist* disposition:
part of a longue durée that might contain many events or periods while
nonetheless having its own historical through-line. With humanism in particular and the coterminous development of humanities in universities,
authors and readers who participated in the literary and historical sphere
could develop over centuries, not just years or decades, a solid sense of

interaction and intersubjectivity – the feeling that what we say, and what we write, has a chance of being *remembered*; that certain selective parts of our works and days can be cognized by individual readers, considered by scholars, recast by potential authors, and carried over with variations from generation to generation. The information we possess and communications we receive instantaneously, in our present digital era, no longer need to be inscribed in books; the information and lifeways are there as long as the electricity flows, but we have yet to reproduce anything approaching the sustained memory – and long-term subjective interactivity – of print publication.

The Longue Durée of Posthuman Prospects

McHale himself has explored the longue durée concept in connection with its advocacy by the Annales group in his *Companion to Twentieth-Century Literatures in English* (2006), coedited with Randall Stevenson. The collection's publisher, Edinburgh University Press, indicates how the chapter authors self-consciously evade periodization: "Far from the usual forced march through the decades, genres, and national literatures, this reference work for the new century cuts across familiar categories, focusing instead on literary 'hot spots.'"

My own contribution to McHale's collection is titled "1991: The Web, Network Fictions" (Tabbi, 2006).

Arguably, over the past half millennium, printed inscriptions promised to preserve our present interactions with others who could focus on the same written archive, into a compelling and continuing bibliographic future. This imagined future, however, is yet another unsupportable narrative in an age like ours "in which omnipresent threats of imminent extinction are also part of the background noise – nuclear annihilation, terrorism, climate change. So we can be blinkered when it comes to tectonic cultural shifts" (Will Self, *The Guardian*, May 2, 2014).

This prognosis is from another contemporary British novelist, Will Self, whose work appears, like Tom McCarthy's, Lars Iyer's, and Claire-Louise Bennett's, in the aftermath of British and American empires that also, in their own ways, supported and were sustained by a humanist and book-oriented ideology. What these writers share is a recognition that conventional, humanist explanations are not enough to assure us that we are not chasing dreams (to paraphrase Italo Calvino, 1998, "Six Memos"); not when the continuation of our own species is now in question, like that of so many plant and animal species obliterated by our technologically empowered and overextended activity. We need to engage not just the pure products on display within our present digital sphere. They've gone crazier than early-twentieth-century poet and New Jersey physician William Carlos Williams could have imagined, and the products are no longer limited to this author's home country. What we need to engage, and Williams with his General Practitioner's knowledge and encyclopedic poetics can be cited as one primary example of this career-long engagement, are the scientific and material substrates that make such knowledge and "tectonic cultural shifts" possible, and possibly narratable. (See the text box on Wordsworth. "The pure products of America / go crazy" is a line from Williams's poem, "To Elsie," 1962.)

The World Is Too Much with Us

The world is too much with us; late and soon,
Getting and spending, we lay waste our powers; –
Little we see in Nature that is ours;
We have given our hearts away, a sordid boon!
This Sea that bares her bosom to the moon;
The winds that will be howling at all hours,
And are up-gathered now like sleeping flowers;
For this, for everything, we are out of tune;
It moves us not. Great God! I'd rather be
A Pagan suckled in a creed outworn;
So might I, standing on this pleasant lea,
Have glimpses that would make me less forlorn;
Have sight of Proteus rising from the sea;
Or hear old Triton blow his wreathèd horn.

William Wordsworth | Poetry Foundation

The transcendentalist writings of American authors such as Emerson, Thoreau, Melville, and Dickinson can be understood as extensions of human imagination into areas that had once been the realm of religion and philosophy. The waning of religion (and the contemporary rise of cities and mass literacies) set the stage for the romantic movement in Europe. But American writers took a somewhat different turn. The commercialized "world" that for Wordsworth (in England, 1802) was "too much with us" was experienced differently in America. We can observe, in American transcendentalism, a conception of *selfhood* determined not by social positions or cultural norms, but by our own independent powers of reason and rationality. In Ralph Waldo Emerson's reinvention of philosophy, for example, human "reason" is said to "prove its power to itself, over itself." As we shall see in the next chapter, Emerson's strange, oblique assertion that "self-reliance is God-reliance" is more about spiritual and conceptual realities, and not so much about self-realization through institutional, political, or economic means.

The rise of commercial culture in England during the First Industrial Revolution caused Wordsworth to lament how "Little we see in Nature that is ours." For him, a once-great deity is reduced to a mere outburst: "Great God! I'd rather be / A Pagan suckled in a creed outworn." The glimpses that would make him "less forlorn" are of deities that predate the humanist and Christian traditions; the "sight of Proteus rising from the sea" and the sound of "old Triton" blowing "his wreathèd horn": these have been taken on by Percy Bysshe and Mary Shelley in their Promethean poetry and fiction that we considered in Chapter 2. "This Sea that bares her bosom to the moon"; Wordsworth anticipates the woman at Key West who "sang beyond the genius of the sea," and thus personifies the power in nature, that is perpetually borne in us. (This is a line from a poem of 1935, "The Idea of Order at Key West" by Wallace Stevens | Poetry Foundation.) For all its lament, Wordsworth's romantic revival is still a humanization of nature. What he, the romantics, and the American transcendentalists could not have anticipated, however was a worldwide expansion of economic activity (and as-yet unimaginable despoliation) that would leave nothing in nature untouched by humans. Wordsworth, Percy Bysshe Shelly, and Mary Wollstonecraft Shelly could still imagine emerging technologies of the early nineteenth century as transformative or (in a Wordsworthian context) restorative. That was not so likely for writers ranging from the mid-nineteenth, early- and mid-twentieth centuries such as Emerson, Thoreau, Melville, Emily Dickinson, William Carlos Williams, and Wallace Stevens, all of whom were writing at a time when cities, plantations, military bases, and ports in the USA were emerging from an unexploited, vast expanse of natural resources (and seemingly unending supplies of indentured labor: European Immigrants in the North and African slaves in the South, and a prior decimation of native populations). For American authors at this transformative time (the late-romantic and modernist periods), the idea that our lifeways could be self-constructed took hold in a powerful way. With the passing of time, however, the exploitation of both human labor and natural resources appears to have reached its limits. As we now observe alterations in nature that could make our world uninhabitable, American writers are rethinking the limits of our own, newfound freedoms, and the limitations of humanist thought itself.

A Relocation of the Literary?

Tom McCarthy is quite explicit about a contemporary literary project that is not so much innovative as it is interactive and informed, allowing us to join in with the universalizing spirit of contemporary science and technology while at the same time resituating earlier, prehumanist forms: "On one side, scientific, evidence-based research; on the other, epic art" (*Guardian*). McCarthy's modern epic, no less than earlier achievements from Goethe to Garcia Marquez, runs against the minimalist textual tendencies in our informatic and data-driven culture, and instead embraces universalizing tendencies implicit in scientific discoveries – and ongoing conceptual disruptions – starting with Einstein, Bohr, and Heisenberg. It is no accident that one of the first literary scholars to announce the arrival of "posthumanism," N. Katherine Hayles, came to this recognition through analyses of experimental fictions of the postwar period, particularly those that engaged with science and technology. Ranging from *Ada* by Vladimir Nabokov to the maximalist fiction of Nabokov's undergrad student at Cornell, Thomas Pynchon, Hayles's *Cosmic Web* (1984) depicts the world – and the emerging world system – "as a mutually interactive whole, with each part connected to every other part by an underlying field" (from the pack cover copy for *The Cosmic Web* at the Cornell University Press). In the opening chapter of this *Introduction*, I have already approached such enactments of scientific field theory in the critical writing of Karen Barad, and we will have opportunities to observe a number of literary enactments of the field concept. These cross-disciplinary literary thought experiments may have been under-recognized, but they are consistent, as we will see in Chapter 8, with posthuman literary developments in Hayles's landmark study, *How We Became Posthuman: Virtual Bodies in Cybernetics, Literature, and Informatics* (1999).

In another, lesser-known but equally crucial professional turn, Hayles would help launch an underlying, interactive field specifically attuned to her own moment with a series of three seminars sponsored from 1994 to 2004 by the National Endowment for the Humanities in the USA. In these seminars, Hayles and more than thirty emerging scholars (myself among them) would explore instances of "electronic literature" or "born digital writing" whose works and self-descriptions integrated digital technologies in nontrivial ways. For a brief period of a decade or two (not more than that), the enabling platforms and programming for this set of nonlinear, interactive literary experiments were fully known and communicated to readers, not kept hidden through copyrighted programs or kept out of circulation behind for-profit subscription services. When such digital narratives reformed in the twenty-teens under the aegis of *Twine*, the interactions were more gamelike than narrative. Their open access, authentically interactive engagement of a geographically dispersed community is, for the most part, unconcerned with formulating movements or avant gardes: communities like these are more about professional interactivity that can make the thought and work of each participant known to others who are working similarly – but without committing any one participant to any given genre or period style. Dispersal is just as likely as interaction. The communities gathered, moreover, are no longer predominantly academic – not like those for first-generation hyper-text, though they might be said to resemble prototypal academic programs such as Creative Writing that are designed similarly by writers for writers: a cohort of watchers, listeners, and readers who are each creating works of their own. A cohort, and an engaged community: not so much of an audience or wide readership.

We can take as given that a scholarly publication like the present *Introduction to Literary Posthumanism* will do well to address a literary audience that is differently composed, more likely to be actively conversing with one another online, and expecting if not to converse with published authors (and publishers) directly, at least to find these personages, too, in designated forums discussing works they have in circulation. We will see in Chapter 6, for example, how Karl Ove Knausgaard (at the Norwegian Literature Festival in 2017) starts off a conversation with Claire-Louise Bennett by asking why it was so hard to find anything about her online. Tom McCarthy's appearances with philosopher Simon Critchley in the (more or less fictional, playfully philosophical) Necronautical Society brought in several authors for focused discussions in multiple venues of the contrarian aesthetic they were each exploring. McCarthy occupied the position of general secretary of the Society; Critchley, chief philosopher. We'll also be engaging, in Chapter 9, with various interactive digital works, like Eugenio Tisselli's "The Gate," that are designed to be read while gaming – in solitude, but also, occasionally at Gallery exhibitions and conference gatherings.

The International Necronautical Society: General Secretary McCarthy, Chief Philosopher Critchly

On the scratchy live recording, the audience coughs nervously and is silent: there is not much else to be done when someone's reading a manifesto at you. The Necronauts continue: through the brief (by now traditional) faux demolition of the Greek idealists, specifically Plato and Aristotle, who believed form and essence to be more real than anything else, and therefore perfect. But "if form is perfect," asks the general secretary,

if it is perfection itself, then how does one explain the obvious imperfection of the world, for the world is not perfect n'est-ce pas? This is where matter – our undoing – enters into the picture. For the Greeks, the principle of imperfection was matter, hyle. Matter was the source of the corruption of form.

Necronauts, as you might guess from the name, feel differently. They are "modern lovers of debris" and what is most real for them is not form or God but the brute materiality of the external world . . . . In short, against idealism in philosophy and idealist or transcendent conceptions of art, of art as pure and perfect form, we set a doctrine of . . . materialism . . . .

(Zadie Smith, "Two Paths for the Novel," *The New Yorker*, November 20, 2008: a review of *Netherland* by Joseph O'Neill and *Remainder*, Tom McCarthy)

Bruno Latour, similarly, has a "set doctrine of . . . materialism" in mind when he frames his Manifesto as something different; something not so doctrinaire. He too approaches creative and critical engagements with both literature and science as an "attempt," a "composition," not an agential conception of science or (in McCarthy's words) an already realized "idealist or transcendent conception of art." And the Necronautical "lovers of debris" are in synch with the modernism of Walter Benjamin's and Paul Klee's Angel of History (see Figure 0.1).

In various ways, the default relations of authors and audiences are displaced in contemporary fictions by authors such as Bennett, McCarthy, and Tisselli, who each in their own way configure alternative literary communities that are more likely to accept narratives and artforms that depart from idealist, transcendental, and lyrical realism. To a degree these alternative literary excursions have been imbricated in media and technologies that have rearranged the way literary communities, and potential audiences, are now forming themselves. Humanism, in the course of its development, had been operating from the beginning through movable type, where (ideally) a single author and unique, contractual publisher could address an audience of mostly uncommunicating individuals with bound books and, later on, through filmic, photographic, and televisual staging. Communications, for the most part, were *broadcast* from one to many. The posthuman, by contrast, constructs itself through media of *reception* that are unlikely to reproduce the kind of public spheres and imagined communities that emerged along with humanism. The promise of current electronic media, as Simone Murray argues in *The Digital Literary Sphere* (2019), is "to collapse distance and provide unmediated access to the intimate thoughts of an author in real time" (51). But this democratization of "mind-to-mind communion between author and reader is revealed to be incrementally commercialized and colonized by corporate interests. Each new platform's vaunted transparency is rendered suddenly disconcertingly visible and economically confected" (51).

At once a democratic and deathlike, necronautical turn in our mediated reception of literary arts?

It remains to be seen if such community-built projects will reinforce current digital enclosures or revive the original promise of the internet; namely, that writing can be created *while interacting*, not in the solitude of Gutenberg-era authorship.

The World System, Epic Poem, and Encyclopedic Novel

The foregoing allusion (at the start of this section) is to Franco Moretti, *Modern Epic: The World System from Goethe to Garcia Marquez* (1996). But we could just as well be exploring the epic poem from William Carlos Williams (circa 1950) to A. R. Ammons a few decades later, Ovid's *Metamorphoses* to Mary Shelley's *Frankenstein*, or independent scholar Steven Moore's two-volume "alternative history of the novel" from Gilgamesh to Margarite Young: the maximalist vein in world literature will be offered (in Chapters 6 and 7 of this volume) as a literary practice particularly well suited to our present posthumanist condition.

The Gutenberg Parenthesis

Graduate and undergraduate Creative Writing (CW) classes (a primary but not exclusive market for current literary arts) have increased markedly over the past few decades, at least in the United States. And posthumanism, far from being an oblique, theoretical specialization in literature and philosophy departments, is becoming recognizable by authors who emerge from CW programs. Unstructured but extensive writing communities have begun to form online. A concatenation of texting and reading has become, arguably, a condition of any literary engagement by the emerging generations. As Lars Iyer acknowledges in his "Manifesto after the End of Literature and Manifestos" (*The White Review*, November 2011), in social life today we are more likely to text than to talk; and in literary forums we are more likely than "ever before ... to comment or write than to watch or listen." If literary scholars recognize this condition and take it to heart – as earlier observers of "the death of the author" in voiceless postmodern performances have done – then it is incumbent on literary artists and scholars to reconceive the audiences we claim to be addressing. For this reason, the present *Introduction to Literary Posthumanism* is not directed exclusively at a conventional scholarly audience; still less is it aimed at the "dying breed" of literary critics, whose devotion to the codex is well described by the British novelist and journalist, Will Self:

> Literary critics – themselves a dying breed, a cause for considerable schadenfreude on the part of novelists – make all sorts of mistakes, but some of the most egregious ones result from an inability to think outside of the papery prison within which they conduct their lives' work. They consider the codex. They are – in Marshall McLuhan's memorable phrase – the possessors of Gutenberg minds. ("The novel is dead (this time it's for real)." *The Guardian*, May 2, 2014)

In literature departments today the mindset is more multimodal, offering opportunities for reading (and conversing) online as often as reading books and also giving aspiring authors in CW programs opportunities to converse with students focusing more on literary studies, rhetoric, and pedagogy. For those willing to walk across campus for the occasional science lecture, Digital Humanities writing workshop, or off-campus poetry reading, the possibility emerges for a post-Gutenberg prototype.

The transformation, then, from human*ism* to the *post*human cannot be framed as yet another new academic or cultural discipline in need of explication for those wishing to enter a functionally differentiated field or practice. It is, rather, a reconstruction and medial relocation of the human mind itself, in relation to other minds and to objects that are newly approached and identified through distributed networks and nonhuman, medial affordances. The timeframe for this larger turn toward a relational, object-oriented aesthetic is best demarcated not by periods but by eras and epochs – including the passing epoch of humanism itself and the sort of mental constructs that arguably emerged with the rise of print, film, and digital media. There will be, of course, much that we can hope to retain from the Gutenberg era – and not least the recording in print of pre-Gutenberg epic art that was, in its own way, oral and community built. As J. B. Hainsworth writes in *The Idea of EPIC* (1991), although neither the format nor heroic action of epic from Homer to Milton have managed to continue into the present, there remain certain strains even in modern literature "where thought and argument were as important as action" (145).

Bernard Stiegler's *Technics and Time: A Becoming Without Future*

Surveying the critical social fissures that index contemporary Western civil society – from 9/11 to the 2002 Nanterre massacre and the 2015 Charlie Hebdo shooting – Stiegler diagnoses our epoch as plagued by the "absence of epoch" (153), whereby computational capitalism and algorithmic governmentality have extirpated the "transcendental imagination" underlying a kind of vital primordial narcissism. In short, these are symptoms of a world increasingly "going mad," in a thousand ways, possible because we are the bearers of "a negative protention of a becoming without future," yet "we prefer not to say so: we do not want to know about it" (173).

From Ekin Erkan's review of Bernard Stiegler's *The Age of Disruption: Technology and Madness in Computational Capitalism* in the peer reviewed journal *Rhizomes: Cultural Studies in Emerging Knowledge* (Issue 35, 2019). The resonance with Melville's "Bartleby," "we prefer not to say so," appears to be coincidental.

Film scholar Patrick Crogan, for his part, draws a clear link between Stiegler's media theory and a "lack of essence," consistent with the "no-thing" we've already observed in recent political and cultural activism (e.g., "Occupy Wall Street") and the necessarily "imperfect" and unpredictable elements that are essential to literary narrative and aesthetics. (See the text box on pages 89–90, "A Distrust in Perfection," written by Jacob Wamberg and Mads Rosendahl Thomsen.)

Crogan's summary of Stiegler's argument is worth quoting in full:

> Stiegler argues in *Technics and Time 1: The Fault of Epimetheus* (1998) that what is essential to the human is precisely the *lack* of an essence. The human is "essentially in default," always already in need of some technical prosthesis in order to survive, to prosper, to improve oneself, so as to realise one's individual and collective goals (1998, 188). . . . The technical prosthesis has always already supplemented the human being, making possible its becoming. Moreover, Stiegler argues that time itself as lived by human beings is constituted in and through this technical prostheticity. Both anticipation of the future and memory of a past not lived become possible with the advent of the tool. The tool is a kind of external memory of the experiences and knowledge of those who devised and refined it and passed it down. To use it is to anticipate the future resulting from its deployment, a future inherited from those past lives of which it is the crystallised exteriorisation. (Crogan, "Essential Viewing," 39)

These epical, cognitive, and argumentative strains have determined the fiction, poetry, and literary essayism that I have selected as the prime examples of an emerging posthumanist literature. The genres themselves are not always clearly demarcated in such works, and while some are born-digital and others written for print publication, all are aware of earlier, preprint eras whose past prospects (realized or not in the present) are not forgotten; even as Mary Wollstonecraft Shelley recollects her romantic and anarchic forebears, and as Shelley herself is imaginatively recollected by her namesake Shelley Jackson, in *Patchwork Girl*. Indeed, their recollection (and literary recomposition) is what constitutes the ongoing literariness of print and digital media, however the book fares in the present, postprint era and whatever visual, aural, and textual forms (and communities for reception) our digital media afford us.

It is, of course, arguable exactly where and how humanism had its start. When it comes to identifying a viable literary future at the other side of the

Gutenberg parenthesis, I am not proposing "posthumanism" as the next best periodization, for reasons I have already articulated in the introduction to this book. Rather, we might better bear in mind some of the reasons we have for taking the long view. I will consider how climate change has scientists thinking in terms of the Pleistocene, the Holocene, and the currently debated Anthropocene. Though, here again, as with the transhuman strains noted (and set aside) at the start of this book, we will want to distinguish anthropocentric strains and tendencies from the broader discourse of posthumanism – lest we end up perpetuating the traditional distinction between the human and its others. Or, worse, we might end up reinforcing the myth of Man's dominion over the natural world, with the new twist that we alone are all that can correct the mass "exterminations, extinctions, genocides, and prospects of futurelessness" that we ourselves have imposed (Haraway, cited in Turner 2017).

That prospect, articulated by Donna Haraway, is worked through in the next chapter.

Haraway's Cyborg, Kurzweil's Transhumanism, and Other Power Fantasies

> By the late twentieth century, our time, a mythic time, we are all chimeras, theorized and fabricated hybrids of machine and organism; in short, we are cyborgs. The cyborg is our ontology; it gives us our politics. The cyborg is a condensed image of both imagination and material reality, the two joined centres structuring any possibility of historical transformation. (Donna Haraway, "Cyborg Manifesto," 1985: 2)

Four decades on, Veronica Hollinger historicizes Haraway's cyborg, on the one hand, as a literary "figure," one that "is responsive to her socialist-feminist politics, to the work of thinking about new ethics and responsibilities as subjects in technoculture, and to the acknowledgement of our close kinship with both machines and animals. But the cyborg," Hollinger continues, can now be

> taken quite literally in the ideologies and projects of transhumanism, which in their most techno-utopian forms – as in the power fantasies of singularity theorist Ray Kurzweil – express a neo-Cartesian desire to transcend the body: human minds might someday be downloaded into more durable technological forms of embodiment or even downloaded into digital virtual worlds. Once again the vulnerable physical body is in danger of being relegated to *alienum*. (Hollinger 2020: 20)

Chapter 4

Posthuman Sublime

The word "Anthropocene" is defined by the *Oxford English Dictionary* as "the era of geological time during which human activity is considered to be the dominant influence on the environment, climate and ecology of the earth." Nobody can deny the extent to which humans have transformed the planetary habitat from the time we put in place private and increasingly secure domiciles: our steps toward agriculture and civilization. The particles and chemicals humans have emitted into the atmosphere are a consequence of our technologies and a shift from arboreal sources of renewable energy to the mining of coal and oil. So are the rock formations that now include "squashed up toys and nappies and all the other stuff that ends up in landfill." And so too are the mass "exterminations, extinctions, genocides and prospects of future-lessness" that humans have imposed on our "many critters across taxa."

These formulations come from Donna Haraway, whose 1985 "Cyborg Manifesto," according to Jenny Turner of the *London Review of Books*, "stands along with William Gibson's *Neuromancer* novels, as a founding text of the late 20th-century cyberculture." Yet Haraway, like many who address our situation with a measure of scientific knowledge, is uncomfortable with our present terminologies. "The problem with the Anthropocene," for Haraway, "is that it is just too anthropocentric." It is the same problem we have addressed, in our opening chapters, of transhumanism as a counterposition to posthumanism – an extension of human agency and rationality rather than its needed resituation. For Donald Worster, a professor of American history, the Anthropocene suggests "the latest version of a very old quest for the domination of nature" (Worster, 2018, 13). The purposely neutral "dominant influence" in the *OED* definition can just as readily be cited in support of the idea that human ingenuity and technofixes are capable of turning our observed damage into activities that are directed, controlled, profitable, and secure. Which is to say, the quest for domination won't be interrupted; it's the only narrative we have now at the global level. But if it's true that we're the lords of all we create, then we can at least do a better job of resource management. "We are as gods and might as well get good at it," in the words of *Whole Earth Catalog* founder

Stewart Brand, who is cited by Worster as "a blatantly Enlightenment Project kind of guy, convinced that technology will always solve everything" – though Worster may be missing the irony bound up in Brand's statement (15).

So the story goes. But a posthuman literary practice, recoverable in the prehumanist, pre-Enlightenment past and getting under way again today, could well be creating the alternative Haraway asks for, namely a "capacity for imagining and caring for other worlds" (*Staying with the Trouble*, 50). In the aftermath of our literary engagement with cyberculture, authors have introduced a cognitive realism that (arguably) better reflects the capacity and extent of nature. By acknowledging that consciousness can only be a very small part of our cognitive makeup and embracing what postmillennial novelist Jeff VanderMeer (2019) calls "entanglements," authors today are finding different ways to engage with natural, medial, and multiple other nonhuman entities. Instead of locating nature as somewhere "out there," in the words of geoscientist Lynn Margulis, we are resituating nature inside us, in our human embodiment and being: a hypothesis that Margulis emphasized by naming it after the Greek Earth Goddess, Gaia. With such geoscientific (and epical) stringencies now in place, VanderMeer's realism and Margulis's naturalism may be closer to the *surrealism* that has always accompanied literary modernist experiments. Louise Economides and Laura Shackelford's edited collection on VanderMeer is titled *Surreal Entanglements* (2021). The editors and their contributors locate VanderMeer's trans-species creatures (known simply as "monsters") in the same lineage as H. P. Lovecraft's turn-of-the-twentieth-century sense of "cosmic horror." Just as Lovecraft's fiction can be understood as a rejection of otherness within human society, his creatures often reflecting racist fears regarding miscegenation and other forms of modern "degeneracy," VanderMeer for his part dramatizes another kind of otherness, with a better justified anxiety at the realization that "the world around us [is] radically independent of our own will and designs" (cited by Economides and Shackelford in their Introduction to *Surreal Entanglements*, 10). These conceptual deviations and excursions from any controlled, directed narrative are no longer secondary, however, as they tended to be in the modern era. No longer are they categorizable as imaginary oddities in an otherwise rational sphere dominated by human consciousness and an environmental stewardship focused on the welfare of human beings.

MacCormack Contra Haraway

Few terms are invoked in posthumanist discourse circa 2020 as often as the word *entanglement*. Whether we are referencing a relationality between the human and animal (in Haraway, notably, and in Cary Wolfe), the colonizer and the colonized individual, or the human "becoming with" its many others, the term upholds a notion that the human might *participate in* a planetary recovery after the Anthropocene. Contra Haraway, Patricia MacCormack (author of *The Ahuman Manifesto*) has rejected entanglement as a false imaginary, a middle ground that is unworkable. "We need to recede, we need to leave be, we need to step aside . . . Our presence in general doesn't help animals, just as the presence of the colonialist doesn't help the non-white other. Just as being mansplained philosophy to doesn't help feminism, and so forth." Rather than engaging in some notional dialogue with our nonhuman others, MacCormack advocates "abolition, withdrawal, grace" and we'd do better if we allowed others to be themselves. Although both MacCormack and Haraway see entanglement as inevitable, where they differ is that MacCormack seeks "a larger radical strategy that would allow the earth to be its own earth. Because I feel like 'listening to the other' and 'hearing the other' who is a nonhuman is a human fantasy and it's almost. . . sentimental" (see https://vimeo .com/397979720; 47:40 – 52:00).

VanderMeer is one of many emerging authors who recognize that intersubjective sensations have always been larger than consciousness, and our fictions might as well reveal just how *many* we are, in our cell and neural makeup which are not at all separate from our psyches. We see, for example, an ecological, but also intersubjective turn in the character Moss in VanderMeer's *Dead Astronauts* (2019):

> Moss against Moss, when it happened, rare, was like intricate garden combat. Between plants. Between obstinate weeds. Pugnacious. Sped up, slowed down. First one in retreat across a dusty yard full of skeletons and then the other. Add a third, a fourth Moss, drawn to the same reality, and there was in the confluence, the flux of outspread filaments and curling grasp nothing but the bliss of tiny flowers and exploding spores. Until, finally, there was no difference between attacker and attacked, and no shame in cease-fire, because Moss could not tell herself from her self.
>
> (69)

This is a marked deviation from the tradition of realist fiction, a countercultural narrative strain that differs also from conventional approaches to how we situate ourselves within changes now taking place in our climate, our habitus, and our geographical epoch. The trouble with the world imagined in most accounts of the Anthropocene (apart from its questionable duration, which I'll address momentarily) is their tendency to channel our newfound power not toward "intricate" (VanderMeer), interactive encounters but rather toward technofixes. And when those don't work, we have only the sad, sad story of the disappearance of our own species, along with everything else. Such an outcome is consistent – and this is no accident – with a deep-seated individualism (of selves a bit too keen on separating themselves from other selves) whose conception of the future extends no further than one's own, personal death. Which is to say, the end of our species, the planet, and our habitat is thought to be something like the end of human life. That's not a prospect that can poll very well or leave those of us who are monitoring the diminishing lifeforms with a narrative that can be pursued by future generations. And few in positions of power from either the left or the right are able to propose broad-based alternatives to the dominant narrative of global destruction, empowered by humankind. "It's a dark force that we're being sucked into and can do nothing about. The politicians and the thinktankers say: 'Oh my God! It's all going to die.'" These are the words of Adam Curtis (director of *The Power of Nightmares* and *Bitter Lake*), in conversation with Adam McCay (director of *The Big Short*, *Vice*, and *Don't Look Up*). And if that dismal end narrative holds sway, we're missing "an opportunity to change the planet in an extraordinary and better way" ("Adam Curtis and Vice Director Adam McKay on how Dick Cheney masterminded a rightwing revolution," MacInnes, 2019).

A New Materialism in Longinus, Sappho, and Other (Proto) Posthumanists

The fact that prominent makers of nonconventional films are echoing critiques in process by novelists like VanderMeer, Bennett, and McCarthy along with scholars like Haraway, Worster, and MacCormick suggests that a change of attitude is in the making. Seeds of this change will be seen also in some of Haraway's literary contemporaries in Chapter 6 ("The Posthuman Imagination in Contemporary Literature"), and we can hope that the stories describing these futures will be, in literature as in the films of Curtis and McCay, recognized more as an opportunity than a "dark force." But for this opportunity to be realized we need to identify powerful, because mostly unconscious, continuations in our corporate sphere of those old narratives of domination that originate, in the West, in our Calvinist religion and colonial history. It is questionable, for example, whether any imagination of other worlds in nature can take hold so long as our corporations and governing powers remain faithful to a long-standing, essentially religious desire to have "dominion" and (in the words of Genesis 1.26, International Standard Version) to be "masters over the fish in the ocean, the birds that fly, the livestock, everything that crawls on the earth, and over the earth itself!"

So "many critters," in other words, across so many categories and contentions: Haraway, who (like myself) was raised Catholic, is under no illusion that the dismantling of such attitudes will be easy – not so long as we remain in the Western imaginary of human (or, more specifically, "Man's") domination over a nature whose fecundity and *otherness* has been feminized, and set up as a realm to be explored, conquered, cultivated, and domesticated. And if we look, for example, to the lofty secular ideals that placed mental creativity in a position of superiority over the wayward webs, ebbs, and flows of the natural world, we see that not only the Western Christian tradition is so disposed. Indeed, the sublime situation of the male rhetor over a feminized audience, "made pregnant" (so to speak) by the speaker's powerful words, predates Christianity by a century, at least. The grandeur and greatness of an author's thought, in Longinus, is said to be "born in a man," but not in the way that Nature bears its offspring. And neither is the sublime "to be acquired by instruction; genius is the only master who can teach it." Longinus asks us to "look at the matter in this way":

> Nature in her loftier and more passionate moods, while detesting all appearance of restraint, is not wont to show herself utterly wayward and reckless; and though in all cases the vital informing principle is derived from her, yet to determine the right degree and the right moment, and to contribute the precision of practice and experience, is the peculiar province of scientific method. (Longinus, "On the Sublime," *Project Gutenberg*)

The twentieth-century term "scientific method" is likely an example of translator H. L. Havell's self-declared tendency to handle Longinus's text "too freely." Yet even then, in the time of Longinus as now, nature may have been subjected to a rational discipline and a powerful narrative. But that did not keep its fecundities from showing forth in our own thought and finding expression in the work of great authors. On such occasions, Longinus notes, "It is natural in us to feel our souls lifted up by the true Sublime, and, conceiving a sort of generous exultation, to be filled with joy and pride, as though we had ourselves originated the ideas which we read" (Longinus, "On the Sublime," *Project Gutenberg*).

"As though," not as *is*. The ideas that we have while reading a text (or listening to an oral performance), the feelings of *sublime and imaginative uplift* are not limited to verbal significations and textual inscriptions. Reading, listening, and other, epical and auratic engagements are ways of both sensing and transcending the material environments that structure our lives: an internalization of significations that are better known to our sensual life experience, *in nature and in the material world*, than to any momentary verbal signification. And this *ad fontes* insight in Longinus (taking us back to the Greek and the Latin Classics) – this transtemporal, epical conversation – arguably is consistent with the emergence of a *new materialism* in more recent, frequently feminist approaches to the posthuman. Might it not be the case that our displacement (and domination) of a feminized nature is a form of compensation, in the rational male, for his inability to bear, in his own being and body, the life that is born naturally by the female? Or by the earth?

Despite the compensatory hierarchy of thoughtful man over a feminized nature, Longinus (in the texts we have preserved) is balanced in his placement of Sappho, a writer of concise poems, on much the same level as Homer, an "author" whose expansive epics were doubtless collaborations by many bards who wandered from city to city, and village to village, reciting from memory and inventing new lines within the constraints of that medium, its formal rhythms, rhymes, and performative gestures. Mythology and mythopoeia, as posthumanist scholar Ivan Callus suggests, are "in so many ways literature's forebears and instigators." In Ovid's *Metamorphoses*, for example, we hear of "the agonies of punitive, gods-decreed change away from a human state, the tales catching on fugitive self-awareness just before the change to, typically, animal or arboreal form" (Callus, "Literature and Posthumanism").

Both Sappho and Homer are celebrated by Longinus, but it is the former, feminine aesthetic of Sappho that realizes a more than human, other than rational aesthetic by bringing the natural world into the poet's inner, affective sphere. In the "passionate manifestations" that Longinus addresses, Sappho's attendance on a "frenzy of lovers" is not limited to the person (or passions) of any one lover. What Sappho selects for emphasis are the material, sensual, and other-than-personal traits. As Longinus says, Sappho "always chooses her strokes from the signs which she has observed to be actually exhibited" by the lover. Not the intentions; not the words spoken. Not these alone. What Longinus identifies in Sappho, beyond the eloquence of her poetry, is how she conveys the nonverbal, material, and more-than-human nature of the sensual experience. Indeed, "her peculiar excellence," for Longinus, "lies in the felicity with which she chooses and unites together the most striking and powerful features" in this poem, which he cites in full:

> I deem that man divinely blest
> Who sits, and, gazing on thy face,
> Hears thee discourse with eloquent lips,
> And marks thy lovely smile.

> This, this it is that made my heart
> So wildly flutter in my breast;
> Whene'er I look on thee, my voice
> Falters, and faints, and fails;
> My tongue's benumbed; a subtle fire
> Through all my body inly steals;
> Mine eyes in darkness reel and swim;
> Strange murmurs drown my ears;
> With dewy damps my limbs are chilled;
> An icy shiver shakes my frame;
> Paler than ashes grows my cheek;
> And Death seems nigh at hand.

Longinus continues with a cogent appreciation of the loss of self and suppression of consciousness in the affective act. "Is it not wonderful," he asks,

> how at the same moment soul, body, ears, tongue, eyes, colour, all fail her, and are lost to her as completely as if they were not her own? Observe too how her sensations contradict one another – she freezes, she burns, she raves, she reasons, and all at the same instant. And this description is designed to show that she is assailed, not by any particular emotion, but by a tumult of emotions. All these tokens belong to the passion of love; but it is in the choice, as I said, of the most striking features, and in the combination of them into one picture, that the perfection of this Ode of Sappho's lies.
>
> (Longinus, "On the Sublime." *Project Gutenberg*)

The "tumult of emotions" is all the more striking to the degree that they take Sappho's sensual passions outside herself and away from her one (of many, potentially) beloved, even as the natural world "inly steals" its way into her own person. Nature is no longer perceived as an externality, as something "out there"; it is inside the lover, as all our awareness is *entangled* within a larger, nonconscious realm. A better realization of the passion she feels is gathered from the "eloquent lips" of the lover, and her smile, as much as anything that is said. (For more on the plurality of the "bundles of relationships" of any one perceived object "to other objects and actors," see the entry in this volume by Dana Bönisch in the Collaborative Glossary of Terms: "Entanglement/Relational Poetics.")

We find a still more intense self-abnegation in another famous poem of Sappho's – this one devoted to "one girl," not many: a friend or (possible) lover who is never plucked away from her natural environment. In neither poem is the object of fascination domesticated – and neither is the singular "one" protected either from the surrounding wilderness, or heedless "passing feet" of shepherds:

One Girl

I

Like the sweet apple which reddens upon the topmost bough,
Atop on the topmost twig, – which the pluckers forgot, somehow, –
Forget it not, nay; but got it not, for none could get it till now.

II

Like the wild hyacinth flower which on the hills is found,
Which the passing feet of the shepherds for ever tear and wound,
Until the purple blossom is trodden in the ground.

(www.poetryfoundation.org/poems/50343/one-girl,
translated by Dante Gabriel Rossetti)

In both poems, it is nature's internal presence that is gathered and conveyed "in all things" bearing "certain constituent parts, coexistent with their substance" (Powers, *Plowing the Dark*, 199) – as we saw near the start of this book, in Richard Powers' reference to the "rhythmic words" spoken by a girl (another "one") reciting a poem by William Butler Yeats. The written words that "might have cast some protecting spell," when they were first written, and read, now have a continuing, retrospective allure: Still, we have in the Yeats poem (as in all poetry) "[s]ounds with meaning, but meaning to no end," none that can be separated from the distinct moments of their reading, in their first appearance in print, and their utterance a century later at a poetry reading party.

"Once out of nature," Yeats had written, "I shall never take My bodily form from any natural thing" (Powers, *Plowing the Dark*, and Yeats, "Sailing to Byzantium," cited in Latour 2008, 268). In the novel by Powers, and in Yeats's poem, an internalization of nature finds its expression, an admixture of posthumous and posthuman articulations much in the way that Longinus describes.

In the following chapters we will see several other contemporary explorations of such epical, *ad fontes* rehearsals. Our imagination of nature and technology, of forces both larger and other than ourselves, can take us beyond conventional binaries of male/female, nature/culture, human/inhuman, and (not least) fact/fiction. These larger than human forces require bringing a bit of imagination into our scientific understanding, and a measure of precision and scientific knowledge into our fictions: "the boundary between science fiction and social reality," for Haraway, "is an optical illusion" (1985, 66). The compulsion, for Haraway no less than Longinus, to engage nature in its multiplicity and untoward, never easily predictable changes, places a limit on our own power as individuals, and any agency we might exert needs to be integrated subjectively with other humans and affectively with our companion species. The role of the rhetor, in Haraway's postmodernist formulation, is "Not to promote the idea of humans living in splendid isolation from material realities, but to help us find words and values for improving the most important relations we have, with the other than human" (1985, 66).

Donna Haraway: A Child of the Scientific Revolution, the Enlightenment, and Technoscience

Haraway herself, who has resisted the term "posthuman," accepts that her own position remains human centered. Whereas Patricia MacCormack, a generation younger, wishes to step altogether outside the exploitative logic of Western technosciences, Haraway addresses these unapologetically "from within" their cultural hegemony:

> Shaped as an insider and an outsider to the hegemonic power and discourses of my European and North American legacies, I remember that anti-Semitism and misogyny intensified in the Renaissance and the Scientific Revolution of early modern Europe, that racism and colonialism flourished in the travelling habits of the cosmopolitan Enlightenment and that the intensified misery of billions of men and women seems organically rooted in the freedoms of transnational capitalism and technoscience. But I also remember the dreams and achievements of contingent freedoms, knowledges, and relief of suffering that are inextricable from this contaminated triple historical heritage. I remain a child of the Scientific Revolution, the Enlightenment and technoscience.
>
> Haraway (1997)

Put this way, in terms of how we might imagine ourselves in relation to a world that is *not us*, a nature whose otherness exceeds and might even *transcend* the limitations of human imagination, the meaning of posthumanism begins to come into focus. Although Haraway avoids the term "posthuman" in both her "Cyborg Manifesto" of 1985 and the *Companion Species Manifesto* of 2003, she does recognize in later work by Cary Wolfe "an original, thoroughly argued, fundamental redefinition and refocusing of posthumanism." Without embracing the term herself, Haraway accepts Wolfe's usage in *What is Posthumanism?* Because this book firmly distinguishes "posthumanism from discourses of the 'posthuman' or 'transhumanism.'"

The *transcendentalism* of authors such as Emerson, Thoreau, and Melville, among others, as a viable alternative to transhuman empowerments and a posthuman situation that holds onto conventional humanist dispositions is a theme of the upcoming section in this chapter, and the next.

Panoramas

Already in the mid-nineteenth century, Henry David Thoreau, travelling to the northernmost parts of Maine to observe a more pristine environment than his industrializing Massachusetts homeland could offer, was discouraged at having observed there, at every turn in the landscape, remnants of trash left by previous explorers. In *Walden*, when he relates his encounters with the squirrels and jays, "whose half-consumed nuts I sometimes stole," as well as his other struggles for basic sustenance, his goal is to "live deliberately" – which is to say, in a way that sustains our individuality in nature and strengthens our free will by separating us from the demands of societal relations. And just how such deliberation plays out, in American frontier narratives is articulated in an introduction by Lisa Swanstrom to a gathering of essays on "Natural Media" that appeared in the *electronic book review* in the Autumn of 2019. Citing Erkki Huhtamo in *Illusions in Motion: Media Archaeology of the Moving Panorama and Related Spectacles*, Swanstrom suggests that an analysis of past literary and medial forms, such as the Panorama, can correct and contextualize our present understanding "by excavating lacunas in shared knowledge":

> Such an excavation ... helps us "reassess" the larger story, by revealing that the "historiographical presuppositions" we have about it require re-examination. What we find in such a re-consideration is that the rhetoric of American expansion is not merely one of divine right or exceptionalism but is also intimately connected to emerging views about what will eventually constitute our conception of "Wilderness."

A change in "historical presuppositions," and not least the supposition that knowledge is centered on what we, as humans happen to be interested in at a particular historical moment or geological epoch, is in fact the kind of perspective that the *literary humanities* has often been particularly good at. As Patricia MacCormack (a contemporary of Swanstrom and Huhtamo) indicates, such literary and aesthetic imaginaries are where the so-called "humanities" have traditionally found their strength – not in the anthropocentric order of knowledge that perpetuates its own claims to truth, nor in the cultivation of individuality and perpetuation of human exceptionalism, but rather (in MacCormack's citation of Jean-François Lyotard's *Differend: Phrases in Dispute*) in that nonhuman, nonincluded other that cannot speak, cannot be heard within the signifying systems and necessary disputations of the human.

Letting the Other Be (Other)

Henry David Thoreau, in *Walden*, like his mentor Ralph Waldo Emerson and successor Walt Whitman, inaugurated a literary imaginary whose transcendence was designed (at its best) not to control or even celebrate the natural world but to bring us closer to nature's mysteries; its powers that could never be challenged or channeled by our own, human powers (and locutions). It is no accident that Cary Wolfe, in his foundational study *What is Posthumanism?*, has a chapter on Emerson; and it is no less significant that "Emerson's Romanticism" in the chapter title is situated along with philosopher Stanley Cavell's "Skepticism," and systems theorist Niklas Luhmann's "Modernity." For Wolfe, posthumanism is less a matter of transcending our own, human nature than embracing the "human" as one form among many, and recognizing that the "humanities," whose beginnings are debatable but by now clearly demarcated, could also, one day, end. By firmly distinguishing present scholarship from the roughly 500-year duration of enlightened rationalism, we might begin to formulate an era that is not so much "new" as it is open to the discovery of continuities in past, even preprint literary modalities. In these pages I have already argued, for example, that posthumanism, arriving as it does with the Internet, takes us to the other side of the "Gutenberg Parenthesis," where the informality of texting and Instagram arguably is returning us to something more like preprint orality; a free-form practice closer to the literary essay than to any more constrained novelistic or poetic practices; a collaborative composition among multiple creative and differently knowledgeable authors that might take the epical bard as a predecessor (see Chapter 7, "Posthuman Epic in the Era of AI," and Chapter 9, "Digital Posthumanism (On the Periphery)"). And if that's so, then the imagination of literature itself will need to take a much longer view than that of novels, poems, and scholarship whose autonomy was reinforced by its containment in the bound text, replicable without variation – or with changes clearly marked – in its printings and editions.

Here again, in this print oriented scholarly practice we can surely find elements worth holding onto – not least the bibliographic curation and classroom circulation of confirmed knowledge and active experimentation, invention, and innovation. But we should also not forget that this valued autonomy, and consistency in conceptual formulation, may have come at the cost of a public silencing; a restriction of the arts to entertainment (via theater, film, and television) and more formal disciplinary thought streams in the academic humanities. Something similar can be said about science and the wealth of environmental knowledge that has been sidelined from meaningful public and political engagement. Disciplinary autonomy, arguably, tends to limit our ability to discover and circulate the facts of our planet, to collectively and imaginatively think about our place here and collaborate at the necessary intercontinental (and interdisciplinary) level in repairing the damage done.

In seeking, by contrast not directly to engage with our many others but rather to let them be in their natural environment, the posthuman imagination, arguably, would circulate more freely and be multimedial in its written, spoken, and visual dimensions. Disciplinary readers might then be more willing to make jumps, to forge relations the way we have learned to do online among facts that had been separated and enclosed by disciplines. Only now, in born-digital writing, might the jumps lead us away from familiar, narrowly human concerns to regions that are not so easily narrativized. Chapter 9 in this volume ("Digital Posthumanism (On the Periphery)") explores ways that authors of born-digital literary and cultural works integrate scientific knowledge (and gaming technologies) into both fictional and documentary narratives. (We might note also, following our discussion of *Patchwork Girl* in Chapter 2, the distributed narratives that Shelley Jackson would go on to produce literally in nature, in the snow outside the author's Brooklyn apartment, or cowritten, word by word and phrase by phrase, on the tattoos of hundreds of Jackson's collaborators worldwide.)

That said, one way that the humanities might embrace their approaching end could be for students, scholars, and creative authors to enlarge our sense of *periodization* in ways that allow us to engage meaningfully with climate and other natural changes that we are now living through. The *Oxford English Dictionary*'s temporal framing of the present Anthropocene as an "era" is itself problematic, and here is an opportunity for humanities scholarship to bring some clarity, and some temporal context, to our present situation. Earlier named epochs (not eras), such as the Pleistocene, extended over periods lasting hundreds of thousands of years from the time when living cells evolved. The more recent Holocene dates back to the last ice age around 12,000 years ago. And the "Great Extinction" we are presently living through – this is counted by authorities as "the Sixth," and it is unlikely that all human life will be extinguished. (No more likely than the billions of human inhabitants presently will be sustainable.)

Overpopulation Awareness

A December 28, 2021 visit to the Overpopulation Awareness website showed the present population to be on the order of 7, 828, 825, 330. It had gone up by 50 or 60, in the time it took for me to type that last sentence. Here is some context given at the site, whose numbers are more trustworthy than the spelling of words translated from the original German:

> The following numbers will show the growing pace of the world population since 1800: only after ten thousands of years its size reached the first billion; the second billion needed slightly more than hundred years, the third thirtythree years, the fourth just fourteen and the fifth only thirteen years;

the sixth billion was reached before the end of the twentieth century, on Oktober 12, 1999 to be precise. Notwithstanding the huge losses of human lives during the wars In the twentieth century the world population has increased that very century from 1.6 to 6 billion. The limits of the sustainable regeneration power of the earth have been surpassed for the first time. Until then humanity could live from the returns of the earth's natural capital. Thereafter we are dipping into the capital itself. The speeding population growth is mirrored by the increase of so-called megacities (more than ten million inhabitants). In 1900 there were only 12, in 1950 the number has grown to 58, in 1975 even to 211 and in 2006 to no less than 408. Among them Mexico City (more than 20 million inhabitants), New York, Istanbul, Caïro, Mumbai and Tokyo.

The unprecedentedly rapid growth of the world population – with an increase of 160 percent between 1950 and 2005 from 2.5 billion to approximately 6.5 billion people and an expected total of more than 9 billion in 2050 – will give rise to a number of negative effects as we all know: of course a deterioration of the environment and the quality of life and a depletion of our global natural resources – to date we have 20 percent overexploitation of the earth's capacity each year. But also an excessive urbanization going together with rural depopulation thus resulting in megacities where more than half of the inhabitants live in slums.

(overpopulationawareness.org)

We have reason to hope, from earlier extinctions such as the disappearance of the dinosaur, that other life forms will remain. Donald Worster, for his part, though he is "wary ... of over-excited media driven labels or slogans or of fashionable names like the Anthropocene," holds out some (modest) measure of hope that we will find a way to "expand old notions of 'history' to include the deep-time dimensions of geology and evolution and to begin seeing human history as part of that broader sweep of time." That's a worthwhile goal that the humanities are uniquely good at addressing. Worster questions, though, whether "we really have the power to kill the full, complex, material reality of nature as a sum of power and creativity, of evolution and change, a force that lies beyond our full understanding and reach".

But is not this acknowledgment of nature as a powerful and creative force beyond human subjugation precisely what Haraway, Wolfe, and many others in the literary/cultural field have been calling for? Neil Badmington, for example, finds in both theorists "a long overdue rethinking of the dominant humanist (or anthropocentric) account of who 'we' are as human beings. In the light of posthumanist theory and culture, 'we' are not who 'we' once believed ourselves to be. And neither are 'our' others" (Badmington 2011, 374). There are parts of liberal humanism that we'd do well to hold onto, as

Badmington, Ivan Callus, Stefan Herbrechter, and many other critical post-humanists would agree: indeed, the location of ourselves on the periphery of settled knowledge and a tendency to remark on the *limits* of all that we do know, about our fellow humans and nonhuman others, is foundational to the literary posthumanism we are exploring in the present volume.

An engagement with multiple others who can never be understood fully, nor perceived as separate totalities, for Hayles opens possibilities that are grounded "not so much on the tension between the liberal humanist tradition and the posthuman but on different versions of the posthuman as they continue to evolve in conjunction with intelligent machines" (Hayles 2005, 2, cited in Badmington 2011, 381). "And other others," as Badmington scrupulously adds, in a concluding sentence that is meant not to give the last word on posthumanism to the technologists. This is part of the reason why Haraway, who is professionally trained and practiced in science, is explicit about the need to integrate fiction into our scientific understanding, and vice versa. There will be nothing apocalyptic about it, as Haraway (ever the Catholic) realizes; nothing narratable in terms that might move us to collective action in the here and now, or the kind of imagined communities that literacy and realist fictions once helped generate. Insects could well be the inheritors of the earth, as William T. Vollmann posits in his ambitious but determinedly nonnarrative first fiction, *You Bright and Risen Angels* (1987). Vollmann, who refers to himself throughout the novel as "the author," was educated as a computer programmer at Cornell, as I was in engineering, in the early 1980s. We never met, but I remember well the transition during my sophomore year from typewriter to computer using Microsoft Word 5.0. Vollmann captures how this writing tool, like the typewriter for Nietzsche, was "also shaping our thoughts" (cited in Kittler (1986), *Gramophone, Film, Typewriter*, 200: see text box "Type Writers").

Type Writers

Through Friedrich Kittler's account of Nietzsche's famous proclamation, "our writing tools are also shaping our thoughts" (Kittler 1986, 200), I came to understand how handwriting had required eyes as much as hands. Working with one of the first mechanical type writing machines, Nietzsche, who was going blind, did not have to see in order to get letters to align; the machine placed the marks one after the other, which meant that what appeared on paper could later be read by a human reader. Like many of the first typewriters, the machine was called a "blind writer" because even a fully-sighted person could not see the writing it produced until the paper was pulled from behind the machine's apparatus. Shortly after their introduction, typing machines were reconfigured to place the letter marks within

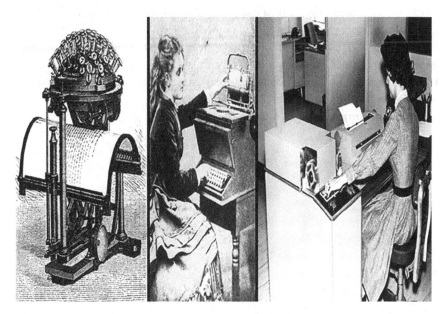

Figure 4.1 Anne Burdick, "Researching Writing Technologies through the Speculative Prototype Design of *Trina*," *electronic book review* 09-12-2021. https://electronicbookreview.com/essay/speculative-trina/.

the typist's line of sight. But trained typists learn to type without looking, programming their fingers to feel the keys and memorize the QWERTY sequence. After taking typing in high school, reading was ruined; I no longer saw word shapes, I saw letters and spaces. The flow of reading that had taken me many years to attain was disassembled as my fingers silently tapped the letters of every word I saw, in every situation, on my denim-covered thighs until sometime in my mid-twenties.

The term, posthumanism, then, is under contention – no less than postmodernism before it, which, as Brian McHale points out at the start of his *Cambridge Introduction to Postmodernism* (2015), was destined to end at its earliest introduction. By contrast, the adoption of a posthumanist perspective is felt, by those who have advanced the term, to be more lasting – even as the reality of climate change, worldwide pollution, and mass extinction lends to the discussion a tone that is not so open to postmodernist ironies. Nor does posthumanism allow, given its thoroughgoing questioning of human agency, for a perpetual embrace of novelty, technical wizardry, and stylistic innovation for its own sake. While recognizing our hand in denaturalizing the world through unbridled acts of conquest, abundance, and consumption, we are no longer so certain that we can do more than mitigate the destructions we have wrought. That these realities have been so well hidden by economic expansion, commercial distraction, and cultural knowingness gives us reason to hope for an awakening of consciousness through a revitalizing of literature and the arts, to its formative context in worlds that are not ours either to embrace or dominate.

Chapter 5

Ah Bartleby, Ah Humanities!
From Transcendentalism to Posthumanism

Conceive a man by nature and misfortune prone to a pallid hopelessness, can any business seem more fitted to heighten it than that of continually handling these dead letters, and assorting them for the flames? For by the cart-load they are annually burned. Sometimes from out the folded paper the pale clerk takes a ring – the finger it was meant for, perhaps, moulders in the grave; a bank-note sent in swiftest charity – he whom it would relieve, nor eats nor hungers any more; pardon for those who died despairing; hope for those who died unhoping; good tidings for those who died stifled by unrelieved calamities. On errands of life, these letters speed to death.
　　　　　　　　　　Herman Melville, "Bartleby, The Scrivener"

This is Bartleby's Wall Street employer speaking. The "Dead Letter Office at Washington," so described, is "rumoured" to have been a previous workplace of the copyist, Bartleby. The employer (and narrator), who is never named in Melville's story, seeks a reason for Bartleby's unexplained abscondence from official duties – his passive refusal to complete the tasks he was hired to do, namely: to proofread, collate, and hand copy mortgage contracts – as well as his refusal to vacate the office in lower Manhattan where he "secretly squats at night" (Edelman, 2013, 100); his refusal to dine after being arrested and housed at the prison known as "the Tombs"; and his passing some days later. Consistently, Bartleby "prefers not to." His abdication of official human agency is unmatched in world literature – though we can find, in nineteenth-century American literature, similarly evasive lifeways by artists such as Henry David Thoreau, Emily Dickinson, and Melville himself in his later career: a disciplined separation from publishing venues and life situations (for Thoreau and Dickinson) whose self-conscious social removal is a condition of works that would *transcend* the everyday, without ignoring its smallest details. (Proust, retired in bed in a cork-lined room to write the *Recherches*; Musil, T. S. Eliot, Wallace Stevens, and William Carlos Williams in the modern era, whose employment by banks, publishers, and hospitals allowed them time enough to write; and postmodern recluses such as Thomas

Pynchon and Claire-Louise Bennett: each in in their own way enact similarly disciplined separations and deviancies from officialdom.)

Bartleby's refusal is significant for literary studies insofar as this Wall Street employee was hired, specifically, to forge handwritten copies of legal documents. Though passive and unreasoned, his refusal is absolute and without the slightest opening for alternative actions. This has been noted by scholars worldwide: by Gilles Deleuze, who remarks on the "formulaic" refusal no less arbitrary than the legal formalisms contained in the documents; by Jacques Derrida, who points out how Bartleby's famous phrase is a "singularly insignificant statement [that] reminds one of a nonlanguage" (Derrida, 1995, 75); and by Lee Edelman, who shows how Melville's story, though it quickly went viral during the 2011–12 "Occupy" demonstrations in downtown Manhattan, offered precisely no alternative social or economic model. Its popular recirculation – no less than its literary recognition as the start of "a subterranean and prestigious lineage" (see DeLeuze in text box "A Subterranean and Prestigious Lineage") – was all the more powerful for that. Powerful as a communicative act, if not a principled or articulated directive for change (*On Curating*, Issue 40).

A Subterranean and Prestigious Lineage

"Bartleby" is neither a metaphor for the writer nor the symbol of any thing whatsoever. It is a violently comical text, and the comical is always literal. It is like the novellas of Kleist, Dostoyevsky, Kafka, or Beckett, with which it forms a subterranean and prestigious lineage. It means only what it says, literally. And what it says and repeats is I would prefer not to. This is the formula of its glory, which every loving reader repeats in turn. A gaunt and pallid man has uttered the formula that drives everyone crazy. But in what does the literality of the formula consist?

Gilles DeLeuze, "Bartleby; or, The Formula" (1997).

One literal answer to DeLeuze's rhetorical question about literality is that the "dead letters" that accumulate by the cartload in America's post offices could just as well be the *alphabetical letters* on a page that have been "assorted" by modernist authors such as Kleist, Dostoyevsky, Kafka, or Beckett. In this respect, Bartleby's mid-nineteenth-century "dead letter office" can be said to anticipate Roland Barthes's postmodern "Death of the Author": an author whose activities (in Barthes's words) are able no longer "to act directly upon reality – that is," the author's actions are "finally external to any function but the very exercise of the symbol" (Barthes 1977, 142). Bartleby, then, is not a metaphor for the literary author so much as its questioning: an early move away from the author as "a modern figure" (Barthes again) who is "produced no doubt by our society insofar as, at the end of the middle ages, with English empiricism, French rationalism and the personal faith of the Reformation, it discovered the prestige of the individual, or, to put it more nobly, of the 'human person'" (Barthes 143). A serial advancement more notional than material, which in due course would approach its end. By now each of these authorial figurations are in doubt, and Bartleby's early, absolute move away from human intentionality and humanist structuring anticipates our present, literary posthumanism where "the voice loses its origin, the author enters his own death, writing begins" (Barthes 142).

We might also note that Melville's story was published anonymously in *Putnam's Monthly Magazine*, under the full title "Bartleby the Scrivener: A Story of Wall Street." Which is to say, the "story" is not so much about one human character, as it concerns the economic activity, vocalizations, and scripting in a particular district at the heart of New York City.

From its start, then, a literary posthumanism situated itself as part of "a subterranean and prestigious lineage" (to again repeat DeLeuze's formulation). That will be the determinedly secondary, outlying, and *peripheral* strain of literary practice that concerns us in this literary study. Explicitly, in the closing chapter, titled "Digital Posthumanism (On the Periphery)"; but implicitly in romantic, transcendentalist, modern, and postmodernist works addressed throughout.)

Like Mary Shelley's *Frankenstein* of the year 1818, Melville's "Bartleby" (1853) has proven itself as a literary work that can be returned to, *rewritten* in filmic and digital contexts, as we saw with *Patchwork Girl*, Shelley Jackson's 2003 hypertext rewrite of *Frankenstein*. The most famous *Bartleby* (1970, Pantheon; https://newrepublic.com/authors/stanley-kauffmann) may have been "a poor film" but the acting in it was "superb," as Stanley Kauffman characterized this version directed by Anthony Friedman (starring Paul Scofield, John McEnery, and Thorley Walters; Kauffman's review appeared in *The New Republic*). A 1969 version produced by the Encyclopedia Britannica is more faithful to the written text of Melville's story. Later, there was a 1976 French version directed by Maurice Ronet, a version directed by Jonathan Parker in 2001, and a 2017 short stop-motion film by Laura Naylor and Kristen Kee, among others. But "Bartleby," because of its indirection and indeterminacy, is also capable of being *re-enacted* in extended protests that receive coverage in multiple media. Thus, Lee Edelman can cite, along with Deleuze, Derrida, and other close readers of Melville's narrative, blog posts by participants in the Occupy movement. These appeared on site in Manhattan and across the nation, in *The Daily Oklahoman*, for example:

> "I would prefer not to." So sayeth Bartleby, the intransigent copyist in a classic Herman Melville short story. To every request to earn his pay, to move on, to do something – anything – Bartleby would reply, "I would prefer not to." ... "Bartleby, the Scrivener: A Story of Wall Street" is

a study in petulant behavior met with inexplicable patience by Bartleby's employer. The story of Wall Street today is one of petulance met with inexplicable patience by authorities dealing with the "Occupy This" movement that's spread from lower Manhattan around the country. Ask the occupiers what they hope to accomplish. They'd prefer not to tell you. Perhaps they don't really know. Who's in charge? They'd prefer not to tell you. Everyone is in charge. Nobody is.

"Goal Remains Fuzzy for Occupy Protestors," *The Daily Oklahoman*, November 6, 2011.

The right-wing journal editors dismiss the Occupy movement as anarchist. Those on the Left might recognize Melville's absolute refusal (in Michael Hardt's and Antonio Negri's words) as "the beginning of a liberatory politics, but it is only a beginning." The left-wing quickly returns to more positive, constructive formulations: "What we need," according to Hardt and Negri, "is to create a new social body, which is a project that goes well beyond refusal . . . Beyond the simple refusal, or as part of that refusal, we need also to construct a new mode of life and above all a new community" (*Empire* [2000], 203–4). Whether constructed by the Left or the Right, however, communities, once identified, can be corporatized. And corporations themselves can be humanized – as US presidential candidate Mitt Romney notoriously remarked to a heckler in the crowd during an August 2011 presidential campaign speech: "Corporations are people too, my friend." The "Occupy Wall Street" protests began a month later, in September.

Richard Hardack's Post to *Critical Posthumanism Network:* "in case some people on the list might be interested in my book . . ."

Your Call is Very Important to Us: Advertising and the Corporate Theft of Personhood is a wide-ranging study of the pernicious idea that corporations are people. It recontextualizes the inordinate influence of corporations and corporate advertising in The US as a legal, political, psychological and sociological phenomenon. [Author Richard] Hardack demonstrates the ways that advertising language helps legitimate a discourse and ontology of corporate personhood – a long-developing form of artificial intelligence – and that its premises have come to supplant human subjectivity in many aspects of US culture. Because corporations were created as "artificial persons" under the law, many pop culture references to artificial and monstrous life contain some corporate residue. For instance, the amorphous and seemingly immortal corporation, revenant in many guises yet always the same, didn't create the alien in the eponymous films – it is the alien. Corporate personhood is part of a zero-sum game, one in which not just wealth, but human rights and traits –

including privacy, legal rights and forms of familial connection and continuity –
are in systematic ways transferred from people to corporations, which are part
of a teleology that ends in, and are themselves [a] form of AI. The assumptions
that foster corporate personhood are drivers and symptoms of a series of
deleterious transformations in US society, and a locus for understanding
systemic changes to our economy and culture.

A press description of the book, *Your Call is Very Important to Us*, sent to
the Critical Posthumanism list on May 20, 2023 by the author, Richard
Hardack.

Preferring neither the neo-Marxism of Hardt and Negri nor the corporative
neoconservative approach, Edelman holds firm to Bartleby's "utter refusal" to
join up for any corporate or political embrace of "communitarian ends":

> Here sounds the doxa whose chorus aspires to incorporate us all: wealthy
> sponsors of the corporate humanities and neo-Marxist critics of global
> empire; the protestors of Occupy Wall Street and Wall Street's CEOs
> alike. Bartleby, in his utter refusal to mean for communitarian ends, can
> possess no value except as a proof of negativity's insufficiency. Hence the
> lawyer who authors Bartleby's tale, unlike Melville who authors the
> lawyer's, must conscript the copyist to the cause of the human by making
> his resistance make sense. His distance from community and his absence
> of anything "ordinarily human" must prove in the end his
> hypersensitivity to the pathos of the human and even his longing for
> a utopian "community" where "good tidings" and "hope" on their
> "errands of life" can neither be errant nor erring. Like Hardt and Negri,
> the lawyer, that is, must refuse "the absoluteness of refusal," forcibly
> wrenching Bartleby from the queerness of preferring not to accede to
> normative reason and sense. (Edelman, 2013, 112)

Edelman, for his part, sees the *queerness* of the Occupy event as a part of its
strength – or, better, its incapacity to be absorbed in *any* identifiable program
or proposition. Like Bartleby's withdrawal, "Occupy Wall Street" is not so
much a movement or political stance as a "threat to community as such." The
protest "teaches us nothing":

> or, more precisely, the place of that nothing, that non, in the politics of
> the human and, therefore, the place of the humanities in the
> performance of every politics. Like the poet, in Sir Philip Sidney's words,
> this humanities "nothing affirmeth," but its queerness inheres in the
> force with which it stubbornly affirms this nothing, insisting, thereby,
> with Bartleby, on its preference for the negative, which is also to say, its
> preference for what the governing orders, the circuits of opinion, the

frameworks of collective reality make invisible, impossible, and, to that extent, unthinkable. (Edelman, 2013, 115)

The very physical appearance of Bartleby – "gaunt and pallid" for Deleuze (68); "cadaverous" for Edelman (99) – situates Melville's creation in the same, necessarily outlying condition as Frankenstein's daemon: a personage recovered from dead body parts. It may well be that the daemon's informal education enables sensitivities and eloquence far exceeding those of his creator. Yet the Frankenstein monster is nonetheless isolated, secluded, and unable to cast his newfound feelings into communal activity or a future – which he wishes literally to conceive through the creation of a female counterpart. This affectless, posthumous condition forecloses any possibility of another, shareable community or humanities project. Both Bartleby and the Frankenstein monster are decidedly apolitical, deadly in demeanor, posthumous, and posthuman in their refusal of subject positioning.

Or, as Steven Henry Madoff and Brian Kuan Wood state (alongside Edelman in their contribution to the Bartleby discussions in *On Curating*, Issue 40): "Bartleby remains, after more than one hundred and fifty years, the nearly mute and implacably sibylline force of an anti-authority as authority, of an eternal gaze into the power of a prodigious and fruitful No-thing" (48).

Sir Phillip Sydney (Circa 1580, Three Centuries before Bartelby)

Now for the poet, he nothing affirmeth, and therefore never lieth; for, as I take it, to lie is to affirm that to be true which is false: so as the other artists, and especially the historian, affirmeth many things, can, in the cloudy knowledge of mankind, hardly escape from many lies: but the poet, as I said before, never affirmeth; the poet never maketh any circles about your imagination, to conjure you to believe for true what he writeth: he citeth not authorities of other histories, but even for his entry calleth the sweet Muses to inspire into him a good invention; in troth, not labouring to tell you what is or is not, but what should or should not be. And, therefore, though he recount things not true, yet because he telleth them not for true he lieth not; without we will say that Nathan lied in his speech, before alleged, to David; which, as a wicked man durst scarce say, so think I none so simple would say, that Æsop lied in the tales of his beasts; for who thinketh that Æsop wrote it for actually true, were well worthy to have his name chronicled among the beasts he writeth of. What child is there that cometh to a play, and seeing Thebes written in great letters upon an old door, doth believe that it is Thebes? If then a man can arrive to the child's age, to know that the poet's persons and doings are but pictures what should be, and not stories what have been, they will never give the lie to things not affirmatively, but allegorically and figuratively written; and therefore, as in history, looking for truth, they may go away full fraught with falsehood, so in poesy, looking but for fiction, they shall use the narration but as an imaginative ground-plot of a profitable invention.

Sir Phillip Sydney. "A Defence of Poesie and Poems," written approximately 1580 and first published in 1595, after his death, edited by Henry Morley, transcribed from the 1891 Cassell & Company edition by David Price. Project Gutenberg.

What we may observe, in the detachment from *human being* by both Bartleby and the Frankenstein creature, can be situated as a determinedly minor strain in world (and world weary) literature. So was Melville's lifework, and that of Henry David Thoreau and Emily Dickinson, perceived in the era of American transcendental-ism, and so it can be observed in a range of contemporary writers who arguably continue in that "minor," "subterranean" but also "prestigious" vein identified by Gilles Deleuze, from the postmodernist experimentation of Thomas Pynchon to the new romanticism of William Gibson and an unnamed, impersonal yet highly self-conscious literary practice that has emerged in twenty-first-century fictions by authors such as Tom McCarthy, Colson Whitehead, Claire-Louise Bennett, and Jeanette Winterson, for example. Each of these authors displays a Bartleby-like impatience with a textual medium – literature – that in Bennett's view is "perhaps the most anthropocentric" of artforms ("On Writing Pond," *The Irish Times*, May 26, 2015). As we shall see in the next chapter, our present posthu-manist aesthetic emerges not so much from a plan of action or participation in a designated movement. What we find instead, in authors like Bennett, is more of a "percipient impulse" ("On Writing Pond"); an encounter with nothingness by an author whose "semi-reclusive existence the tales revolve around" (as Andrew Gallix notes in a *Guardian* review [2015]). Bennett's narrative generates in readers "an immersive experience" that (for Gallix) "aims at... nothing short of a re-enchantment of the world." In Bennett's own vocabulary, her authorial figure becomes something "numinous," a being who emerges from our present, "reduced circumstances." (According to Webster, "numinosity" is a term derived from the Latin numen, meaning "arousing spiritual or religious emotion; mys-terious or awe-inspiring.")

Bennett herself, or her narrator, after having wasted "many thousands of words" on a doctoral dissertation, stages her own departure from the human-ities much as Dr. Frankenstein had done, by departing from the protocols of the academic and human sciences of his era. Though Bennett (or her anonym-ous persona in *Pond*) had once received an invitation to speak at "an eminent university across the water upon a subject I was very interested in indeed," she departs from academic formality:

> I ignored the usual critical frameworks which were anyhow quite incomprehensible to me and instead pilfered haphazardly from the entire history of Western literature in order to strengthen my argument, which I cannot now recall. It had something to do with love. About those adventitious souls who deliberately seek out love as a prime agent of total self-immolation. Yes, that's right. It attempted to show that in the whole history of literature love is quite routinely depicted as an engulfing process of ecstatic suffering which finally, mercifully, obliterates us and delivers us to oblivion. Dismembered and packed off. Something like that. Something along those lines. (*Pond*, 20–1)

"Dismembered and packed off." The resonances, and shared academic experience, in Dr. Frankenstein's, Mary Shelley's, and Shelley Jackson's patchwork constructions are again worth underlining.

Bennett's is an aesthetic whose wonderous dimensions are part of an "abandonment" that can be said to emerge out of the transcendentalism of Ralph Waldo Emerson, whose thought (and its contemporary, posthumanist applications) we shall now explore.

An Austere, Bartleby-like Calm

Ralph Waldo Emerson's biographer, Robert D. Richardson Jr, notes in Thoreau "an austere, Bartleby-like calm – the calm of a tomb . . . . He was also capable [like Bartleby] of bitter all-out negation; in this he was more like Carlyle than Emerson. He had little ordinary warmth, not much of the common touch, no concessions to ordinary human weakness and appetite. An important part of his inner core was a deep capacity for renunciation, an agility to do without, which was all the more impressive for seeming to be effortless. The ability to say no, to prefer not to, created a wall around Thoreau." (Emerson: *The Mind on Fire*, 463)

To Be Rid of a Scrivener's Table Altogether: From Bartelby to Claire-Louise Bennett

I began to write – not to make sense of things, the opposite in fact. I wrote in order to keep rationality and purpose at bay, to prolong and bask in the rhythmic chaos of existence, and luxuriate in the magnificent mystery of everything.

(Claire-Louise Bennett, *Pond*, 20)

The way of life is wonderful. It is by abandonment.
(Ralph Waldo Emerson, "Circles," 1819)

Indeed, there is much that is wonderful in the abandonment Melville would depict in "Bartleby." And much to wonder *about*, three decades after Emerson's statement in the essay "Circles." Melville, in his canonical story, presents us not only with Bartleby as a singular outsider. Melville as author sketches, rather, a veritable cross-section of white male corporate America that is *incapable* of integrating with humanist structuring or affective commitments (and it is only men who sought employment in law offices at this early establishment of the American legal system). Besides Bartleby and his employer, there are three others in the office: the copyist, a young man nicknamed Nippers, who gets nothing done in the mornings; his co-worker, the rather elderly Turkey, who generally stops working after a liquid lunch; and the twelve-year-old boy known as Ginger Nut (after the cakes he brings daily to the office workers). Each one registers more moderate, less absolute refusals than Bartleby's. Although one, Turkey, is a man "of self-indulgent habits" and the other, Nippers, is "of a very ingenious mechanical turn," neither one can subordinate the object world to their own human purposes. Neither Turkey nor Nippers ever can adjust their table heights to suit them. Each can be said to share, halfway, the nihilism that Bartleby presents in full: "Nippers knew not what he wanted. Or, if he wanted any thing, it was to be rid of a scrivener's table altogether." Turkey, for his part "would gobble up scores of these cakes, as if they were mere wafers – indeed they sell them at the rate of six or eight for a penny – the scrape of his pen blending with the crunching of the crisp particles in his mouth."

Base Materialism

Lest our preoccupation with particulate matter in "Bartleby" should appear of passing interest, an oddity specific to Melville's violently comedic characters, we might contextualize the "scrape of pens," "ingenious" adjustments to the desktop height and orientation, and "crisp particles" crunching in Turkey's mouth. These mid-nineteenth-century literary excursions arguably anticipate a defining trend of the literary modernism that would become apparent with the 1922 publication of James Joyce's *Ulysses*. As Tom McCarthy has noted, this canonical modernist work is "comically . . . packed to overflowing with such things: in it every concept, no matter how intangible or rarefied, is transformed into something lowly, degraded, abject – and the more so the more elevated it held itself to be. Poetry turns into snot; nature, and the contours of the romantic sublime, into a bowl of sluggish vomit."

Citing Georges Bataille on "base materialism," McCarthy identifies what he sees "as one of the central thrusts of literature as it moves into and through the 20th century." A thrust that carries on from literary modernism into McCarthy's own literary strain that abandons realist characterizations and enters fully into the expansive, object-oriented un-worlding of the human nonconscious. McCarthy extracts from a transnational and aesthetically diverse Modernist grouping a viable list of posthumanist predecessors (extending Gilles Deleuze's mention of Kleist, Dostoevsky, Kafka, and Beckett, in this chapter's first text box: "A Subterranean and Prestigious Lineage"; or my own listing of Proust, Musil, Emerson, Eliot, Williams, and Stevens):

> You see it emerging in late Yeats, as his lofty esoteric icons are downgraded to a clutter of rag-and-bone-shop trinkets in "The Circus Animals' Desertion"; you see it, later, in the *proêmes* of Francis Ponge, where he celebrates the endomorphic thingliness of things, the way their sheer material facticity breaches the limits of every attempt to contain them conceptually or aesthetically; or in Wallace Stevens, in his plum that "survives its poems," oozing, and rotting beyond and between their lines; in visual art, you see it in the thick, muddy canvases of Dubuffet, where materiality far overtakes mimesis; or, later, in the unformed mounds of fat slapped down in front of us by Joseph Beuys. But *Ulysses* is where the process fully plays itself out, whirring and clunking and splatting and squelching. *Ulysses* matters most, because it makes matter of everything. Everything in *Ulysses* is *déclassé*, or (to use a term of Joyce's) "netherfallen." Things aren't even things in *Ulysses*, at least not in any quasi-autonomous sense, monadic entities with subjective sovereignty: they are abject, broken, the excreta of other things. Everything is a by-product of something else. Cheese isn't just self-consuming, it's the "corpse of milk"; jackets, soap, and margarine are corpses of corpses, the offslew of the hide, hair, and horns disgorged by slaughterhouses, what Bloom, brilliantly, calls "the fifth quarter": the one that's surplus to a thing's integrity, to mathematics itself, a remainder.

We might take note of the indirect self-reference to McCarthy's own novel of this title: "remainder." An imaginative exploration into the cognitive nonconscious that (as we will see in Chapters 6 and 7) takes its start where mathematics and numerical rationality ends. Here we have, in the thought stream of Joyce's character Leopold Bloom, an excursion worthy of Bartleby into the materiality of printed letters. As McCarthy notes:

> Bloom assesses the written word, too, solely in terms of its by-products: the blotting paper that he used to sell, that he blots [his penfriend] Martha's name with, hatching an idea for a detective story in which blotter-residues lead a sleuth to solve a crime; the giant sheet of it that he proposes the stationer Wisdom Hely parade through the streets; or the equally enormous ink bottle he also pitches Hely, "with a false stain of black celluloid" (Claes Oldenburg's entire career opens and closes in the space of that throwaway); or the actual ink, the "encaustic pigment" he recalls Molly

leaving her pen in, "exposed to the corrosive action of copperas, green vitriol, and nutgall." His own compositional effort ("I am a...") also gets bogged down by the material he writes on, as his stick sticks in the mud and thus becomes the very thing it tries to represent.

Tom McCarthy, "'Ulysses' and Its Wake," *London Review of Books* (36.12, June 19, 2014)

Writing and eating become ways of processing particulate matter. More than this, the scriveners cannot control. Their employer considers how, "amid the stillness of my chambers, Nippers would sometimes impatiently rise from his seat, and stooping over his table, spread his arms wide apart, seize the whole desk, and move it, and jerk it, with a grim, grinding motion on the floor, as if the table were a perverse voluntary agent, intent on thwarting and vexing him." No better anticipation could be cited for the "object-oriented ontology" that would come to characterize our present, posthuman turn in literary studies. The employer can "plainly perceive that for Nippers," unlike Turkey, "brandy and water were altogether superfluous." The agential presence of objects is enough to channel their energies into the very things a literary author struggles to represent (to invoke Tom McCarthy on James Joyce's *Ulysses*, in text box "Base Materialism").

In comparison with the everyday dehumanization of his coworkers' chambers, Bartleby's refusal is not unique. It is only taken to the full degree. Indeed, we may find in the aforementioned work of Claire-Louise Bennett a self-presentation that resonates with the detached and largely solitary lifestyles depicted in each of Melville's characters (and some similarly deflecting literary styles, in Melville's time and continuing to the present). Like Bartleby, Bennett prefers a solitary, unstructured way of being: "In solitude you don't need to make an impression on the world," Bennett explains to readers of *The Irish Times*, "so the world has some opportunity to make an impression on you. When that impression fails to materialise," in the story titled "A Little Before Seven," Bennett's protagonist (like Nippers in "Bartleby") presses down on her worktable to give herself "a little more density" (*Pond*, 60).

Objects, places, and particulate matter(s): these are the items, the many "prodigious and fruitful" No-things (Madoff and Wood, n.d.), that now emerge as central in a specific, posthumanist vein of literary writing.

A Distrust in Perfection

The aesthetic value of imperfection is not only a matter of turning values upside down and claiming the ugly to be beautiful. Rather, the imperfect

> should be seen as a key element of narrative, and of aesthetics more broadly, since it is hard to imagine interesting stories that do not include mistakes, bad intentions, accidents, and other less than ideal events that stir up the world. Dystopian visions of the future sometimes prove this negatively, by portraying worlds where societal control eliminates the unpredictable and thereby impoverishes human life. The emphasis on imperfection in narrative thus seems to be bound up with a quality of life, at least as we have come to know it.

So write Jacob Wamberg and Mads Rosendahl Thomsen, in their focused exploration of "The Posthuman in the Anthropocene: A Look through the Aesthetic Field" (2016). While their work includes sustained critiques of the positivist, transhumanist approaches, their interest in a *literary* posthumanism gives us a further reason to embrace the more sidelined, subjective and "imperfect" phenomena that are found in emerging strains and "several glimpses of posthuman desires." These, for example:

> Apart from visual popular culture, an increasing number of non-science fiction writers incorporate elements of human enhancement into their novels, most notably cloning in Kazuo Ishiguro's *Never Let Me Go* (2005) or the creation of a new, benign, and dull successor to the human race envisioned in Michel Houellebecq's *The Elementary Particles* (2000). David Mitchell's *Cloud Atlas* (2004) tells a sweeping story of humanity's evolution, meandering between the 1850s, the present, and what is clearly a dehumanized posthuman world, followed by a post-apocalyptic return to a more primitive state. And while the fantasies are not developed into a fully described fictional world, two of the most seminal American writers, Thomas Pynchon and Don DeLillo, have provided several glimpses of posthuman desires, always accompanied by a distrust in perfection. (Wamberg and Rosendahl Thomsen, 2016)

We've now observed in some detail what are meant to be suggestive through-lines going back from Claire-Louise Bennett to a number of anticipatory posthumanist texts: notably, Mary Shelley's *Frankenstein*, Ralph Waldo Emerson's "Circles," Percy Shelley's "Defense of Poetry," William Wordsworth's "World is too Much With us," and Herman Melville's "Bartleby." Going forward, we will be extending these connections, no doubt, to many of the "usual critical frameworks" that Claire-Louise Bennett herself found "quite incomprehensible" during her post-graduate forays into the literary humanities (*Pond*, 20–1). The application of an object-oriented ontology to the various worktables in both Melville's "Bartleby" and Bennett's *Pond* is an assignment ripe for integration into Masters level curricula. But such humanist formulations are precisely what each of these authors is *refusing*. Not because there is anything wrong with the recognition, *ad fontes*, of thematic, conceptual, and subjective continuities through the centuries. But the classroom assignment of so many authors to fixed fields of knowledge discourages individual, never fully organized engagements with literary canons that both students and prospective authors themselves have discovered during their own literary and intellectual explorations. Emerson's unconventional engagements with literary and philosophical traditions (in China and Turkey no less than contemporary French and Germanic approaches) were always, in every instance, acts meant to *extend* his own self by placing his thought within a field that is larger than any momentary act of expression. The same can be said of all the posthumanist authors, that share in a *resistance* to their own prospect of being included in a formulaic canon of literary precursors.

The thing about Bartleby is that, in his absolute refusal, negation, and comic violence, he too is a transcendentalist. But he also serves to remind us that this term (transcendentalism), when it was first applied to Emerson and his cohort in the USA, was itself a kind of joke: a putdown for the overreach found in Thoreau, Emerson, and some others. Melville, for his part, invents a violent comedy of his own that works not through our institutional, official world, but thoroughly *against* the world. (See Deleuze on Melville's "violently comedic characters" in "Bartleby; or, The Formula.") And this is consistent with what Emerson's biographer, Robert D. Richardson, Jr, has to say about "the highest, most trustworthy knowledge" in transcendental thought emerging from "intuitive graspings, moments of direct perception," and "free mental acts of cognition and recognition, a series of mental activities that," as Emerson realized when he left the clergy, "could be summed up by the word *reason*." Richardson continues:

> Customarily he used visual imagery for these acts of knowing, calling them insights, perceptions, or visions. What he was now doing, with [Joseph de] Gerando and with all of his reading henceforward, was looking for traces of the momentary outbreaks of reason – these flashings forth of the intuitive truth as Melville called them – down through history. And already he was recognizing his own ideas reflected back to him in the ideas of Confucius, Pythagoras, and Heraclitus . . . So strong was this sense of validation while working on Gerando in 1830 that Emerson could write, in language he would later use for the essay "Self-Reliance,"
>
>> that when a man has got to a certain point in his career of truth he becomes conscious forevermore that he must take himself for better or worse as his portion, that what he can get out of his plot of ground by the sweat of his brow is his meat, and though the wide universe is

full of good, not a particle can he add to himself but through his toil bestowed on this spot.

Emerson: The Mind on Fire (1995): 104–5. On Joseph de Gerondo: "a continuing influence on RWE," Richardson cites John B. Wilson, "A Fallen Idol of the Transcendentalists," in *Comparative Literature* 19 (1967): 334–40 and H. H. Clark, "Emerson and Science," *Philological Quarterly* 10 (July 1931).

What characterizes Emersonian self-reliance, as Richardson shows on practically every page of this biography, are acts of reading that extend back to pre-Socratic philosophers – Anaximander, for example. And in Anaximander's mastery (and alteration) of what his teacher, Thales, had to say. Attention was to be paid as well to Anaximander's own teachings (and further dissemination, and transformation) by his pupils Anaximenes and (possibly) Pythagoras. Self-reliance is thus in the first instance a reliance on a line of communication within a recognized literary and philosophical tradition and its dissemination through a sustainable educational structure. The act of reasoning cannot be reduced to unreflective citations of facts or liturgies. Arguably, Emerson's own departure from his clerical position in the First Church of Boston (occupied before him by his father) was a means of freeing himself from what had become formulaic sermons and opening a space for the self-reflective, experimental, and free-ranging essayistic endeavors that secured his place in literary history.

Emerson's departure from the ministry was not a rejection of faith. As Richardson points out, Emerson "praised Christianity as progressive because it had managed to throw off Calvinism, reject the idea of this world as the "scaffold of divine vengeance," and abolish other "austere and macerating monkish observances." What the move away from the ministry enabled was the exploration of the meaning of human life, which for Emerson was discoverable through "individual education." But even this was partial, and momentary. As he wrote to his Aunt Mary in 1827, only "a portion of truth, ... bright and sublime, lives in every moment in every mind" (*Emerson: The Mind on Fire*, 79–80, 82).

Thinking with Emerson (Cavell, Wolfe, et al.) in Cognitive Environments

Arguably, what struck mainstream authors, scholars, orators, and clerics as violently comic and dangerously isolating in the time of Emerson, Melville, Thoreau, and (a bit later) Emily Dickinson has been precisely what has made the work of these authors lasting. Rather than trying to change the world,

Emerson himself accepts, in the words of the twentieth-century philosopher, Stanley Cavell, "that the world exists as it were for its own reasons" (2003, 79). Cary Wolfe further extends Cavell's arguments to show that Emerson's advocacy of self-reliance is anything but a celebration of individualism and extended human agency. Indeed, its embrace of "passivity" – Wolfe's terms for Emersonian cognition – could be read as another instance of the Bartleby theme. "Thinking with Emerson," Wolfe writes,

> becomes not active apprehension (prehensile grasping of the world by our concepts, as it were) but an act of *reception*, a reception in which passivity – because it consists of a capacity to be affected by the world in manifold ways that cannot be contained by the choked bottleneck of thought as philosophy has traditionally conceived it – becomes, paradoxically, a maximally *active* passivity. (*What is Posthumanism?* 241–2)

In a word: this is Bartleby.

The passive preference *not to* grasp a copyist's pen and platform, and a refusal to perform exclusively in a business environment is also evident in Wolfe's reading of Emerson:

> This process is everywhere testified to in Emerson's work from beginning to end, from the "Transparent Eyeball" passage in *Nature*, to the seemingly paradoxical assertion in "Self-Reliance" that "self-reliance is God-reliance," to his assertion in "Experience" that "all I know is reception. I am and I have: but I do not get, and when I fancied I had gotten anything, I found I did not … When I receive a new gift, I do not macerate my body to make the account square, for if I should die I could not make the account square. The benefit overran the merit the first day" (*What is Posthumanism?* 242, Wolfe is citing *Emerson's Prose and Poetry*, 212)

The gift of life itself is diminished when it is subjected to a business-like, cost–benefit analysis. Better to embrace the *nothing* that both precedes us, as living humans, and will return with humanity's collective removal (following its many material macerations during an anthropocentric passage that cannot be expected to have the duration of previous epochs – over millennia, not centuries or decades).

A Transparent Eyeball (Emerson)

> Standing on the bare ground, – my head bathed by the blithe air, and uplifted into infinite space, – all mean egotism vanishes. I become

a transparent eye-ball; I am nothing; I see all; the currents of the Universal Being circulate through me; I am part or particle of God. The name of the nearest friend sounds then foreign and accidental: to be brothers, to be acquaintances, – master or servant, is then a trifle and a disturbance. I am the lover of uncontained and immortal beauty. In the wilderness, I find something more dear and connate than in streets or villages. In the tranquil landscape, and especially in the distant line of the horizon, man beholds somewhat as beautiful as his own nature. Emerson, *"Nature"* | Project Gutenberg

Chapter 6

The Posthuman Imagination in Contemporary Literature

"The development of the novel in the period [since 1945] is arguably characterised by the lapsing of the human as the dominant figure for civilised life, and the emergence of a posthuman rhetoric and aesthetic, which shares much with the other postal compounds that shape cultural life in the later decades of the century – such as postmodernism, poststructuralism, postcolonialism, and so on. – Peter Boxall
("Science, Technology, and the Posthuman," 2015, 130)

"If there is something comforting – religious, if you want – about paranoia, there is still also anti-paranoia, where nothing is connected to anything, a condition not many of us can bear for long." – Thomas Pynchon
(*Gravity's Rainbow*, 1973, 506)

In Chapter 3, I discussed Tom McCarthy's deviation from transhumanism's "naive escapist fantasy (of individual self-expression, or the transcendent human spirit, or art-as-redemption and so forth)" (*The Guardian*, March 7, 2015). In this chapter, I wish to address a minor (but compelling) lineage of novelists, McCarthy among them, who are part of a more object-oriented – and lasting – posthumanist turn in literary practice.

We have already seen in Claire-Louise Bennett a related impatience with mainstream literature as "perhaps the most anthropocentric" artistic medium. Bennett mentions this phrase (with attribution to Italo Calvino) in both her essay in the *Irish Times* (May 26, 2015) and an interview with Philip Maughan in *The Paris Review*, titled "The Mind in Solitude" (July 18, 2016). Bennett's contrarian aesthetic emerges not so much from a plan of action or participation in a designated movement. Consistent with both Bartleby's refusal of *any* contract, social or legal, and McCarthy's call to his fellow writers to "remap their entire universe," Bennett's approach has a certain tone of withdrawal: "My own nails are doing very well as a matter of fact . . . If you must know I painted them in the kitchen last Wednesday after lunch" (*Pond*, 17).

Reading Bennett is in some ways like reading Bartleby, in that her unabashed solitariness is only reinforced when a reader's presence is acknowledged. Bennett's writing also resonates with the "Cosmic Web" that I have referenced and will further explore in the scholarly work of N. Katherine Hayles, as well as Thomas Pynchon's postulation of paranoid connectivity as a corporatized and enumerated replacement of communal and transcendental aspirations. "It was, after all," for Bennett "the whole cosmos I felt a part of and wished to respond to – not just my small portion of it, the here and now of my specific, increasingly circuitous, circumstances – but everything, everywhere, always" (*The Irish Times*, May 26, 2015).

In her desired approach to a "more transcendent reality," Bennett likewise echoes Bruno Latour's "Parliament of Things" – and (closer to her own generation) Graham Harman's (2018) and Ian Bogost's (n.d.) object-oriented ontology – when she observes how "objects are not simply insensate functional things, but materials, substances, which have an aura, an energy – even, occasionally, a numinosity" (*The Irish Times*, May 26, 2015). There are few better examples, in literature, of the new materialist integration of our human concerns with nonhuman objects. But we should not mistake the self-conscious material engagements of Bennett and McCarthy as a "posthuman" movement or generic novelty: these works find continuities in the systems novels of the postwar period, and further back in the transcendentalist fictions of Melville along with earlier epical precursors of posthumanism (as we shall see in Chapter 7). Their experimental forays have more to do with rediscovery, haphazard pilferings (*Pond*, 20), and the continuation in changing circumstances of established literary genres than with any innovative pretensions or aspirations toward novelty.

Numinosity, percipience, peregrine displacements (see text box "This Boundaried and Stable Self . . . The Social Being – Doesn't Concern Me Much"): these distinctly contemporary terms are reserved for a heightened and immersive affective being that has replaced the language of religion in earlier literary formations. Given her admission that "[h]uman beings and the stunts they pull" had always been "a minor constituent" of her world view, Bennett offers a viable alternative to self-expressive and personalized fictions. ("On Writing Pond," *The Irish Times*.) Her determination, along with Italo Calvino, to "give the slip" to "Anthropocentric parochialism" places her more in line with the first wave of posthumanist literary authors whose work I'll be exploring in this chapter: a literature that gives us less domesticity, fewer filled out characters, and more world.

**"This Boundaried and Stable Self . . . The Social Being –
Doesn't Concern Me Much."**

At the start of a public conversation at the Norwegian Literature Festival in the
summer of 2017, Karl Ove Knausgaard mentions to Bennett how hard it was to find
any personal information about her, online. Knausgaard's own moment by
moment, day in day out, year by year documentation (exclusively in print) of his own
lifeworld has seemed, to some commentators like a literary correlative of the real
time documentation of everyday lives through blogs and social media.
(Knausgård møter Bennett. See also Rettberg et al., 2018)

Bennett offers another response, no less aware of the presence of online lives but
protective of the privacy and immersive presence needed to explore a different kind
of self-construction. What we have in mainstream fiction, "[t]his boundaried and
stable self," as Bennett notes in her *Irish Times* essay on writing *Pond*, "the social
being – doesn't concern me much. What I want to delve into and express in my
work is the peregrine self – the being who is fluid, exotic, and nebulous." The
destabilizing of selfhood in Bennett's writing, and that of other contemporary
authors treated in this chapter, marks a surprising departure from the socially
mediated presence that has come to define our online lives. Without denying the
immediate usefulness of all that is made available to us by digital media, the
posthuman situation of selfhood, in a writer like Bennett, might be more in line with
Thomas Pynchon's lifelong avoidance of any personal appearance in public media –
except for one cameo in *The Simpsons*, where the cartoon version of Pynchon
appears with a paper bag over his head. (But the voice is his.)

Some Singularities

Although posthumanism arguably preceded "the decentering of the human
by its imbrication in technical, medical, informatic, and economic networks"
(Wolfe 2010, xv), no account of the posthumanist turn in contemporary
literature can neglect the enhancement and near ubiquity of our technological
environments, nor the corporatization of our lives. We have already seen (and
set aside) the tendency to ground transhumanist thought in singularities:
hoped-for transformations emerging from a furthering (and continuous
updating) of technological infrastructures. Indeed, I'll be suggesting that
one feature of a literary posthumanism is its ability to reconceive other-than-
human narratives, without projecting God-like qualities onto either individual subjects or collective machinations. Now, as always, our technologies are
more Promethean than God-like, even as the bringing of fire and civilization
to mortals could just as easily cause our destruction. There is simply no reason
to assume, or hope, that a disembodied, digitized, or algorithmic intelligence

will do more than enhance and automatize agencies that we already have in place. The *messianic* approach that was said, for example, to characterize Nick Bostrom's and Zoltán Boldizsár Simon's embrace of the singularity, is brought out (and questioned) in the more self-aware, explicitly *pseudo*-religious, and unapologetically *paranoid* fictions of Thomas Pynchon, whose work exemplifies both the prevalence and the cognitive complexity of a posthuman literary aesthetic.

Indeed, the inherent unknowability of our technological "imbrication" (Wolfe 2010, xv) might be best grasped in the opening line of Pynchon's *Gravity's Rainbow* (1972, p. 3):

> A screaming comes across the sky. It has happened before but there is nothing to compare it to now.

The scream is from a V2 rocket approaching faster than the speed of sound in a region of wartime London – which means that the rocket, if we hear it, has already exploded somewhere else. Those who are hit would not have heard it coming. The rocket's unknowability is representative of a novelistic setting and narration after the singularity has occurred. Pynchon's narrative does not in any way purport to depict the singularity: rather, it is presented, like so many unknowable conditions in both the physical and cognitive sciences, as an opportunity for imaginative engagement. Pynchon depicts a condition of *not knowing* how much we can ever know about, or influence, what takes place in our material world – and in the course of our everyday lives, of not having to think about the vast nonconscious activity that makes our thought possible.

As Pynchon continues, in his World War II setting experienced through the eyes and thoughts of the as yet unnamed character, Pirate Prentice:

> It is too late. The Evacuation still proceeds, but it's all theatre. There are no lights inside the cars. No light anywhere. Above him lift girders old as an iron queen, and glass somewhere far above that would let the light of day through. But it's night. He's afraid of the way the glass will fall – soon – it will be a spectacle: the fall of a crystal palace. But coming down in total blackout, without one glint of light, only great invisible crashing. (3)

Both networks – the technological and the intersubjective – are entangled as the mind-to-mind communication (from author to reader) is purposefully *enacted* throughout the text of *Gravity's Rainbow*. Pynchon describes a crowded train moving through the streets of wartime London and ambiguously arriving at another structure from an era now passed, that of a "vast, very old and dark hotel, an iron extension of the track and switchery by which they have come here . . ." (4). The ellipses, here and throughout the novel, are Pynchon's: a literal gesture toward the emptiness we have seen in earlier, transcendental literatures from the time when such anti-authoritative "No-things" were first thematized: a "prodigious and fruitful" built environment of both matter and data that exceeds consciousness and individual agency (see Madoff and Wood – alongside Edelman et al. – in their contribution to the Bartleby discussions, *On Curating*, Issue 40).

Media and Informational Multiplicity (John Johnston)

More consistently than perhaps any other US scholar, John Johnston has brought the range of poststructuralist theory to bear on American fiction's most discussed experimental texts. Specifically, *Information Multiplicity* (1998) takes its key terms – "assemblages," "multiplicity," and "machinic phylum" – from Gilles Deleuze and Felix Guattari: theorists who have also influenced the new materialism of posthumanists such as Rosi Braidotti and the coeditors, Madoff, Wood, and Edelman of the special issue of *On Curating* on Bartelby (number 40). Equally important for Johnston are the "discourse networks" or "writing-down systems" (*Aufschreibsysteme*) of Friedrich Kittler, who decisively generalizes the notion of medium, applying it to all domains of cultural exchange in the social environment no less than in processes of psychological individuation. Like the works by Kittler and Deleuze dealing specifically with literary texts, Johnston's criticism resituates the scholarly discussion by drawing attention to the impact of media themselves – that is, the interdiscursive networks that link writers, archivists, addressees, and interpreters. Johnston uses the term "mediality" to indicate the ways in which a literary text inscribes in its own language the effects produced by other, nonliterary media. Johnston's critical mission is to ascertain how these media effects – our culture's technological unconscious – are narrativized or how they can be seen to condition conscious awareness as a "reading effect."

Johnston's narrative, because it is situated in specific technological transformations rather than a generalized epistemological shift, describes historical changes among novelists and from one work to another. Indeed, where many critics find nonhierarchical and nonlinear structures liberating, Johnston argues that such flexible structures largely redefine power (be it male, female, or otherwise) within "the military-industrial complex born from World War II" (*Information Multiplicity*, 63). Specifically, Johnston's master narrative works in three stages, proceeding from (1) a time of separate and separable media (registered in such works as *Gravity's Rainbow*); to (2) "a condition of partially connected media systems" in Pynchon's *Vineland* (where differences in media, as in the transition from filmic to digital registrations, still offer spaces of resistance to newly aggregated structures of corporate power); to (3) the prospect, in cyberpunk fiction, of media's "disappearance" into "a totalized, global information economy" in which "cyborg culture becomes the only culture" (*Information Multiplicity*, 233–4).

Ellipses and elisions are present throughout *Gravity's Rainbow*, suggesting an *emptiness* that cannot possibly be filled, let alone by the reader. Pynchon's description of a train filled with evacuees moving through the streets of wartime London is also an accurate metaphor for the narrative we are about to begin reading:

> No, this is not a disentanglement from, but a progressive *knotting into* – they go in under archways, secret entrances of rotted concrete that only looked like loops of an underpass . . . certain trestles of blackened wood have moved slowly by overhead, and the smells begun of coal from days far to the past, smells of naphtha winters, of Sundays when no traffic came through, of the coral-like and mysteriously vital growth, around the blind curves and out the lonely spurs, a sour smell of rolling-stock absence, of maturing rust, developing through those emptying days brilliant and deep, especially at dawn, with blue shadows to seal its passage, to try to bring events to Absolute Zero . . . (3; ellipses in the original)

"To try": the processual, uncertain course that retains a tangible, sensual memory of "days far to the past," of smells that still mark an absence, "rolling stock" that in peacetime (the time of uninterrupted commerce) has been carried along the same tracks and traceries that the evacuation now follows. Pynchon's narrative is structured in ways that turn past occurrences and departed personalities into active presences and impersonal forces that exceed human control and defeat any sustained character development. Yet, at the same time, there are many approaches to "Absolute Zero," some of them announced in the Calvinist and Puritanical language of Pynchon's American forbearers. We might consider, for example, the many ways of tracking the course taken by evacuees on the train as it begins its intercity journey: "It is a judgment from which there is no appeal" (4). After the evacuees are "taken in lots" on the elevator, to unlit rooms they sometimes share but mostly occupy alone, the Absolute absence has been interiorized: "Each has been hearing a voice, one he thought was talking only to him, say, 'You didn't really believe you'd be saved. Come, we all know who we are by now. No one was ever going to take the trouble to save *you*, old fellow . . .'" (4).

The evacuation, however, and the theater of war described in the opening, turns out to be all in the mind of an army captain by the name of Geoffrey ("Pirate") Prentice. And there are equally religious, if less apocalyptic versions under way among his actual house guests and military comrades, awakening as "London light, winter and elastic light" (4) begins to pour in through the windows: "All these horizontal here, these comrades in arms, look just as rosy as a bunch of Dutch peasants dreaming of their certain resurrection in the next few minutes" (4–5). Prentice, waking early, catches a glimpse of an incoming Rocket, which he will soon be called on by his military superiors to investigate. But first, he must put together a breakfast for his guests – a tradition that he has established after planting bananas on his building's rooftop. This activity, like many incidental and purposeless actions in the novel, is consistent with natural, recurrent but never fully knowable settings and life situations that typify the many social, but at the same time other-than-human contexts in *Gravity's Rainbow*:

> Messmates throng here from all over England, even some who are allergic or outright hostile to bananas, just to watch – for the politics of bacteria, the soil's stringing of rings and chains in nets only God can tell the meshes of, have seen the fruit thrive often to lengths of a foot and a half, yes amazing but true. (5–6)

An apocalyptic judgment from which there is "no appeal," or a banana breakfast that Prentice concocts for his "messmates": who exactly is speaking here? Was the earlier, indeterminate opening scene of a population to be evacuated "to salvation" (3) nothing but a dream? Were we then, and are we now (a few pages later) in the mind of Pirate Prentice? The characters in the novel, first among them Tyrone Slothrop (his name, a play on entropy), will eventually be "scattered all over the Zone" of Postwar Europe (712). From the start, as the narrational voice "begins, and continues throughout much of the novel with an outside, perhaps ironically detached, posture" (Arlett 1996, 134), a certain authorial distance is maintained between the reader and our third-person narrator. Such perspectival shifts, however, can also occasion direct, often ironic and sometimes irritated, modes of personal address – consistent with those we have seen in Claire-Louise Bennett, a generation or two after Pynchon. For example, one section of *Gravity's Rainbow* opens with the line "You will want cause and effect. All right" (663). Bennett likewise imparts self-descriptions grudgingly, with phrases, such as "if you must know" (*Pond*, 164), "I may as well menion" (22), "for your information" (28), "Can't you see!" (75), "I'm determined you see" (76). The distancing effect may be consistent, in Pynchon's case, with his own dislike of public and critical attention, which has led most critics and scholars to assume that Pynchon is "compelled to 'hide' himself in his fiction as he does in life" (Arlett 1996, 141, citing Schwarzbach 1978, 65). But, as Robert Arlett has suggested in his chapter on Pynchon in *Epic Voices*, plentiful

> intrusions of the author, through and beyond Pirate's fantasy management, signal that Pynchon's personality is one with the surrealistic excursions . . . that permeate the narrative. Indeed, the

> narrative survives only by a series of absurd chase and escape scenes that
> undercut the validity of character as action, except to assume that the
> action of the narrative takes place within the author's phantasmagoric
> self. (*Epic Voices*, 141–2)

By weaving in and out of his narrative, by giving his characters Puritan ancestors
consistent with his own family history and thematizing the *managerial* tactics
that corporate powers have applied to our innermost thoughts and desires,
Pynchon can be said to enable a much more direct voicing of his authorial
disposition than most critics and scholars have perceived. By contrast, Robert
Arlett, having listened closely to the *epic voices* throughout *Gravity's Rainbow*,
celebrates "the achievement" (while noting the unavoidable corporatist compli-
cities) "of the novelist to manage and display the consciousness of others (his
characters)" (*Epic Voices*, 139). Where a world grounded in continued technological development fragments and forgets, literary texts weave together in the
manner of textiles: touching on common themes across timeframes, periods,
eras, and epochs, and communicating not via an abstract network of proprietary
technologies (the mode of today's social media) but by imagining human minds
in relation to other minds, and (many more) nonconscious cognitive assemblages. Moreover, it is this *intersubjective*, at once "Inner and Global Impulse"
(to cite Arlett's subtitle) that links Pynchon, and his pre-eminent posthumanism, more to the long tradition of literary epic than to the realist novel.

The Apprentice Author As Fantasist-surrogate

Pirate's "famous... Banana Breakfasts" (*Gravity's Rainbow*, 5) and his London
hothouse with "foot and a half" long bananas – surely a collective English fantasy
during the war – are, the previously ironic speaker assures us, "amazing but true"
(6). Despite this assertion, it is possible that, while the initial dream sequence ends
early, a larger Pirate-related dream remains as narrative impetus.... [Pirate's] most
"amazing" quality is that he can, the speaker "might as well mention here" (11),
"get inside the fantasies of others" (12). He is useful to "the Firm" because he can
unburden others – very important people in the Firm's scheme – of their
"exhausting little daydreams." This he does in his role as "fantasist-surrogate" (12).

> Arlett (Epic Voices, 138–9) goes on to say more about how the Firm's
> surrogation of the psychological disposition of people they wish to control
> is comparable to Pynchon's own not infrequent shifts away from his
> character's consciousness into his own authorial presence:

It is as though the [ap]prentice pirate[r] (writer/printer) is an authorial
surrogate.... Pirate's fantasies seem to be the key to the phantasmagoric
transitions in the narrative. If we are told of Pirate's Mendoza gun, on the next page
we will zoom back to the seventeenth century to consider an ancestor of

[twentieth-century wartime character] Katje shooting dodoes to extinction with his haakbus. And if it seems inappropriate for, say, a [positivist and instrumentalist character such as] Pointsman to be assigned an inner consciousness that reaches poetry, we may attribute it to the reverie of Pirate/Pynchon. The rendition of Pointsman's "mad exploding of himself" (*Gravity's Rainbow*, 143) belongs less to that "scientist-neutral" Pointsman, so identified by Jessica, than to that inner sensibility reached by Pirate's old commando trick: it is the achievement of the novelist to manage and display the consciousness of others (his characters).

Without too much of an imaginative stretch, then, we might identify the Prentice character as a surrogate for (the notably private) Thomas Pynchon's authorial enactments. As a character, Prentice exists "primarily as a conduit to the inner beings of others" (*Epic Voices*, 138). That, after all, is the achievement of any novelist or epical vocalizer who presents us with the imagined subjectivity of fictive characters, in settings that are no less imagined because they can be only partially observed and observed *differently* by perceivers in different settings and moments in time. And once our narratives are fixed in print, on film, or in digital media, it becomes possible to preserve our cognitive interactions. The *medial turn* in contemporary literature offers multiple ways of transforming these passing moments into epical narratives of human lifetimes, stories, and histories. Such imagined self-awareness and dispersed characterizations are what impart to Pynchon's narrative a sense of experiential otherness and *a presence of other times* that, for Mikhail Bakhtin (for example) was a primary concern carried over from epic to modern fictions. That carry-over, once it becomes grounded in a novelistic genre, might take the form of "exhausting little daydreams" of powerful and (self-)important people (*Gravity's Rainbow*, 12). But there can also be more long-term, deep, and retentive enactments that, in philosopher Bernard Stiegler's terms (of primary, secondary, and tertiary *retentions*), are held onto over time and among many subjectivities through the generations and across media. It is precisely such intersubjective and intertextual linkages that determine how we, as readers, experience the reality (or surrealism, or epical heroism) of a literary work in our own time.

The Idea of EPIC (J. B. Hainsworth)

Heroism, empire, destiny, and faith are all necessary myths that have been sustained and sometimes created by art. The art was that of heroic poetry at the beginning of literature, when heroic poetry reached society as a whole.

So writes J. B. Hainsworth in *The Idea of EPIC* (1991, 148). He points out how "In those times society *listened*," whereas in the late twentieth century "society *views*." Film, not poetry is for Hainsworth (and Pynchon) "the modern heroic medium." But a dispersed, mediated society no longer listens, its members don't remember for long, and its own heroic, imperial, generational and religious qualities are no longer presented without a measure of skepticism and irony. It is no accident, for example, that digital authors Eugenio Tisselli and Rui Torres call for a turn away from postmodern cynicism to a different, arguably posthuman disposition that they describe as *kynicism*, namely: "a rejection of official cultures by means of irony and sarcasm, confronting the normalized ideologies masked by cynicism" (Torres and Tisselli, 2020).

Such is the promise of Pynchon's subjective interactions, archival intersections, and ranging imaginative excursions. What makes these excursions compelling, yet also strange and disturbing, is the ease with which they are discovered and then taken over by the "higher echelons" of an emerging, post-World War II corporate culture (*Gravity's Rainbow*, 14). Prentice (Pynchon's primary authorial surrogate), for example, is said to possess an intuitive grasp of other people's dreams: "He had known for a while that certain episodes he dreamed could not be his own. This wasn't through any rigorous daytime analysis of content, but just because he knew" (13). This ability is something he keeps, understandably, to himself (and maybe one or two trusted acquaintances), but it is only a matter of time before Prentice's corporatist and military superiors find out about his talent and create for him a position as "fantasist-surrogate" (12), allowing Them to access, control, and redirect the visions and dreams of enemies and competitors. ("They," the unnamed, unknown third-person powers that be, are capitalized throughout *Gravity's Rainbow*.)

Retention and Surrogation: Primary, Secondary, and Tertiary (Bernard Stiegler)

Here at the start, and throughout Pynchon's narrative, we have a clear example of what philosopher Bernard Stiegler would later call "retentive enactments": a sensibility that is sustained "when the same temporal object occurs twice in a row," and so "it produces two different temporal phenomena" (Stiegler 2014: 34). A primary retention is simply a recollection we may have of things we see and hear in the world where we live. What Stiegler termed "secondary" retention, was the way an experience brought to our sensory attention – for example, a melody we "might have heard yesterday" – can then be recalled, watched, felt, and listened to again "in imagination through the play of memory" (52). In this way, sensations we experience at a given moment become a "filter" that releases what is held in memory and thus constitutes a flow of consciousness that determines continuities of our life experience.

Stiegler's example of a remembered melody is particularly appropriate as a lens through which to observe the closing scene of *Gravity's Rainbow*, where a projected readership is addressed along with the depicted audience at the Orpheus Cinema in Los Angeles, California: "Now everybody –". The word "sing" is unspoken – though of course it will be heard in the mind of every reader of *Gravity's Rainbow*, as we close the book in a present moment we might share with the author at the time when he was writing the novel. Through this, a collective, collaborative destiny is conveyed – a *protention* and anticipated completion of the contract and connectivity Pynchon has established with his readers as he and his audience join together in song. (See the text box "Song in Gravity's Rainbow.")

Song in Gravity's Rainbow

Throughout Pynchon's novel, there are many songs to choose from, ranging from the silly to the salient, from the "obscure sanjak" to the authorial "Hand," at the end, that turns the time:

> There is a Hand to turn the time,
> Though thy Glass today be run,
> Till the Light that hath brought the Towers low
> Find the last poor Pret'rite one. . .
> Till the Riders sleep by ev'ry road,
> All through our crippl'd Zone,
> With a face on ev'ry mountainside,
> And a Soul in ev'ry stone. . .
> Now everybody –

The omnipresence of song in Pynchon is addressed in a 2017 essay by Anahita Rouyan, who references a collection of "twenty-eight songs included in *Gravity's Rainbow*." This "peculiar CD project" was assembled, a few months before the publication of Pynchon's sixth novel, *Vineland*, by "a group of Portland State University students under the name of The Thomas Pynchon Fake Book." Rouyan continues:

> Bringing Pynchon's lyrics to life provided an opportunity for reactivating the value of language in vocal performance, perhaps what had been intended to happen with every reading of the novel. The last words of *Gravity's Rainbow*, "Now everybody – " (760), invite the reader to join the performance, a readerly act which Pynchon seems to covertly suggest every time he offers one of his zany, parodist, or disturbing lyrics. In their compelling study of the theme of domination in *Gravity's Rainbow*, Luc Herman and Steven Weisenburger remark that "one ought to stop, recognize the known or likely melody, and sing

> the text, feel its powers as a performance in a mock musical" (176). Songs do not only add to the entertainment value of *Gravity's Rainbow* but are integral to the novel's preoccupation with cultural dominance, expressed in the systematic nature of language and the order it imposes on human experience. (Rouyan 2017)

Stiegler argues that "[i]n the flux of what appears to your consciousness, you make selections which are personal retentions; these selections are made through the filters of secondary retentions which are held in your memory and which constitute your experience" (Stiegler 2014, 52). Stiegler's terminology responds in part to a concept of "deep attention" that originated with N. Katherine Hayles. Like Hayles, Stiegler recognizes a "generational shift in cognitive styles that poses challenges to education at all levels, including colleges and universities" (Hayles 2007, 187; cited by Stiegler 2012, 73). The continuities so produced in the mind of any one person across the generations sustain the continuity of consciousness that is necessary for our own continuing sense of selfhood. But what Pynchon offers with his conception of a fantasist-surrogate is more in line with what a *literary author*, like himself, brings to his readership. Though such surrogation is imagined, in *Gravity's Rainbow*, as a sharing of dreams, these can be realized among literary authors who are inspired in the first instance by other authors; by interacting readers, watchers, and listeners through material means: print or digital publication, filmic depiction, or the orality of preprint epic.

Such collective memories communicated through the generations are what Stiegler designates as *tertiary* retentions – which is to say, intersubjective and multimedial communications. A song's recording, a photograph's placement in a family album or, what is most significant from a literary standpoint, the printed word on paper or (more often at present, circa 2022) on screens in digital media. Depending on how they are implemented and curated, these tertiary retentions have the capacity to make us mindful of occurrences that we have not ourselves experienced directly. At this level, we can also extend our memories beyond our personal retentions toward resonant, *intertextual* linkages that operate on a larger cultural, conceptual, and historical plane of comprehension.

Intertexts: Pynchon, Gibson, McCarthy, Whitehead, and Winterson

I have presented, in the previous two sections, close readings that take us from the opening sentence in *Gravity's Rainbow* (1973) to its open-ended closing, inviting "everybody" to join in song, a gesture (as we've also seen) toward an intersubjective and, as I will now show, intertextual condition in literary strains from epic orality to posthuman projections. Pynchon is not alone in his literary resistance to machinic automaticity. And his use of metaphors, juxtapositions, nonlinear narratives, and accidental occurrences convey realities that are both larger than consciousness and resistant to quantification or programmed, algorithmic conveyance. Let us now compare Pynchon's famous first sentence ("A screaming comes across the sky . . . .") with four others, produced over the succeeding decades, sequentially.

This one is by William Gibson, at the start of *Neuromancer* (1984):

> The sky above the port was the color of television, tuned to a dead channel.

The second comes at the start of Colson Whitehead's *Intuitionist* (1999):

> It's a new elevator, freshly pressed to the rails, and it's not built to fall this fast.

This one, at the start of Tom McCarthy's *Remainder* (2005):

> About the accident I can say very little. Almost nothing. It involved something falling from the sky. Technology. Parts, bits. That's it, really. All I can divulge. Not much, I know.

And a fourth, also skyward, from Jeanette Winterson's *Frankissstein* (2019):

> What we could see, the rocks, the shore, the trees, the boats on the lake, had lost their usual definition and blurred into the long grey of a week's rain.

Screens "tuned to a dead channel" – whether a grey field of fluctuating static in Gibson's America of 1984 or the small black rectangle of today's handheld digital devices – can only reinforce the feeling that our ongoing evacuations, as we saw at the start of *Gravity's Rainbow*, are "all theater." All carry a mixture of transcendental promise and a falling apart into material bits and pieces (and, in Winterson's case, "every solid thing" is shown to have "dissolved into its watery equivalent," another gray, particulate dissolution in which we might hear an echo of Karl Marx, "All that is solid melts into air" [chapter 1 of the *Communist Manifesto*]).

Each line in this series of literary posthumanist explorations enacts a measure of *unknowing* and incapacity to communicate, "divulge," or explain what is happening. All share the theme of environmental and technological breakdown. We cannot say for certain whether Gibson, Whitehead, and McCarthy are intentionally alluding to Pynchon. In Winterson's case, we have a book-length rewriting of Mary Shelley's *Frankenstein*, in parallel stories set in rain-soaked Lake Geneva during that novel's composition in the summer of 1816, a speculative rewriting that is paired with a gathering, in the twenty-first-century present of "transgender medical professionals," some of whom are "transhuman enthusiasts" as well (*Frankissstein*, 104).

Self-consciously intertextual, or coincidental, it's safe to say in each instance that the wartime "evacuation" depicted at the start of *Gravity's Rainbow* "still proceeds" into late-twentieth- and early twenty-first-century bookish encounters with singularities: things falling from the sky; the sky being looked at as though it were a tv screen; elevators that sometimes fill and sometimes empty tall buildings; and what Mary Wollstonecraft and Percy Bysshe Shelley could discern in the mists above Lake Geneva, 1816.

In peacetime, as in Pynchon's Second World War setting, entire city neighborhoods can be abandoned – in a way that gives Whitehead's main character, Lila Mae Watson, a feeling that her own "city had been evacuated" (*The Intuitionist*, 3). Communication hardware in Gibson, a falling elevator in Whitehead's modern high rise, falling rain in Winterson's waterlogged setting or the falling parts in Pynchon's V2 rocket and McCarthy's drone era – these technologies and environmental realities are mostly ignorable before the object falls or the city is evacuated. We don't think about the dangers they contain until their supporting infrastructure is gone – or gone awry.

The Intuitionist

In a deftly plotted mystery and quest tale that's also a teasing intellectual adventure, Whitehead traces the continuing education of Lila Mae Watson, the first black woman graduate of the Institute for Vertical Transport and thus first of her race and gender to be employed by the Department of Elevator Inspectors. In a "famous city" that appears to be a future New York, Lila Mae compiles a perfect safety record working as an "Intuitionist" inspector who, through meditation, "senses" the condition of the elevators she's assigned. But after an episode of "total freefall" in one of "her" elevators leads to an elaborate investigation, Lila Mae is drawn into conflict with one of the Elevator Guild's "Empiricists," those who, unlike Intuitionists, focus their attention on literal mechanical failures. *Kirkus Reviews*, Nov. 15, 1998 (review posted online May 20, 2010: www.kirkusreviews.com/book-reviews/colson-whitehead/the-intuitionist/).

Few fictions have set out a conflict that so clearly parallels the oppositions we have seen between an affective and intersubjective posthumanism on one side (Whitehead's Intuitionists), and a transhuman technicity on the other (Empiricists). And few so clearly embrace a guiding predecessor at the start of their career – as did Pynchon himself, for example, in his early short story "Entropy." There, the character Calypso in 1950s Washington DC is drafting his own personal biography in the third-person mode of *The Education of Henry Adams* (written *by* Henry, 1907). Regarding Whitehead, the *Kirkus Review* presents *The Intuitionist* as a "dizzingly-high -concept debut of genuine originality, despite its indebtedness to a specific source" namely: Ralph Ellison's classic *Invisible Man*. Whitehead's reviewer in the *New York Times* notes the Pynchon connection: "He's obviously trying to do for second-generation elevator transport what Thomas Pynchon did for alternative mail delivery in 'The Crying of Lot 49' – using it ironically as a metaphor for a radical new way of restructuring the accepted reality." Gary Krist, *New York Times*, February 7, 1999.

As we have seen with Shelley Jackson's self-conscious rewrite (and remediation) of Mary Shelley's *Frankenstein*, the posthumanist strain in literature is less a matter of "originality" than it is (like the longer epic tradition discussed in the next section) a commitment to *growth*. Specifically, the growth in Whitehead's fiction is achieved not through building and accumulation but cognitively, by his character Lila Mae's *sensing* the condition of the elevators she inspects. In this way, we can observe in Lila Mae another literary enactment of the new materialist concern with bringing the objective, built world into her inner, affective sphere – although, in this case, the elevation takes on much more literal dimensions than has been experienced in earlier sublime and transcendental enactments in literary works.

Through the high-speed transition from one era to the next – depending on which technology emerges at any given time – we have a literary continuity that can help us to perceive a commonality. We can find, for example, numerous continuities that run through our present, posthuman era, while hearkening back to preprint, epical strains. The intertext is what I hope to have suggested, in this section's collocation of opening lines from Pynchon in 1973 and further along in Gibson's mid-1980s cyberpunk and Whitehead's, McCarthy's, and Winterson's more recent, carefully staged re-enactments of narratives that can no longer be contained in everyday human consciousness. In these "percipient" fictions (which for Claire-Louise Bennett are more about moment-by-moment perception than preconceived human subjects), subjectivity circulates among many characters and authorship is projected onto multiple and, at times, other-than-human surrogates. Francisco Collado-Rodriquez finds, for example, in the work of William Gibson, a "cybernetic surrogation" that might be said to carry Pynchon's idea of the "fantasist-surrogate" into computational realms that anticipate our current digital era. There, in the "path-breaking novel *Neuromancer*" (1984):

> Gibson used the expression "To leave the meat behind" in a McLuhanian reference to the process by which his hackers switch themselves into the computer and enter cyberspace, in this way leaving their flesh (meat) behind and letting the mind ride free in the Web. But in his novel Gibson also foresaw the dystopic and commercial possibility of riding cyberspace – which he termed the matrix – to occupy somebody else's emotions. The process, which he called SimStim or Simulated Stimulation (*Neuromancer*, 1984, 55), featured soon in cyberpunk literature and also in films such as Kathryn Bigelow's *Strange Days* (1995). In these works, the process of occupying somebody else's emotions is frequently linked to the notion of commodification: SimStim has a commercial use and it also becomes addictive. In an ultimate manifestation of McLuhan's theories, the user of this device extends her or his self by entering the consciousness of another self, thus expanding towards the other, feeling pleasure, or pain or both. Collado-Rodríquez, "On Human Consciousness and Posthuman Slavery," 2018, 132.

(McLuhan notably advanced his theories of media addiction during a Tomorrow Show interview with National Broadcasting Corporation host Tom Snyder in the year 1976: "Marshall McLuhan Speaks," https://marshallmcluhanspeaks.com/soundbites/difficult-to-understand)

The theme of surrogation, explicitly named in Pynchon and Gibson, is also implied in Tom McCarthy's novel from the start, when the unnamed narrator is enriched with an £8.5 million settlement by the company responsible for the "technology," "parts," and "bits" that caused his injury. As noted by Sydney Miller, "the whole text is bound by the same nondisclosure agreement," and yet the novel is not an investigation of "what has happened" but rather what comes after – that which remains, in memory and the narrator's cognitive, physical, and psychic lapses ("Intentional Fallacies," 2015, 639):

> The Settlement. That word: *Settlement. Set-l-ment.* As I lay abject, supine, tractioned and trussed up, all sorts of tubes and wires pumping one thing into my body and sucking another out, electronic metronomes and bellows making this speed up and that slow down, their beeping and rasping playing me, running through my useless flesh and organs like sea water through a sponge – during the months I spent in hospital, this word planted itself in me and grew. *Settlement.* It wormed its way into my coma. (*Remainder*, 5–6)

What McCarthy's narrator has lost is not his conscious awareness but something larger: what N. Katherine Hayles terms "nonconscious cognition," which was taken for granted prior to the accident. To fill "the no-space of complete oblivion" (*Remainder*, 6) that the narrator has entered, he spends most of his wealth and highly focused attention on *re-enactments* of entirely ordinary settings and unremarkable, habitual human activities. Hayles's depiction of the narrator's first re-enactment, a crack on a bathroom wall, "illustrates the peculiar combination of chance and fanatical exactitude that characterizes his projects, as if he were channeling John Cage's 'chance operations' while gulping amphetamines." Hayles (*Unthought*, 90) continues:

> His imagination, growing outward from the crack, conjures an entire building, a mishmash of memories, second-hand anecdotes, and fantasized encounters. We know, for example, that the arrangement he dictates for the courtyard comes not from his own experience but from his friend Catherine's account of the place in her childhood where she felt most authentic, "swings, on concrete... And there was a podium, a wooden deck, a few feet from the swings' right" (*Remainder*, 76). The narrator appropriates her account to re-create this exact scene (*Remainder*, 122).

Narrators appropriating accounts by characters in the service of the author's own purpose: We have noted Pynchon's use of Pirate Prentice as a "surrogate" for his own authorial acts of imagination. Sydney Miller observes McCarthy's narrator functioning similarly, "as a surrogate not for the reader but the author – the imaginative Everyman whose command of his creation extends only through its completion, who dictates every detail of a text only to relinquish interpretive control to the critics awaiting its publication" ("Intentional Fallacies," 634–5). The surrogation, in *Remainder*, can thus be said to take readers further into cognitive realms than the imagined, personal fantasies found in Pynchon and Gibson. McCarthy, for his part, extends authorial powers into the more than human, cognitive environment that conditions our posthumanity: What would life be like if you had to think about every move you made? How to walk across the room, take a seat or grab hold of something? The defamiliarizations that McCarthy imposes are not just about his particular authorial dispositions: they bring to a reader's awareness the power of our own nonconscious experience. And our take is neither a realistic nor hysterical worldview but rather a better appreciation – through the detailed depiction of a neurological injury – of what it means to think, and the many contingencies, cracks, and nonconscious ecosystems that surround us and enable our actions, and our thought.

Frankisssstein

Frankisssstein: A Love Story is a holistic tribute to Mary Shelley's *Frankenstein; or, The Modern Prometheus* (1818). Through the double first-person narrative of Mary Shelley and her 21st-century reincarnation Ry Shelley, Winterson weaves an intricate trans-temporal and trans-spatial multiplicity, the coding of which is governed by Shelley's masterpiece, and particularly by the *topos* at its core: Frankenstein's Monster. On the literal level, Winterson recreates the motif of a humanoid composite brought to life by scientific intervention through the lens of contemporary scientific possibilities and the prevailing discourses on the nature of identity and humanness (most notably, queer theory, transhumanism, and posthumanism). One of the main protagonists, Ry Shelley, is a transgender physician who identifies as "not one thing. Not one gender. I live with doubleness" (Winterson, 2019, 89). His lover Victor Stein, an artificial intelligence savant, is instrumental in an even more literal evocation of Shelley's central motif. He conducts experiments with body parts Ry supplies from his hospital. Another prominently featured twist on the Monster topos are the AI-run sexbots that one of the characters develops and sells. Mojca Krevel, "The Monstrous Cosmos of Jeanette Winterson's Frankisssstein" (2021, 86)

Krevel's mention of a "humanoid composite" resonates with Bruno Latour's compositionist manifesto and the compositional effort in McCarthy's *Remainder* that in both authors is material and literal as much as it is literary.

The respective openings that we've explored in this section carry us over, without interruption, from Pynchon's V2 Rocket cartel at the end of the Second World War, to Gibson's televisual, mass-mediated moment, and into Whitehead's and McCarthy's more object-oriented, digitized era of technological parts and informational bits (and bytes), whose divulgence is closely monitored by the (unnamed, never fully known) powers that be: Pynchon's "They." The series of moments that we experience in these one-line narrative openings signal a continuing, high-speed transition from one era to the next. Depending on which technology emerges at any given time, we have a literary continuity that can help us to perceive a commonality, and numerous continuities that run through our present, posthuman era, while hearkening back to preprint, epical strains that I will address in the next chapter.

Transhumanist and Posthumanist Approaches (in Whitehead)

We might find further instances of *unknowing* in Hayles's account of the singular, unexplained crashing of Elevator No. 11 in Whitehead's narrative. Rationally and politically, the Empiricists and the Intuitionists are keen on deciding which intellectual camp is responsible for the elevator's fall. As Hayles indicates: "Empiricism investigates the soundness of elevators using measurable variables and arrives at results that can be verified empirically," whereas Intuitionism, by contrast, "relies on intuition, internal visualization, and feelings to arrive at judgments expressed not through measurements but subjective feeling." The Empiricist/Intuitionist opposition parallels the structure of Transhumanist and Posthumanist approaches, even as the *undecidability* is shown by Hayles to re-enact the indeterminacy that one finds in both Bohr's modern physics and Alan Turing's machine, which placed a "conceptual limit to what computation can accomplish" (*Unthought*, 186).

Hayles observes how Lila Mae's own investigations parallel those of modern science, when, for example, Whitehead's character

> discovers the elevator's secret when she returns late at night to the Fanny Briggs building. Although No. 11 is now smashed to bits, she re-creates her experience of it with No. 14, using the elevator's ascent to remember, as vividly and in as much detail as possible, her intuitive grasp of No. 11's performance. As she rises, "The genies appear on cue, dragging themselves from the wings. All of them energetic and fastidious, describing seamless verticality to Lila Mae in her mind's own tongue . . . The genies bow and do not linger for her lonely applause. She opens her eyes. The doors open to the dead air of the forty-second floor. She hits the Lobby button. Nothing." (*The Intuitionist*, 227)

Forensics, Lila Mae intuits, offers nothing to account for the accident, and neither do the Empiricist and Intuitive standpoints, so long as they are advanced as disciplinary or political positions. And it is precisely this region of indeterminacy and unknowability that both the literary and scientific imagination inhabit, *differently* depending on circumstances.

Chapter 7

Posthuman Epic in the Era of AI

Shelley is improving my Greek and Latin. We lie on the bed, him naked, his hand on my back, the book on the pillow. He kisses my neck as we manage new vocabulary. Often we break off for love. I love his body. Hate it that he is so careless of himself. Truly he imagines that nothing so gross as matter can oppose him. But he is made of blood and warmth. I rest on his narrow chest, listening to his heart.

Together we are reading Ovid: *Metamorphoses*.
– Jeanette Winterson, *Frankissstein* (59–60)

No clearer opposition can be found, for the replacement of a romantic, male, transcendentalist neglect of "matter" with an ever-emerging, multigendered, multigeneric, and intertextual materialism. And no literary activity addresses this materialism more fully than a shared, unabashedly sensual engagement with new vocabularies and the intertextual renewal of earlier literary accomplishments. Winterson in this passage is imagining the convergence of sensual and mental experience that moved Mary Shelley toward a life-changing literary engagement. It is an aesthetic projection by Winterson, in her own fictive work, on the same order as Mary and Percy Shelley's shared reading (and Mary's rewriting) of Ovid's classic. This line, for example that Winterson adds to the many headnotes that separate sections of her novel:

> Nor dies the spirit but new life repeats
> In other forms and only changes seats. Ovid, *Metamorphoses*
> (Winterson, *Frankissstein*, 315)

Ovid himself, who was twenty-four years old when his Roman predecessor, Virgil, died (19 BCE), was careful (and capricious) enough not to repeat too closely the achieved epical format embodied in the acclaimed and finished generic form of the *Aeneid*. Ovid knew, as well as those who emulated Virgil and Homer, how much the epic's necessary myths depended on realizations, in writing, of "heroism, empire, destiny, and faith" – the generic forms that provided a model for Rome's ambitions as an empire. But in the *Metamorphoses*, as J. B. Hainsworth noted in *The Idea of EPIC* (1991, 116–17),

Ovid's own intentions were more narrative than Virgil's, his verse structure more elegiac, and the roughly 250 stories in Ovid's *Metamorphoses* more numerous – and not so definitive and heroic as what we find in the traditional, epical format. As his title suggests, Ovid is more open to changes, unexpected and even inconsequential metamorphoses in the events and narrative structuring. Both Ovid in the first century and Mary Shelley in the nineteenth anticipate narrative structures that would now be termed "novelistic." And we can see quite clearly the emergence of this modern genre in the thoughts, and in the written words of Mary and Percy Shelley, as recounted by Jeanette Winterson:

> Shelley read out to me from Ovid the story of the sculptor Pygmalion, who fell in love with the statue he had carved himself. So deep in love was he with his creation that women were nothing to him. He prayed to the goddess Athena that he might find a living lover as beautiful as the lifeless form on his bench. That night, he kissed the lips of the youth he had created. Hardly believing what he felt, he felt the youth kiss him in return. The cold stone warmed. (*Frankissstein*, 60)

Percy Shelley also notes a recurrence of Ovid's theme in Shakespeare, "when the statue of Hermione comes to life" at the close of *The Winter's Tale*. "She steps down. She embraces her husband, Leontes, the tyrant. Through his crimes, Time itself had turned to stone, and now, in her movement, Time itself flows again. That which is lost is found" (60).

It must be, says Shelley (in Winterson's re-enactment) "that Shakespeare had such a picture in mind" (60). But the recovery of lost time is not simply a theme that recurs (with variations) in Ovid, Shakespeare, and the writings of Mary and Percy Shelley. The recovery of these dispersed narratives, and their present *rediscovery* by Jeanette Winterson, enriches literary history with a distinctive through-line of recurrent fictions, with variations and reimaginings that run from epical origins to our own time. Winterson asks herself, as Mary Shelley must have done when devising her Frankenstein novel, whether or not there is "such a thing as artificial intelligence?" (61). Or artificial life. The statue that wakes and walks. About this, Winterson is doubtful. "Clockwork has no thoughts. What is the spark of mind? Could it be made? Made by us?" (61).

The question, as Mary Shelley knew, had already been asked by Shakespeare in Sonnet 53:

> What is your substance, whereof are you made,
> That millions of strange shadows on you tend?

One answer, arguably, is that the re(dis)covery and rewriting by contemporary writers of past works is itself a revitalization of our imaginative powers, in narratives that do not remain fixed, formally (as epics tend to do), but that take on continually new formats – a tendency that Ovid had already anticipated with his title: *Metamorphoses*. But not until Mary Shelley's time in the early to mid-nineteenth century would the literary arts break free of the earlier epical constraints and be designated with the name that has been given to this emerging literary genre – namely, the *novel*.

Ada Lovelace and the Analytical Engine

It is desirable to guard against the possibility of exaggerated ideas that might arise as to the powers of the Analytical Engine. In considering any new subject, there is frequently a tendency, first, to *overrate* what we find to be already interesting or remarkable; and, secondly, by a sort of natural reaction, to *undervalue* the true state of the case, when we do discover that our notions have surpassed those that were really tenable. The Analytical Engine has no pretensions whatever to *originate* anything. It can do whatever we *know how to order it* to perform. It can *follow* analysis; but it has no power of *anticipating* any analytical relations or truths. Its province is to assist us in making *available* what we are already acquainted with.

Augusta Ada King, the Countess of Lovelace, 1843, cited by Mark Halpern in "Artificial intelligence isn't as intelligent as you think," *The American Scholar*, March 2, 2020.

Ada, daughter of Lord Byron, is widely recognized as the first computer programmer, and Halpern rightly directs our attention to how Ada's first words "demand and repay close reading." The computer, Halpern reiterates:

"can do whatever we *know how to order it* to perform." This means both that it can do *only* what we know how to instruct it to do, and that it can do *all* that we know how to instruct it to do. The "only" part is just as important – it explains (for those open to explanation) why the computer keeps performing feats that seem to show that it's thinking, while critics, like me, continue to insist that it is doing no such thing.

The same can be said of the many critical posthumanists who, like Halpern (and Ada Lovelace), insist on the analytical engine's *lack of imaginative power*. Though our present-day computers are now capable of executing millions or billions of steps, this does not mean that they are thinking: unlike the billions of neurons in a human mind, "the computer never behaves mysteriously, never appears to have volition." And that, Halpern claims, is the source of its value: being unable to "think for itself," the computer is

the perfect vehicle for and executor of *preserved human* thought – of thought captured and "canned" in the form of programmed algorithms. And we must not be so thunderstruck at our success in building a perfectly obedient servant that we take it for our peer, or even our superior. Jeeves is marvelous but is, after all, a servant. Bertie Wooster is master.

From Metamorphoses to Media Multiplicity

The generic distinction between epic and novel that I have set out here is far from original. Famously, M. M. Bakhtin asserted that the epic and the novel are at opposite poles: the former "an absolutely completed and finished generic form," the latter "the sole genre that continues to develop" (*The Dialogic Imagination*, 15, cited in Arlett, *Epic Voices*, 11). For Bakhtin in the mid-twentieth century, "epic discourse is infinitely far removed from [novelistic] discourse of a contemporary about a contemporary addressed to contemporaries" (*The Dialogic Imagination*, 3, cited in Arlett, *Epic Voices*, 11). This definition would certainly exclude Dante's *Divine Comedy*, Wordsworth's *Prelude*, or Whitman's *Leaves of Grass* from epicism. Arlett, for his part, aligns his own approach to "certain novels written in the third quarter of the [twentieth] century," *Gravity's Rainbow* among them, "with that of Brian Wilkie" – who had suggested:

> following the lead of such earlier epic liberals as Voltaire, Schelling, and Fielding... that the "basic law of epic throughout its history has been growth" and that, although the epic tradition may be rooted in the past, "the partial repudiation of earlier epic tradition is itself traditional." Thus [Wilkie] asserts that "no great poet has ever written an epic without radically transforming it or giving it new dimensions, and often that intention is explicitly declared." (Arlett, *Epic Voices*, 10–11, citing Wilkie, 1965, 10–11)

Gravity's Rainbow (1973), published a generation after Bakhtin's "Epic and Novel" (1941; in Bakhtin, 1981), no doubt would be excluded from epical traditions were it not for the widespread recognition throughout Pynchon scholarship of epic's "basic law" of growth: an accrual that is more ecosystemic than economic, and more of an *internalization* than a mere exploration of the world and its entangling objects. We have seen how this novel's opening sequence not only resonates with authors Pynchon's age (in the postmodern era) but also speaks to younger contemporaries exploring a growth that is unabated from one decade to the next (if somewhat displaced from rocket technology and nuclear threat to ever smaller, more personalized gadgets). Relevant books, articles, and chapters abound on both cognitive and corporate growth that is enacted in Pynchon's own thought streams. Tom LeClair's "systems novel" (1989), Franco Moretti's *Modern Epic: The World System from Goethe to Garcia Marquez* (1960), Frederick Karl's *Mega-Novel*, and my own *Cognitive Fictions* (2002) are each absorbed (with revisions) into Stefano Ercolino's try at a definitive description of a transnational, contemporary *Maximalist Novel: From Thomas Pynchon's* Gravity's Rainbow *to Roberto Bolaño's* 2666 (2014). Also referenced by Ercolino are John Johnston's "novel of information multiplicity," Edward Mendelson's "encyclopedic novel," and N. Katherine Hayles's "Cosmic Web" (which fills out the scientific and technological extensions that typify Pynchon's writing specifically). Like Arlett in *Epic Voices* two decades earlier, Ercolino aims at a summary term in the aftermath of a sustained but not yet historically integrated set of approaches, which together demonstrate epic's tendency toward growth (of consciousness and actively shared memories, not a settled human-centered history or mere extension of factual knowledge).

Encyclopedic Narrative from Dante to Pynchon

Encyclopedic narrative identifies itself not by a single plot structure, but by encompassing a broad set of qualities. All include a full account of a technology or science. A complete medieval astronomy may be constructed out of Dante, a full account of Renaissance medicine out of Rabelais. Don Quixote is an adept at the science of arms. *Faust* expounds opposing geological theories and anticipates evolutionary biology. *Moby-Dick* is an encyclopedia of cetology, and there is a detailed account of embryology embedded in the "Oxen of the Sun" chapter of *Ulysses*. *Gravity's Rainbow* is expert in ballistics, chemistry, and some very advanced mathematics. Encyclopedic narratives also offer an account of an art outside the realm of written fiction: the carved bas-reliefs in the *Purgatory*, the puppetry of *Don Quixote*, the Greek tragedy of *Faust*, the whale-paintings in *Moby Dick*, the musical echoes in *Ulysses*'s "Sirens," film and opera in *Gravity's Rainbow*. Edward E. Mendelson (1976), "Encyclopedic Narrative: From Dante to Pynchon," 1270–1

The integration of visual, sonic, and touchable "art outside the realm of written fiction" has been observed already in Shelley Jackson's hypertext fiction and will be a defining feature of more recent works that we'll explore in Chapter 9 ("Digital Posthumanism (On the Periphery)").

We can discern, then, in the reception of Pynchon's fiction in particular, a distinctive strain of epical narrative that is now running through our present, posthuman era. It is worth pausing to consider the ways that our current media of reception might be even further inclined toward epical formalisms. In the wake of novelistic, and determinedly *new*, never finished generic forms (to again reference Bakhtin on the novel), we may now be re-*turning*, going back and working variations on epical literary forms. No longer are we assembling narrative fictions in a single, print medium; we are now more inclined toward a vast compilation of observable, measurable, interconnected but never completely cognized elements and objects.

As Pynchon himself recognized early in his career, there is almost a mysticism that accompanies our self-made human enhancements. A feeling that "the highest condition we can attain is that of an object – a rock," as the character Esther (in his first novel of 1963, *V.*), recalls from her vague memory of "one of the Eastern" religions: she feels herself "drifting down, this delicious loss of Estherhood" as her nose is operated on for cosmetic purposes (*V.*, 106). And this insight into objectivity, and pseudoreligious belief in bodily improvement, brings Pynchon closer to the new materialist strain of more recent literary posthumanisms, as literary scholar Amy Elias notes in a 2015 presentation (at the International NARRATIVE conference in Chicago):

> Object oriented ontology (abbreviated OOO) is a developing branch of theory associated with what is called "the new materialism." There are numerous versions of TRIPLE O, but all make ontological claims: all are realist philosophies that assert that a reality actually exists independently of the human mind. ... Sometimes referenced as "thing theory," this theory asserts that objects have presence, even agency, within the complex macrosystems or "hyperobjects" constituting reality.

Pynchon scholarship, Elias points out, has "long noted the use of catalogues, lists, and animated objects in Pynchon's novels – talking clocks, ball lightning, mechanical ducks, glowing Indians, Lambton Worms, runaway cheeses, Gardens Titanic, angels, sentient tornadoes, etc." There is also, as I have here noted, substantial, encyclopedic background that has been addressed by Pynchon scholars. What Elias herself brought to the conversations, in her paper on Pynchon at the Chicago conference, is a convergence of this object-oriented, systems approach in Pynchon with an emerging literary posthumanism in contemporary fiction.

Two Slide Shows (One Real, One Fictional)

Some premises of Object-Oriented Ontology (OOO) and [Jane] Bennett's "critical vitalism" that are important to *Gravity's Rainbow*:

1. Reality is not discourse. It is real. It is living, creative vitality, as are all objects in it. Correlationism is false.
2. All animate and inanimate things are equally things/objects. Anthropocentrism and biocentrism are false.
3. Philosophies that impose hierarchies upon the real are false. OOO levels violent hierarchies (such as subject / object) and eliminates moralities imposed upon being (such as Elect / Preterite).
4. Things resist cognitive mastery: things have "allure," "vibratory intensity," and immanent properties but are "withdrawn" from other objects, from presence. We cannot ever penetrate or fathom the full being of something else.
5. All object relations distort the things that are in relation; things can't relate fully to each other's thingness. "No object relates with others without caricature, distortion, or energy loss" (Graham Harman, "The Well-Wrought Broken Hammer," 188).
6. [Jane] Bennett (not Harman or Morton): Objects / things (including living things) form temporary aggregates or Deleuzian "agentic assemblages," and then disperse to reform again: life is actually flow and affective relation, not subject / object relations of domination.
7. [Jane] Bennett (not Harman or Morton): The world can be re-enchanted by realization of (the real) élan vital that flows in and as all things. Materiality itself is raised in status. "The Subjunctive" – as a realm of being where the time and space of consensus reality are suspended and ontological hierarchies are flattened – actually is monistic Reality.

> Amy Elias, University of Tennessee Short Paper delivered at "NARRATIVE: An International Conference" Roundtable "Reading Rainbow: Pynchon's Narrative Poetics Revisited," with Brian McHale, Kathryn Hume, Luc Herman, John Hellman. Chicago, IL, March 2015 "Pynchon, Gravity's Rainbow, and OOO, that Mysterious Rag."

While we are transcribing slides shown by a contemporary scholar, we might consider this one, in Winterson's *Frankisstein* (72–3) set out in a (fictive) TED talk by a leading transhumanist scholar, entrepreneur, and "Gospel Channel scientist," Victor Stein:

> He has a nice, clear graphic up on his screen:
>
> **Type 1 Life: Evolution-based.**
> Victor explains: Changes happen slowly over millennia.
>
> **Type 2 Life: Partially self-designing.**
> This is where we are now. We can develop our own brain software through learning, including outsourcing to machines. We update ourselves individually and generationally. We can adapt within a generation to a changing world – think of toddlers and iPads. We have invented machines of every kind for travel and labour. Horses and hoes are a thing of the past. We can also overcome some of our biological limitations: spectacles, eye-

laser, dental implants, hip replacements, organ transplants, prosthetics. We have begun to explore space.

Type 3 Life: Fully self-designing.
Now he gets excited. The nearby world of AI will be a world where the physical limits of our bodies will be irrelevant. Robots will manage much of what humans manage today. Intelligence – perhaps even consciousness – will no longer be dependent on a body. We will learn to share the planet with non-biological life forms created by us. We will colonise space.

His manner of presentation has a "sex-mix of soul-saving erudition. His body is lean and keen. . . . Women adore him. Men admire him. He knows how to play a room. He'll walk away from the podium to make a point. He likes to crumple his notes and throw them to the floor. . . ." (*Frankissstein*, 73)

Like the modern-day transhumanist scholars we have explored in Chapter 2 of this volume, Professor Victor Stein and his technological forays are presented by Winterson, for all their rhetorical cogency, as essentially speculative, and messianic:

He's a Gospel Channel scientist. But who will be saved? (*Frankissstein*, 73)

We might also, when recognizing (or re-*cognizing*) established literary genres, discover a much wider range of material and cognitive exploration than we had noticed before. In Charles Dickens, for example, scholars are now rediscovering contexts and backgrounds that have tended to be ignored – like the cracks in a bathroom wall and other, inconsequential "remainders" that Tom McCarthy self-consciously brings to the fore. Or the fingernails we've observed in Claire-Louise Bennett's *Pond*, painted "in the kitchen last Wednesday after lunch" in a shade called Highland Mist, which "is a very good name, a very apt name, as it turns out. Because, you see, the natural color of my nail, both the white part and the pink part, is still just about visible beneath the polish, it hasn't been completely obscured" (17).

Really a Crash, "Eureka" Book

In a 2008 interview McCarthy explained how he stumbled into writing *Remainder*: It "was really a Crash, 'eureka' book. I was at a party and saw a crack on the wall in the bathroom and had a moment of deja-vu – exactly like the protagonist; and within twenty or forty minutes I'd written an outline of the whole book on the back of an envelope or something. It was really a happy accident." ("What's Left Behind," 2008)

What remains, when human character is presented in all its limitations and powerlessness by McCarthy, Bennett, and (before them) Dickens, are an endless (but also focused) assemblage of environmental elements that have a vitality wholly unrelated to the lives and lifeways of a novel's protagonists. Particularly cogent are Claire-Louise Bennett's detailed presentations (of bananas, arrangements of fruit bowls on a bare window ledge, porridge, sliced almonds that resemble fingernails): these are some of the clearest current examples in contemporary fiction of an object-oriented literary practice. Described by *The New York Times* as "witty misanthropy," Bennett's disposition might be something more than this. It can be said to embody, in prose fiction, the way that actor–network theory urges us (in the words of Robert S. Emmett and David E. Nye) to see people (and ourselves) "not as sovereign individuals but as parts of complex systems that are structured to move in certain directions and to express certain values" (*The Environmental Humanities*, 2017, 143).

These nonhuman, environmental actualities, which were certainly sensed in Dickens's contemporaries (and famously dismissed, by George Orwell, a century later), have only recently garnered sustained, scholarly attention – in what we might now identify as a *new materialist, object-oriented* scholarship. (See the text box "Dickens's Epic Melodramas.") Pynchon's own obsession with bananas at the start of *Gravity's Rainbow* prevented his influential predecessor, Norman Mailer, from reading beyond the first chapter. Both Orwell and Mailer might appear in retrospect to have over-valued a personalized, humanistic counterforce to social and political systems that they (rightly) found oppressive. Pynchon, in his own depiction of a WW2 corporatization that was successfully carried forward by all sides in the war (German, American, Japanese and, eventually Russian), has little patience with left/right political factions that, in Amy Elias's words, were only pitting "dominant culture" against "resistant counter-culture." These human-centered, cultural emphases are readily absorbed into commercial schemes. Their mostly expressive self-positing "will only create a violent hierarchy within a conceptual system and make 'counter-culturalism' a subordinate Other to dominant reality." A subordination, not a structured political opposition. For Elias, however, an OOO approach asserts a more proactive political orientation in which "Pynchon distinguishes between systems (associated with Them) and agentic assemblages (associated with open affiliations) and advocates the latter. Agentic assemblages are created and dissolved spontaneously, are constantly shifting, are antiteleological, and are non-deterministic. In other words, starting with OOO, the openness of assemblages is realism, not counter-symbolization" ("Pynchon, *Gravity's Rainbow*, and OOO, that Mysterious Rag").

What we will not have, in Bakhtin's term, is an "absolutely completed and finished generic form" in the literary novel. And neither will we find such generic uniformity in the mega-novels of an author such as Thomas Pynchon or the remediations and intertexts of authors such as Shelley Jackson and Jeanette Winterson. An emerging posthuman epic is unlikely to produce "the definition or the celebration in absolute terms of a shared system of values and domains of knowledge, as was the case for the Homeric epic or for the didactic epic of Hesiod" (Ercolino, *The Maximalist Novel*, 31). We won't have a universally shared religious faith or a synthesis of knowledge from diverse disciplines and ways of life. Our philosophical and political paradigms will be inflected increasingly by other-than-human objects and life forms. Yet we might still have, in literary writing, "a deep and ineradicable need and illusion of being able to order, and thus master, the chaos and madness of existence. Whatever Lyotard may have to say, not all grand narratives came to an end with the advent of the postmodern," or (more recently), the posthuman. "Not at the aesthetic level, at least" (*The Maximalist Novel*, 32).

Dickens's Epic Melodramas

What most distinguishes Dickens's novels from those by almost any other, and from life, is that hardly anything in them ever recedes entirely into the background. Dickens fought long and hard against the human tendency to focus exclusively on what is of immediate pressing concern in any given situation. His often anodyne protagonists have to compete for our attention with the idiosyncratic vitality possessed by the dozens of minor characters who surround them (hundreds, if there's a riot in progress). After a while a glazed expression seems to settle on their face, as it dawns on them that they will never become the sort of person their creator most liked to describe. Less often acknowledged is the fact that the "worlds" these minor characters inhabit, while ascertainably mythical, have almost without exception been *sensed*: seen and heard, in all cases, and sometimes touched, tasted, or smelled.

David Trotter (December 17, 2020) reviewing "The Artful Dickens: Tricks and Ploys of the Great Novelist" by John Mullan, *London Review of Books* 42.24.

There is more than artfulness at work in the sensual world that overtakes, enlarges, and arguably outlasts the sentimental and (by now) established humanism of Dickens's fictional characters, whose inner lives are less engaging. George Orwell was not the only twentieth-century author to notice, in Dickens, the overuse of "unnecessary detail." As David Trotter goes on to say:

Orwell had in mind the "baked shoulder of mutton and potatoes under it" on which the company is feasting in *The Pickwick Papers* while Jack Hopkins tells the story of the child who swallowed a necklace. Dickens couldn't stop sensing. "His imagination overwhelms everything," Orwell concluded, "like a kind of weed."

A better anticipation could scarcely be found for a posthumanist aesthetic in the novel genre: specifically, the "epic melodramas" in Dickens that might not display the sophisticated subjectivities of a character in George Eliot or Henry James, but which nonetheless can be "exacting" in its own way. A "sheer copiousness of imagination," along with much "formal daring" and "experimental verve," are said (by John Mullan in *The Artful Dickens*) to have transformed the novel as a genre. And this transformation has much to do with the material circulation of the print novel (in installments both in London and across the Atlantic to an eagerly awaiting American audience) and the cultivation in readers of a capacity for *remembering*: "Serial publication," Trotter observes, "meant that Dickens had to find ways of enabling his readers to identify characters they might not have encountered for weeks or even months. No wonder, then, that he made especially effective use of the devices in novels dedicated to the 'strange operations of memory', including *Great Expectations* and *David Copperfield* where smell, for example, is said by Mullan to reveal 'the presentness of what is lost' (but not to Dickens)."

Much of the physical, embodied sensuality – of smell, touch, and taste more than conscious thought – can be understood in retrospect as a foray into the world of "unthought" that a posthumanist theorist such as N. Katherine Hayles would explore in contemporary fiction of the early twenty-first century. And it is probably no accident that John Mullan, in his 2020 rediscovery of Dickens, observes techniques, ploys, and fantastic analogies that exceed any character's conscious awareness, while having brought "new powers to fiction."

Chapter 8

Interlude

N. Katherine Hayles and the Cognitive Turn in Literary Posthumanism

My own first hint at the intellectual framework for understanding posthumanism might have reached me as an undergraduate when I opened *The Cosmic Web* (1984) by N. Katherine Hayles and found this statement:

> We are living amid the most important conceptual revolution since Copernicus argued that the earth was not the center of the universe. ("Preface," 9)

What allowed Copernicus (1453–1543) to decenter the earth in the cosmic scheme was a combination of rational argument and technological affordance – primarily, the telescope that enabled humans to perceive the cosmos apart from the flat earth that was previously conceivable. Dramatic as this change was for humanity's self-awareness, still it worked as an extension of human perception, agency, and individuality – which is to say, the decentering of the earth became a foundation for an emerging humanism. By contrast, Hayles in *The Cosmic Web* could move past this still human-centered cosmos by referencing the "field concept" of early-twentieth-century science whose implications and resonances, by now known to scientists, had not yet been recognized and reformulated by literary scholars for their own, aesthetic purposes. After Copernicus (for another four or five hundred years) we may have persisted in the belief that we humans ourselves remained central to life on earth, and capable of absorbing what we know from scientific observation into narratives of our own. That was no longer the case in the mid-1980s; and by this time, too, after the earth was no longer thought of as the center of the universe, the humanities were no longer at the center of the university.

"Perhaps most essential to the field concept," Hayles noted in 1984, "is the notion that things are *interconnected*" (9). As we now approach a moment when these interconnections (cross-disciplinary, intertextual, and multimedial) are becoming more and more evident, it is worth returning to Hayles's early innovations in literature and science and tracing their continued development right up to our present moment of new materialisms: not least the materiality of cognition, the "continuities and discontinuities between a 'natural' self and cybernetic posthuman," and the emergence of worldwide digital interaction (Hayles, *How We Became Posthuman*, 1996, 5).

Hayles, then, arguably is *the* scholar whose work current posthuman theorists continually go back to. Given the range and interconnectedness of the field concept, it is important for us to trace the evolution from her early innovations in literature and science right up to the emergence of today's digital posthumanism.

It is worth citing Hayles's definition of the field concept in full:

> The field concept, as I use the term, is not identical with any single field formulation in science. For the men and women who work with the various scientific field models and theories from day to day, they have highly specific meanings and applications. The term "field concept," by contrast, draws from many different models those features that are isomorphic, and hence that are characteristic of twentieth century thought in general. (*The Cosmic Web*, "Preface," 9)

Another notion that Hayles puts forward at the start of her career has to do with "the *self-referentiality* of language," which means that it's not just themes and theories that are interconnected. The language we use to formulate our themes and theories is itself a web of linkages and intersubjective communications. And these linkages, moreover, between words and things, the arbitrary signifiers we use to reference actual objects and experiential events: that structural web of linkages is as much our subject as the sciences we bring into contact with literary scholarship.

Seeing the Interconnection of the Whole

> Physics will never replace [Homer's contemporary] Hesiod, *because it does not confront the same questions.* And vice versa: so long as the need is felt for a "unitary world-view," modern science will have to yield to those "systems which apply to everything... and answer all questions." Francois Jacob, "Evolution and Tinkering," *Science* 196 (June 10, 1977), 1161; cited in Moretti, *Modern Epic*, 37 and Ercolino, *Maximalist Novel*, 32.

Like Hayles, Jacob and his successors recognize a tendency for science to fragment into "highly specific meanings and applications" (*The Cosmic Web*, 9). What Hayles brings to the discussion with the "field concept" is a perspective more in line with the modern physics of Bohr and Heisenberg, the systems theory of second-order cybernetics, and (as literature relocates in digital spheres) an algorithmic narrativity that promises to realize and enlarge the "structural web of linkages" that Hayles in 1984 had already identified in Pynchon's *Gravity's Rainbow*. There, everything is placed "at an equal distance from the reader, so that background and foreground collapse into the same perceptual plane" (174). And Pynchon's refusal "to make the distinction between the meaningful event and the 'irrelevant' detail" (174) further displaces human character and consciousness from larger, environmental conditions.

With everything "at an equal distance from the reader, meaning can no longer be achieved," as it is in structural linguistics, "by discerning difference. Rather, it emerges as a result of seeing that everything is at the same distance" (175). Hayles continues: "Meaning thus becomes a function not of difference but of similarity, arising not from distinguishing parts but from seeing the interconnection of the whole" (175). Here, too, Hayles, like the many new materialist scholars she anticipates and influences, departs from the Structuralist and Psychoanalytic perspectives of her time. That said, she does make some initial gestures, in a footnote, toward a cognitive perspective in early forays by, for example, Ulric Neisser in *Cognitive Psychology* (Englewood Cliffs: Prentice Hall, 1967) and M. Toda's nontechnical account in "Time and the Structure of Human Cognition," in *The Study of Time II*, edited by J. T. Fraser and N. Lawrence (New York, Heidelberg, Berlin: Springer-Verlag, 1975, 17ff).

As an undergraduate engineering major studying the relations of literature and science, what I appreciated about Hayles, and what she brought to the early meetings of the Society for Literature and Science (founded in 1985), was a seamless integration of poststructuralist theories, without collapsing the different contexts that the physical sciences can bring to a literary discussion. Sure enough, poststructuralism was something everybody in English departments was talking about, but Hayles, unlike others, never lost sight of the materiality of language itself. She had a way of bringing literary theory into a larger, scientific conversation and field view (be it a disciplinary or natural "field") where "everything is connected to everything else." And language, whether spoken, typed or (already, in the mid-1980s) flickering on a screen, is itself no less complex than the physical and worldly relations it describes and brings to awareness:

> Because everything, in the field view, is connected to everything else by means of the mediating field, the autonomy assigned to individual events by language is illusory. When the field is seen to be inseparable from language, the situation becomes even more complex, for then every statement potentially refers to every other statement, including itself. (*The Cosmic Web*, 10)

Words referencing words; statements referencing other statements (and referencing themselves): What keeps Hayles from falling into the hermeticism that sometimes infects literary theory is her appreciation of the imaginative qualities of scientific and technological developments. Hayles is able to recognize this convergence of materiality and literary imagination in the placement of historical characters in imagined settings, such as the scene in *Gravity's Rainbow* where Walter Rathenau's ghost makes an appearance. In Hayles's reading, our ongoing technological issues of "control and synthesis" are affected (or "perverted") by imaginary "bureaucrats on the other side":

> As Rathenau suggests, the issues of control and synthesis are central to understanding our perversions of the field view. In Kekulé's dream, the bureaucrats on the Other Side try to bring dreams within Their control. But in Rathenau's seance, control itself is revealed as a dream. The bureaucracy aims to reinforce pre-existing patterns of consciousness by reassuring the self-conscious mind that even its moments of unconsciousness are controlled by "switching-paths"; but the spirits from the Other Side insist that even moments of supposed self-awareness are an illusion. "Caught in the Web: Pynchon" (in *The Cosmic Web*, 173)

Walter Rathenau, who is recognized by historians as "prophet and architect of the cartelized state" (*The Cosmic Web*, 172) appears in a séance staged by Pynchon in *Gravity's Rainbow* (164). Such perspicuous analysis of passages that mainstream contemporaries of Pynchon were prone to label as "hysterical" (Wood, 2000) distinguish Hayles's encounter with Pynchon's aesthetic. What Hayles perceived in this early encounter that few others would notice prior to the cognitive turn in literary criticism was a replacement of conventional, self–other conceptions of cognition by "an appreciation for the synchronicity of Nature in which humans do not stand outside as originators of pattern but take their place within already existing harmonies that include and subsume them" (173). Like so many who have noticed Pynchon's surrogation of his own authorial powers and subordination of character to nonhuman characteristics, Hayles regards "the narrator's obliteration of pattern" as "an attempt to create another kind of pattern, a pattern that is holistic rather than sequential, synchronous rather than causal, natural rather than specifically human" (173).

Object Orientation (and Latour) Revisited

While philosophers used to see direct knowledge of the objective world as unproblematic, authors since Kant have problematized this idea: our knowledge of the world is always mediated, by the categories of our understanding according to Kant, or by language, anonymous structures or ideology according to more recent authors. How, then, can one make room for things? How can we ever know what things really are or want, when we are buried under representations, social constructions, ideologies or power

relations? In opposition to the "prelinguistic stance" of earlier thinkers, where knowledge of the thing in itself seemed possible, we are children of the linguistic turn: nothing is known without mediation through language.
– Massimiliano Simons, *The Parliament of Things and the Anthropocene: How to Listen to "Quasi-Objects"* (2017, 2)

As we've seen earlier in discussions of Einstein's and Heisenberg's physics, our modern epoch demands a different response to the events we observe in nature. Like Karen Barad, Massimiliano Simons shows that traditional conceptions of science and technology as direct, nonlinguistic "responses to nature cannot be maintained, and that purely linguistic approaches are unable to conceptualize" natural events such as climate change (for example), since the "science of climatology offers us a picture completely different from that of a science of certainty by direct contact with the facts themselves or a complete technological control" (Simons, 2). Rather, in the words of Bruno Latour "the very notion of objectivity has been totally subverted by the presence of humans in the phenomena to be described – and in the politics of tackling them" (Latour 2014, 2).

Writing in 1984, Hayles included in her chapter on Pynchon an apt reference to C. G. Jung, whose exposition of synchronicity as a world model, she notes, "was greatly influenced by quantum mechanics and the Uncertainty Principle through correspondence with [physicist] Wolfgang Pauly, who was one of his patients" (Jung 1973, cited in *The Cosmic Web*, 173 n. 6), In the mid-1980s, psychoanalytical models were still in full force in literary studies. But readers in the succeeding decades are more inclined now to connect the characteristically multidisciplinary descriptions in *The Cosmic Web* to Hayles's later elaboration of a posthumanist framework, especially in *How We Became Posthuman* (1999) and *Unthought: The Power of the Cognitive Nonconscious* (2017). The Jungian passage from *The Cosmic Web* would not be out of place among these later, more cognitive approaches: "Psychologists," Hayles writes, "have shown that this subordination of perceptual data into background is an essential element of cognition; it is what allows us to 'tame' the incoming signals so that we are not constantly overwhelmed by a mass of detail" (*Cosmic Web*, 174). Arguably, it is precisely this amassing of detail that situates Pynchon's posthumanist fictions in the realm of Hayles's cognitive nonconscious. The "masses of detail" that can be safely ignored by our conscious awareness is also a rich field for *imaginative exploration*. This background is real, if never fully cognized, and it offers an untamed, plentiful field of nonconscious exploration that both Hayles and Pynchon would pursue over long careers that have kept pace with the breakthroughs (and never fully graspable accumulations) in the sciences.

Bureaucracies of the Other Side

It was nice of Jung to give us the idea of an ancestral pool in which everybody shares the same dream material. But how is it we are each visited as individuals, each by exactly and only what he needs? Doesn't that imply a switching-path of some kind? a bureaucracy? Why shouldn't the IG go to seances? They ought to be quite at home with the bureaucracies of the other side. (Gravity's Rainbow, 410–11)

The IG Farben, *Interessen-Gemeinschaft Farbenindustrie*, or the "Community of Interests" of chemical dye-making corporations, was a German chemical and pharmaceutical conglomerate dismantled after the Second World War, though it was quickly reconfigured in such transnational postwar German chemical corporations as Bayer, BASF, Hoechst, and others.

The cybernetic and information theory, for example, that Hayles explored in her definitive revisiting of the Macy conferences in Chapter 3 of *How We Became Posthuman* (1999), brought together such predecessors as Norbert Wiener, Gregory Bateson, Margaret Mead, and computer scientist Warren McCulloch. Hayles was already observing how these scientists, anthropologists, and cybernetic originators were engaged as much with the media of communication as with the scientific information that was circulating at these conferences. "In the wake of World War II," Hayles argues in *How We Became Posthuman*, the development of information theory had left poststructuralist theorists and scientists alike with "a conundrum: even though information provides the basis for much of contemporary US society, it has been constructed never to be present in itself. In information theoretic terms ... information is conceptually distinct from the markers that embody it, for example newsprint or electromagnetic waves. It is a pattern rather than a presence" (25).

Rather than separate either the physical world of the sciences or the conceptual worlds of thought from the language we use to live in the world and to think about it, Hayles joins a distinctive tradition of scientific and philosophical practitioners who grounded their knowing not exclusively in Copernican rationalism and individualism but in Heisenbergian reflexivity, paradox, and uncertainty. This *conceptual grounding* in atomic and energetic phenomena that cannot be observed directly is shareable across literary and scientific disciplines. The uncertainty and *unknowing* nature of human thought and observation becomes the foundation of an ethical and also, in particular strains of literature, epic sense of interconnectivity broader than humanist disciplinary segregations allow.

From this foundation, at once groundless and fully embodied in our senses and in neural networks that cannot – none of them alone – account for consciousness, Hayles was able to extend her interest in cybernetics to another new materialism – namely, the newly understandable materiality of cognition. Her previous exploration of field theory, I would suggest, enabled her *recognition* that thinking, along with the media that underly and shape our thought, is what enables us to act within, and adjust our immersion in, the world.

Here is Hayles's articulation of still further anticipations of posthumanism in our more experimental and adventurous strains of literary modernism:

> In the late nineteenth and early twentieth centuries, movements such as surrealism and practices like automatic writing sought to crack open the conscious surface and let something else – less rational, less dedicated to coherence – emerge. In the late twentieth century, this tendency began to assume sharper edges, honed by neuroscientific research on brain traumas and other neurological anomalies and benefiting from improved diagnostics, particularly PET and fMRI scans. Popular accounts of neurological deficits, such as Oliver Sacks's *Man Who Mistook His Wife for a Hat* (1998) and Antonio Damasio's *Descartes' Error: Emotion, Reason, and the Human Brain* (1995), called attention to the crucial role of nonconscious processes in supporting normal human behavior and the inability of consciousness, stripped of these resources, to carry on as if nothing had happened. (*Unthought*, 86)

The same "improved diagnostics" that enabled an expansion of our understanding of both consciousness and its needed, nonconscious environment were being applied, during the 1980s and '90s, to emerging, born-digital literary forms. We've seen these in our account of the classic hypertext by Shelley Jackson, and it is no accident that Hayles extends her attention from experimental literature in print (such as Thomas Pynchon, Tom McCarthy, and Colson Whitehead) to an emerging strain of electronic literature, which I will introduce in the following section.

Digital (Post) Humanities

> Narrative fiction, being itself a model of life experience, must wrestle with the unexpected and the random to incorporate as affect the things, events, and processes outside human meaning-structures ... We manage to make some sense of experience, despite the noise, indeterminacy, and randomness. But we also use these very chaotic processes to our advantage in making sense.

Will Luers, "Affect and Narrative in Recombinant Fiction" (2020)

At the start of Hayles's career in the mid-eighties, changes were afoot, for sure – culturally no less than conceptually – and none would be more transformative, nor could they have been more directly in line with the *new materialist* approach Hayles had set out. Already by 1993, Hayles had written an influential essay on the "flickering signifiers" we'd begun to observe daily, many of us on the desktop computers we were starting to use for our note taking and essay writing. And some of us, who attended the first of two National Endowment for the Humanities seminars organized by Hayles during this period in her then home institution, UCLA, were making other, more literary objects – as well as programs, platforms, and literary databases. Projects like Michael Joyce, John B. Smith, and Jay David Bolter's *Storyspace*, which brought computation and author/reader interactivity into the literary work itself, were producing a first generation of electronic literary arts. This enabled Hayles, for example, to address "The Invention of Copyright and the Birth of Monsters: Flickering Connectivities in Shelley Jackson's *Patchwork Girl*" (2000). After having explored (in *The Cosmic Web*, 1984) the ways that words and things, stylistic forms and human natures were interconnected in print works by D. H. Lawrence, Nabokov, Borges, Pynchon, Phillip K. Dick, and Robert Pirsig, Hayles was able to extend her researches into a larger "textual ecosystem," the term ecocritic Eric Dean Rasmussen (2016) used to describe the self-made, self-published *Keyhole Factory* by William Gillespie, an electronic literature author and founder of the independent press, Spineless Books. (See text box "Further Flickering Connectivities.")

Further Flickering Connectivities

Not coincidentally, Hayles's essay on Shelley Jackson was published in the journal *Postmodern Culture*, one of the first entirely web-based journals capable of including "still images, sound, animation, and full-motion video as well as text."

pomoculture.org/about/

William Gillespie, for his part, has described *Keyhole Factory* as "a mosaic of 22 narrative shards. Characters recur but are barely recognizable from each other's points of view. (Like many of us, they don't narrate themselves the way others would narrate them.) Characters differ, their experiences differ, their interpretations of events differ, the literary styles and forms in which they are rendered differ, but, most deliberately, the plausibility that their stories can even be told differ."

keyholefactory.com/keyholefactoryfactory/

Ecocritical scholar Eric Rasmussen cites Hayles in his description of Gillespie's literary (and life) work:

> *Keyhole Factory*, a conceptual, constraint-based novel that can seem dauntingly esoteric if readers don't practice both close and hyper readings of the codex book and the digital text and consult the web-work map ... that constitute the *Keyhole Factory* textual ecosystem. These three components comprise a larger "Work as Assemblage, a cluster of related texts that quote, comment upon, amplify, and otherwise intermediate one another" (Hayles 2005: 105). And when *Keyhole Factory* is read as part of an even larger, deliberately designed literary ecosystem, including texts published by Gillespie's press, *Spineless Books*, it provides an exemplary model and working platform for collaborative, conceptual, and countertextual literary writing across media. As with other recent Work as Assemblage (WaA) novels, such as Steven Hall's *The Raw Shark Texts* (2007) and Mark Z. Danielewski's *Only Revolutions* (2006), in *Keyhole Factory* the codex book becomes a transmedial artwork that integrates other media forms to form a "distributed literary system" that resists "the putative decline of narrative." (Citing Hayles, 2012: 15, 172–3; see also Manovich (2002) on narrative as a residual form supplanted by databases.)

Notice how seamlessly Rasmussen's description of Gillespie's transmedial work, in all its newness, takes in a term introduced by Hayles – one of many such that have entered the academic-literary vocabulary. Terms like "flickering signifiers," "media specificity," "deep- and hyper-attention" come to mind as having guided literary explorations in digital media in particular. Each is consistent with the disciplinary and ecological field concept that was introduced in Hayles's debut critical writing. When I read the phrase "Work as Assemblage," I'm reminded of still another essay that Hayles presented in Dubai in 2018, published in the *electronic book review* under the title "Literary Texts as Cognitive Assemblages: The Case of Electronic Literature" (2019). And then I'm reminded of the response to this essay, also presented in the *electronic book review* by early career scholar Dani Spinosa (who in 2018 published a book with University of Alberta Press titled *Anarchists in the Academy*). The community of scholars Hayles has assembled in her own colloquia and conference agendas is ongoing and diversifying. There are many terms advanced by Hayles that circulate similarly, among networks of readers, each one interacting with the others in both academic journals and emerging Open Access literary networks. The networks begun with her NEH seminars continue in digital projects of my own and these will be presented, in my closing chapter, "Digital Posthumanism (On the Periphery)," as one model for a literary future in the (post)humanities.

Another contemporary model is articulated by William Paulson in his major, though overlooked, book *Literary Culture in a World Transformed: A Future for the Humanities* (2001): "recent literary culture's distrust of the global and the synthetic," Paulson suggests, "its emphasis on local knowledge, tactics, opposition, and resistance – can usefully be complemented by an engagement with strategic, systemic, large-scale, and long-term perspectives" (108). If literary scholars wish to engage the nonacademic world, not to mention the mostly nonhuman ecosystems, technologies, and communicative networks that determine our situation, we had better use the power at our disposal to renew the forms of *narrative*: what the German sociologist and systems theorist Niklas Luhmann has called "the public description of time," and the French literary theorist Bernard Stiegler, as we have seen, has termed "retentive enactments."

For Luhmann and Stiegler, as for Paulson, the present is known only narratively, not through a sequence of events so much as a continually moving boundary, "the differential of the past and the future" (Luhmann, 1997). Neither the critique of past evils nor a programmatic future are available *as* present knowledge, where outcomes (in the words of German novelist W. G. Sebald) are "decided in movement, not in a state of rest" (*Austerlitz* 2001: 20). The future must remain uncertain, and what we know of our present situation is known only reflexively, in a process of feedback that seeks neither affirmation nor resistance but stability in the interaction with the world "so as to modify it and be modified by it" (Paulson 2001: 118). Any intervention in the natural ecology, for example, must damage the environment and expend energy in the pursuit of alternatives or protective measures; any act of resistance or subversion must involve risk to the actor. The fact that present action can happen only from a specific location within the system that supports us is our tactical reality. We can never observe the foundations for action – even as eyesight cannot observe its own blind spot. But recognizing those limitations does not mean giving up on strategic projects in our literary, cultural, and aesthetic studies.

Taken together, these early encounters with our world-transforming digital media can help to ensure that the present turn in academia toward a digital humanities is not without precedents. The digital networks initiated with the NEH seminars in the mid-1990s and the Electronic Literature Organization that Hayles hosted for some years at UCLA continue in the ongoing projects undertaken by generations of literary scholars who are bringing a field-oriented and ecocritical literary practice into the media where current generations are now doing most of their reading.

Chapter 9

Digital Posthumanism (On the Periphery)

Our writing tools also are working on our thoughts.
> Frederick Nietzsche

Nothing in education is more astonishing than the amount of ignorance it accumulates in the form of inert facts.
> Henry Adams

Flocks of books open and close, winging their way webward.
> J. R. Carpenter

Literature – etymologically, "things made from letters" – is American novelist Robert Coover's starting point in a 2018 essay that does not forecast so much as inhabit "The End of Literature." This essay by Coover, like his overall career and lifework, exemplifies a kind of writing that is "all over" – in the double sense of being finished but also dispersing, even as the printed word itself is displaced into and reconfigured within digital media. Indeed, there is today an emerging recognition that computation and universalized digitization might be regarded not as a displacement of writing so much as its continuation and expansion. As Serge Bouchardon and Victor Petit have argued, "the computer is a multi-faceted and complex machine which has at least one very clear consequence: the extension of the domain of writing, in the same way as our possibilities for calculation have been enhanced and multiplied." Indeed, if we can revisit, resituate, and *extend* our understanding of generic terms like novel, narrative, poem, and (not least) the digitally inscribed *essay*, we might approach digitization not as a prospective "end" of literary production but its renewal: continuous with the same long history of "practices developed in Mesopotamia five millennia ago" (Bouchardon and Petit, 2019). And consistent, also, with the *epic* tendencies that we identified, in earlier chapters, as an increasingly powerful attentiveness to nonhuman objects in an environment that has no clear connection to predominant human plots or agential characters.

We have already seen, in our various encounters with *transhumanism*, many contemporary recurrences of the Sumerian demigod Gilgamesh who (according to the World History Encyclopedia [2018]) is "generally accepted" as "the historical 5th king who ruled in Uruk, widely regarded as the birthplace of writing in the west, circa 2500 BCE." The hero of the epic, "according to the poem felled the great trees of the Cedar Forest with his friend Enkidu to build the mighty gates of the city and journeyed far to find the secret of eternal life from the seer Utanapishtim." Throughout the epic narrative, the oldest on record, Gilgamesh tries to achieve immortality by attempting (and failing) not to sleep for six nights straight, and by eating a plant that is said to ensure immortality. (The plant is devoured by a snake before Gilgamesh can get to it.) His collaboration with Enkidu, giving each of them a shared power (and a prospective future) is disrupted by Enkidu's death, which makes Gilgamesh himself aware of his own mortality:

> How can I rest, how can I be at peace? Despair is in my heart. What my
> brother is now, that shall I be when I am dead. Because I am afraid of
> death I will go as best I can to find Utnapishtim whom they call the
> Faraway, for he has entered the assembly of the gods. (Sandars 1960, 97)

The mainstream immortality narrative, evidently, was already set aside at its earliest formation; and instead of Gilgamesh entering the assembly of gods, the series of failures in his quest for immortality was (successfully) *written down* by the authors and archivists of a more expansive and more critical narrative presence. For Gilgamesh, a demigod, the realization gradually emerges that our material being cannot be shared across the generations; not without being preserved and transferred through letters written in stone and other materials that are unconnected to our living bodies. While this material reality cannot be overcome by Gilgamesh or any of the partly god-like heroes of this pre-Christian epic, it is nonetheless possible to project immortality onto *the text of the epic itself*, which was (historically) printed on marble stones that were recovered from the destroyed library of Knut, after being buried there for a period of 2,000 years.

In a moment when the preservation of digitized performances (in Storyspace, Flash, and so many other outdated formats) is so precarious, our ability to share narratives across the generations is again in doubt. As if "literature itself," in the words of Robert Coover, may be turning into "an outmoded technology and fast declining into an archival state of primary interest only to scholars and hobbyists." Coover does not anticipate new literary forms in the next, newest digital technology: rather, he sets up his prospective literary future (as we might do here, in this book) via a glance back to the earliest literary work we have on record:

> Some 33 all-too-brief centuries ago, the 13th-century BCE redactor of the then-500-year-old Gilgamesh epic, our oldest known sustained literary narrative, added a frame story that pretends to locate, hidden within a copper foundation box under the legendary ramparts of Uruk, themselves by his time long since fallen into dusty ruin, a text engraved on lapis lazuli and perhaps inscribed by Gilgamesh himself upon his return from his adventures, which presumably is the story about to be told – a modernist, if not postmodernist, metafictional contrivance right at the very beginning of what we call literature. Which at the time was itself a new experiment, so new that the author of the original epic didn't even have an alphabet with which to compose. (Coover, 2018)

At present, the first generation of born digital literature (exemplified in our earlier chapter by Shelley Jackson's hypertext fiction *Patchwork Girl*), had a run of about two decades before its disc format was outdated. That was an effect of a valorization of the continual updating (and consequent obviating) of digital formats in a field where medial innovation supersedes aesthetic, conceptual, and cultural experimentation. Going forward, the ecological costs of our unlimited and ever-renewing electronic services render unlikely literary promises of generational legacies (like those that originated at the very start of our epic literary excursions). The most cogent among the emerging born-digital literary works that we'll be observing in the present chapter are more geared toward narrative ends than new beginnings in updated technology; and the awareness among digital authors of the need to preserve and archive the written work itself is consistent with what we find in the oldest of our epic traditions.

The Eternal Life of Gilgamesh

These scribes attribute the original source of the story to Gilgamesh himself who, allegedly, inscribed his great deeds and adventures on a huge stone by the gates of Uruk. In the words of the anthropologist Gwendolyn Leick, Gilgamesh thus "became immortal by making a significant contribution to the greatness of his city by availing himself of the city's ultimate cultural invention: writing" (56).

Through the written word, the story of Gilgamesh and his pride, his grief for the loss of his loved friend, his fear of death and quest for eternal life, the great king does, in fact, conquer death and wins his immortality each time his tale is read.

Joshua J. Mark, *The Eternal Life of Gilgamesh*, World History Encyclopedia (April 10, 2018)

Figure 9.1 Part of Tablet V, the *Epic of Gilgamesh*,
Osama Shukir Muhammed Amin. Wikimedia.

But in the present *Introduction to Literary Posthumanism*, we have also
caught glimpses, on the periphery, of smaller, dispersed object-orientations in
the work of mainstream authors (like Dickens) and more experimental, yet
also canonical writers such as Musil and Pynchon, along with emerging
authors such as Shelley Jackson, Tom McCarthy, and Claire-Louise Bennett.
Indeed, Bennett's situation "on the most westerly point of Europe, right next
to the Atlantic Ocean" is but a literalization of our posthumanist positioning
on the periphery: "as close as we get" to her first-person narrator, "and as
much as we need," in the words of her reviewer, Andrew Gallix. We do not
even know the name of the narrator, "whose brain and body we inhabit" and
whose "semi-reclusive existence" we share at the time of our reading
(*Guardian*, November 18, 2015).

Having explored such self-consciously peripheral performances in the late
age of print, we might now set out some anticipations of a posthuman
fulfillment of these personal displacements in current, and recurring, strains
of multimodal, born-digital writing. Once we recognize the "overall" extension of writing's domain, we might also discern a longer, loosely structured, at
present minor tradition whose exemplars are more essayistic than narrative,
more audible than legible, and more epic than epochal. Such born-digital
writing is less likely to be caught up in the humanist scheme of enlightenment,
transcendentalist, modern, and postmodern periodizations. Such works, now
emerging in multiple media, are neither novels nor poetry so much as *poiesis*:
a processual "making" that extends to the materiality of one's vocal, print,
and/or digital delivery. This can be less of a linear, end-oriented project than

a "swerve" away from conventional form which Language Poet Joan Retallack defines as "sometimes gentle, often violent out-of-the-blue motions that cut obliquely across material and conceptual logic," providing "opportunities to usefully rethink habits of thought" (*The Poethical Wager*, 1). Or, still further, the digital swerve might allow readers to rethink "the status quo organized, the world configured, by the thought interrupted as narrative's central, moving element." So writes Jason Childs, in his contribution to *The Essay at the Limits: Poetics, Politics, and Form* (2021, chapter 12, 184). There Childs explores the essayistic turn in contemporary literary practice in print, in modern authors ranging from Milan Kundera and J. M. Coetzee to John D'Agata, Claire de Obaldia, David Shields, and Karl Ove Knausgaard: a gathering that Mario Aquilina regards as an important strain of "novelistic essays" or "essayistic novels" that can be said to comprise an "anti-genre" of its own (*The Essay at the Limits*, 165).

Humanity (and the Humanities) As a "Thing Made from Letters"

> Montaigne speaks of "science humaine" (II, 12, *passim*) and Bacon of "human knowledge" or "humanity" (which follows the knowledge of nature and God). Through these expressions, they refer to the study of human nature. Emiliano Ferrari (2016, 214)

The convergence of the human with the scientific, arguably, is a foundation of what we would now term the *Humanities*, which were at least nominally an institutional location where the arts and sciences could cohabit and communicate. For authors like Eugenio Tisselli in *The Gate, A Game-Essay on Coexistence and Spectrality in the Anthropocene* (2020), J. R. Carpenter in *The Cloud*, and Anne Burdick and Janet Sarbanes in *Trina*, such essayistic, gamelike, and born-digital modalities are channeled quite differently within a public sphere that uncomfortably incorporates business, military, and educational concerns.

Anne Burdick herself points out that she "originally launched *Trina* to take up a challenge" that she and her coauthors made in a landmark 2012 collection, *Digital_Humanities*: "Building tools around core humanities concepts – subjectivity, ambiguity, contingency, observer-dependent variables in the production of knowledge – holds the promise of expanding current models of knowledge" (104). And not only concepts and models, but the materiality of their designation, so that the underscore in the title, *Digital_Humanities*, might convey – as much as anything written in the book – how any relation between digital arts, literature and the humanities must needs be a thing "made from letters" (to again cite Robert Coover, *American Scholar*). Burdick's and Sarbanes's *Trina: A Design Fiction* asks us to look at letters similarly – as objects in themselves as much as they are signifiers. Indeed, the re-emergence in digital writing of the idea of the signifier as a material object can disrupt, in a radical way, the thinking of the essay – and its seamless integration into both fictions and graphic designations – as a conduit for human wandering and reflection (though the so-called "lyric essay" in print has been known to play with these aspects too).

I will explore, in this closing chapter, an example of *digital essayism* by contemporary programmer, writer, and researcher Eugenio Tisselli.

A Fruitful Capitulation

If an essay is essentially a trial, an act of weighing and balancing a certain kind of conceptual matter, then its outcome is strictly *open-ended*. If an essay is considered to be a kind of writing in which the author plays experimentally with ideas by submitting them to previously untested procedures, then the act of encoding and rendering an essay as a game is not only a plausible, but perhaps a desirable alternative to its traditional linear form based solely on written language. The historical, linearly written form of the essay could be regarded as a sort of betrayal of its full potentiality: instead of allowing the essay to branch out into the different possible outcomes typical of a trial experience, linearity inevitably guides the reader towards a single, predetermined ending, after having followed a path that will never be different from itself. The traditional essay is a step-by-step development that excludes variation, deviation or even fruitful capitulation. Under this perspective, only a multilinear narrative form, such as a game, would do full justice to the essay's open-ended endeavor. Yet, while the form proposed here, that of the *game-essay*, does not imply that the form of the traditional essay needs to be discarded in favor of an *upgraded*, game-based version (for doing so would be an unforgivable and ultimately futile exercise in arrogance), it does explore the essay's historical limitations precisely by attempting to overcome them though the usage of the strategies and dynamics of gaming. – Eugenio Tisselli, Preface to THE GATE, a game-essay on coexistence and spectrality in the Anthropocene (2020)

Arguably, the nonlinear "form proposed here" by Tisselli can be contrary to mainstream literary and academic traditions in print, but there are other, more elusive traditions. The digital "essay" here under consideration, titled "The gate, a game-essay on coexistence and spectrality in the Anthropocene," is closer to the original, determinedly nonlinear experiments set forth by (for example) Michel de Montaigne, who in the sixteenth century speaks his meaning "in disjointed parts" (*The Complete Essays*, 824), or Robert Musil, who in the 1930s describes essayism in fiction and in critical writing as the taking of a "thing from many sides without wholly encompassing it" (*The Man Without Qualities*, Volume 1, 270). Tisselli clearly shares this unmethodical looseness, not least in the many variations on capitalization in the work's title: THE, The, or the gate, Gate, and GATE. At the same time, there's also an acceptance of "fruitful capitulation" (to a certain degree) to more stringent disciplinary and societal requirements.

The Need for a Constrained Community

Eugenio Tisselli V. on Twitter: "Congratulations to the @tdrbark team for the launch of the inaugural issue! And special thanks to @wluers for his careful editorial work Enjoy playing/reading 'The Gate,' among other born-digital essays by people whose work I love and admire https://t.co/OmVZg80Tbn"

Twitter: https://twitter.com/motorhueso/status/1271157277618319360

Tisselli, who, as we will see, is harshly critical of forums such as Twitter and FaceBook, and who for a time ceased writing works of electronic literature (e-Lit), nonetheless makes use of the forum for concise notification among a defined circle of contacts who are, or might become, affiliated with those whose work he loves and admires. Here is how he defines the necessarily constrained community that he wishes for, in the e-Lit field:

It has become all-too-common to find the notion of community being uncritically summoned as a purifying lotion even in the most unexpected environments, such as corporate marketing or the financial sector. But we must be cautious: it is precisely because this notion is undergoing such a thorough abuse that we run the risk of readily assuming that we know what a community is. But what is a community? Or, perhaps more interestingly, what forms of existence can a community bring forth?

Of the many possible definitions of community, the one I prefer is that which says that a community is a group of people who share a common set of symbols, but not necessarily a common set of meanings (Cohen 1985). Contrasting with other notions of community which focus on social structures, I find that this symbolic approach offers a high degree of flexibility, and therefore allows us to understand communities as ever-shifting spaces of exchange. According to this definition, members of a community agree on common symbols, but are not required to agree on what those symbols mean. Thus, the detachment of symbol and meaning opens up the possibility of thinking about heterogeneous communities, formed by individuals with possibly contrasting views who are, nevertheless, bonded together through mutual agreements that need to be

> constantly renewed. We, as a community, gather periodically to take care
> of the symbols we have in common. We also discuss their meanings, and
> we may agree to disagree without disrupting our common body.
>
> Tisselli, "The Heaviness of Light" (14–15)

"The Gate" is presented by Tisselli explicitly as "a *game-essay* about the Anthropocene." Conceptually, the game-essay framework directly engages with posthuman themes, as can be seen in the author's introductory remarks:

> The theoretical basis of "The gate" draws from Donna Haraway's
> suggestion that, in order to "stay with the trouble" in the Anthropocene,
> we must learn to coexist and form all kinds of allegiances with the most
> unlikely non-human creatures. But how can these bonds be forged, if the
> languages spoken by these beings are fundamentally *strange* and
> inaccessible to us?

Tisselli goes on to cite noted posthumanist scholar Timothy Morton, novelist Antoine Volodina, and Romanian fiction writer, philosopher, and historian Mercia Eliade, who present our natural environment (and our posthuman narrative setting) as a *spectral place*, one whose ghosts "are neither dead nor alive: a quality forced upon us all by the imminence of catastrophes such as mass extinction and global warming." Tisselli is quite up-front about his narrative predecessors, literary contemporaries, and scholarly compeers who have helped guide him in the (re)presentation of languages and embedded circumstances that we cannot hope to translate into human language. The same can be said about the disappearance of species that we know about abstractly: impending extinctions that we can forecast and measure but not experience afterwards as events any more than we experience our own individual deaths.

By embracing the activity of digital gaming, which by now initiates and shapes the literacy of current generations much more than printed texts (and classroom textbooks), Tisselli recognizes that any inclusive, *collective* literacy will be multimedial in its formation, gathered with nonhuman objects and ecological assemblages, and codeveloped by artists and scholars, programmers and performers from multiple disciplines and specialized spheres of activity. Indeed, Tisselli's description of "The Gate," together with his collective engagements with the emerging e-Lit community (and one noteworthy, momentary withdrawal), might be taken as a reformulation of an *epical* genre for the current age: one whose community and other-than-human, mediated communications can be conceived differently from oral

Figure 9.2 The Gathering Cloud // J. R. Carpenter (https://luckysoap .com/thegatheringcloud/). The row of birds emerges from below, and then hovers over the text (and the two human observers).

and print epics and moves the act of narration into alternative, antirealist and antigeneric models. Given the impossibility of internalizing and communicating the masses of data generated by computational programs, we need to face up to a cognitive dissonance in our cloud-like, immaterial conception of computational activity. There is, notably, an emerging body of born-digital literary design writing that conveys the ubiquity of our technologies, and how they contribute to our present exhaustion of resources and depletion of species.

Tisselli mentions, for example, that as he and his e-Lit colleagues gather at conferences around the world, "the clouds gather too, as the poet JR Carpenter has warned us." (See the accompanying reproduction of Carpenter's Frontispiece; Figure 9.2.) Indeed, Carpenter states in *The Gathering Cloud* that "The scale of the cloud should fill us with urgency." "The fog," Carpenter writes, "comes on cute pics of little cat feet," and we're told how the four million feline photos shared each day "track carbon footprints across The Cloud." More generally, against a background row of specimens of stuffed birds, we're advised that "The cloud is an airily deceptive name connoting a floating world far removed from the physical realities of data."

At the 2017 Electronic Literature Organization meeting where he delivered his keynote essay on "The Heaviness of Light," Tisselli quoted Jussi Parikka's listing of physical realities that impart "a metallic taste to our i-clouds. The average smartphone, for example, contains 13.7 grams of copper, 0.189 of silver, 0.028 of gold and 0.014 of palladium per 100 grams of material, together with other significant minerals such as cobalt, lithium, nickel, tin, zinc, chrome, tantalum and cadmium" ("Heaviness," 12, summarizing Parikka 2014, *The Anthrobscene*). Another artist mentioned by Tisselli, Joana Moll "reminds us in her piece CO2GLE," how "the seemingly harmless act of navigating the digital cloud results in measurable quantities of greenhouse gases, emitted by servers located throughout our planet. So, how," Tisselli asks, "do we connect the disruption of the Earth's ecosystems, as carried out by the extractive industries in the Congo, Mexico and elsewhere, or as provoked by our daily online activities, with electronic literature? Let's explore these interconnections together" ("Heaviness," 14; see the text box on Moll's CO2GLE).

CO2GLE

GOOGLE.COM EMITTED 191944.77 KG OF CO_2 SINCE YOU OPENED THIS PAGE

This was clipped about ten minutes after my opening of Joana Moll's CO2GLE page on November 13, 2021. The emission after a few milliseconds was around 1,000 kilograms; by the end of my writing session, three or four hours later, we'd reached half a million.

Moll, in her project description, states that *"CO2GLE* is a real-time, net-based installation that displays the amount of CO_2 emitted on each second thanks to the global visits to Google.com." The project, Moll continues, "was created from an urge to highlight the invisible connection between actions and consequences when using digital communications technologies."

Tisselli and his colleague and collaborator, Rui Torres, for their part identify the "very physical ways" that our daily, hourly interactions with technology also affect our "capacity for thought." Citing an article by James Bridle in the *Guardian*, they find that "Rising carbon dioxide levels – the main driver of climate change – aren't just a hazard to the earth and other living creatures, they're also affecting our thinking. At higher levels, CO_2 clouds the mind: it makes us slower and less likely to develop new ideas, it degrades our ability to take in new information, change our minds, or formulate complex thoughts" (Bridle 2018).

After surveying the intricate environmental implications of AI systems that have been mapped by numerous scholars, Tisselli and Torres ask, "isn't it ironic how, as we build machines that mimic thought and language in ever more persuasive ways, the very energy that fuels those machines is making us ever more stupid?" (Torres and Tisselli, 2020).

The invitation to his readers to "explore . . . together" is not entirely rhetorical. Tisselli's repositioning of a literary practice to its technological mediation is highly personal, following an earlier decision that Tisselli communicated to the e-Lit community:

> As of today [November 25, 2011], I have decided to temporarily stop creating new works of e-Lit. I feel that the issues involved in creating artworks with computers are too important to be ignored. So I call for a truly trans-disciplinary, cross-sector research on electronic literature: one that also involves a profound understanding of its environmental and economic effects. One that doesn't ignore the social and cultural contexts which are being effectively destroyed for the sake of our technology. I am thinking specifically about Africa, and many other places around the world in which land is being grabbed and exploited, and where societies are being condemned to suffer so that we, the lucky ones, can remain connected. (Tisselli, 2011)

Tisselli's engagement with communities in Africa eventuated in a 2016 dissertation, titled "Reciprocal Technologies: Enabling the Reciprocal Exchange of Voice in Small-Scale Farming Communities through the Transformation of Information and Communications Technologies." By the summer of 2017, when (on the invitation of Rui Torres) he delivered a keynote address at the Porto meeting of the Electronic Literature Organization, many of the e-Lit scholars and artists were now said to be gathering in much the same way as the clouds gather in the writings of Carpenter, Parikka, and Moll: "They loom ever darker over our heads, beneath our screens. They shift shape, morphing from allegory and metaphor into the concrete, breathable cloudness of gasses and suspended particles" ("Heaviness," 13–14).

The shift in *The Gate* from figurative and fictive shapes to lived (and endangered) experience is conveyed in the lines beneath the Screenshots, which ask us to enact an affective awareness of the rhythms and sounds of life and death, actual and imagined, in us, and in the natural world:

> If you must listen, don't use your ears. Let your whole body resonate.
> The forest is dripping with sweat.
> The fox has become extinct.
> The agricultural gods are dead and gone.
> Sound enters through the cracks of your skin
> No sound. Head throbs violently. World whirls around wildly.

Such lines, and Screenshots that I have herein spliced from "The Gate," are in synch with a disposition that I cited by N. Katherine Hayles near the start of this book. For what we are seeing here is a literary work that seriously sets out to construct a posthuman subject-ivity of our own, out of what Hayles terms "a distributed cognition located in disparate parts that may be in only tenuous communication with one another" (*How We Became Posthuman*, 3–4). A cognition in which sound enters the cracks of our skin, and the worlds we imagine whirl wildly, so that our attention is turned to an author's self-conscious wor(l)dings. Though tenuous, and subject to a range of technological restraints, these distributed cognitive interactions are in communication with our natural environment, whether we know it or not. And this communicative extension and communal exploration is what defines our *emerging literary communities*, which Tisselli for his part brings to the fore in his unabashedly scholarly prologue and "brief note" that accom-pany his creative work *The Gate*'s publication in *The Digital Review* (a journal dedicated to literary works that combine critical scholarship and creative design-writing).

Extending the E-Lit Community

The text (and context) of Tisselli's "Gate" explores the material implications of electronic reading and writing in the Anthropocene. It does so by briefly examining the consequences that the production and usage of electronic devices has on ecosystems and social contexts and our own mental predis-positions. Three perspectives on how a reader or writer may deal with the negative effects of sociotechnical systems are specified: restraint, pharmaco-logical awareness, and togetherness. Such perspectives can be transformed into reading and writing tools for the Anthropocene that may allow readers and writers of electronic literature to realize "not an infinite, ungraspable canon of works, but rather a mode of circulation and of reading" – to again reference David Damrosch's 2003 volume, *What Is World Literature*. (See text box "Electronic Literature as World Literature.") No less than print during the Gutenberg era, this shared medium of digital circulation, whether or not it generates agreement or discord, might still be capable of forming extended communities – those that enact intimate and paradoxical complicity with nearby and remote humans and nonhumans and invite them into the digital text.

Electronic Literature as World Literature

> Electronic literature is not just a "thing" or a "medium" or even a body of "works" in various "genres." It is not poetry, fiction, hypertext, gaming, code work, or some new admixture of all these practices. E-Literature is, arguably, an emerging cultural form, as much a collective creation of new terms, keywords, genres, structures, and institutions as it is the production of new literary objects. The ideas of cybervisionaries Paul Otlet, Vannevar Bush, and Ted Nelson, foundational to the electronic storage, recovery, and processing of texts, go beyond practical insights and can be seen to participate in a long-standing ambition to construct a world literature in the sense put forward by [David] Damrosch (*What Is World Literature*, 2003): "not an infinite, ungraspable canon of works but rather a mode of circulation and of reading ... that is as applicable to individual works as to bodies of material" (5). The model for such constructions, however, may be not the global literary commerce envisioned by Goethe and adopted by Karl Marx, not the romantic tradition of poets as "unacknowledged" world legislators (Percy Shelley), and adopted in this essay. The model, rather, is the literary practice of writing under constraint, developed long before the Internet but suited to its computational impositions and game-like literary presentations.

This essay of mine, "Electronic Literature as World Literature," appeared in a Special Issue on Constrained Writing (edited by Jan Baetens and Jean-Jacques Poucel) in *Poetics Today* 31.1 (Spring 2010). The essay's advocacy of *constraint*, arguably, is consistent with Tisselli's more recent acceptance of literary practices of *restraint*, and the community of artists devoted to an emerging, geographically, racially, and aesthetically diversified *world literature*.

The pharmacological attitude toward technology, which we've seen in Thomas Pynchon's detailed imaginative engagement with IG Farben in wartime Germany and (by implication) its successors in postwar Big Pharma, is carried over by Tisselli into electronic literature. Specifically, Tisselli enacts in his essayistic narrative the theories of Bernard Stiegler, who (in Tisselli's words) "argued that we are living through a multifaceted crisis, largely triggered by a breakdown of the relation between technology and society." Tisselli continues:

> Such a crisis brings about a pharmacological consciousness, in which we become aware of the toxic nature of technology (Stiegler 2015). This consciousness quickly becomes more and more acute and widespread and should eventually give rise to a pharmacological attitude through which, instead of adapting ourselves to a technological environment, we become capable of adopting it. We often feel that the experience of adapting to the ever-increasing array of technologies is an imposition. According to

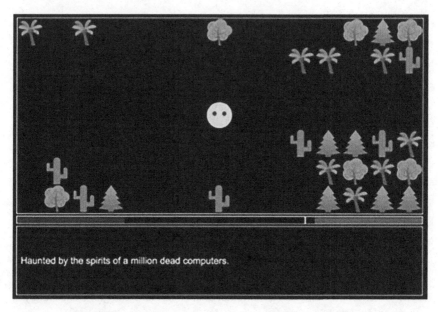

Figure 9.3 Game credits: Concept, programming, and text: Eugenio
Tisselli; Sound: Eugenio Tisselli; Graphics: https://thedigitalreview.com/
issue00/the-gate/index.html. Publication: *The Digital Review*.

Stiegler, when I adapt myself to a technology, I become proletarized, that
is, I progressively lose my autonomy and ability, or savoir-faire, by
delegating significant aspects of my existence to the dark machinations of
the black boxes (Stiegler 2015). But rather than simply rejecting this aspect
of technology, I can reverse its proletarizing effects by adopting it: by
becoming one with the wound it inflicts, by recognizing that technology is
the human wound. Therefore, by refusing to adapt to the toxic religion of
Silicon Valley, by leapfrogging the impoverished social rationalism of
Facebook, and by dismantling the black boxes of Google, we produce
bifurcations: we learn to live with the digital: not against it, but with it, in
a different way. ("Heaviness," 17)

We have already seen in our discussion of contemporary print fictions
(Chapter 6), how Stiegler channels our collective memory through media that
enable intersubjective, as well as multimedial, communication; enabling contact
among those who share an experience (of song, melody, or memories) that define
one's membership in a community rather than merely being connected. What we
are observing here, in Tisselli's "game-essay," is the construction, through
a combination of moving images, sonic vibrations, and text, of a potential *future*

Figure 9.4 Screenshot from Tisselli, "The Gate," *The Digital Review*.

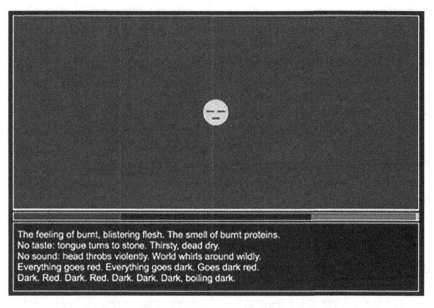

Figure 9.5 Screenshot from Tisselli, "The Gate," *The Digital Review*.

Figure 9.6 Screenshot from Tisselli, "The Gate," *The Digital Review*.

memory that will come (and go) in the ordinary course of individual lives. But such long-term communitarian enactments come at a cost, for e-Lit as much as any other materially mediated communication. What is needed, to generate a grounded community, are not fragmented, ephemeral social media posts but sensual experiences that can be rehearsed and remembered: not by all but by those who actively participate and communicate over extended periods of time. For this to happen, our writing needs to be implemented and curated by the community of scholars and artists. And this is one reason why we find, embedded within the design writing of an author such as Tisselli, a sustained engagement and explicit citation of literary and cultural scholars on the order of Donna Haraway and Bernard Stiegler. The cocreation of literary arts and scholarship, indeed, is by now a primary characteristic of the most robust endeavors within an emerging digital (post-)humanities across many nationalities and aesthetic orientations.

Tisselli, writing from his position as an academic with Mexican roots who is actively engaged with those who are not so "lucky," recognizes too well that creative and scholarly works will rarely reach the sizable audience for day-to-day social media posts. And his "Defense of the Difficult," cowritten with Portuguese artist, author, and Po.Ex database curator, Rui Torres, is also a detachment from third-generation electronic literature that too warmly embraces the "toxic," "impoverished," and dark practices of Silicon Valley, Facebook, and Google (to again cite "Heaviness"). What is needed, "if we want to follow the pharmacological path and cultivate solidarity with our extended community," is a "native" disposition with a "capacity to trace connections of causality between planes of existence" (17).

We adopt technologies in order to coexist with them, but in a different, more actively communicating and transformative way. But, above all, cultivating a pharmacological consciousness in our digital world implies both an intellectual and a practical journey in search of the right dose. In much the same way that drugstore pharmacology studies the interaction between the pharmakon and the organism, technological pharmacology investigates the ways in which technological artifacts cure or harm our individual and collective minds, bodies, and soul.

Epilogue:
Platform (Post?) Pandemic

> It was about the beginning of September, 1664, that I, among the rest of my neighbours, heard in ordinary discourse that the plague was returned again in Holland; for it had been very violent there, and particularly at Amsterdam and Rotterdam, in the year 1663, whither, they say, it was brought, some said from Italy, others from the Levant, among some goods which were brought home by their Turkey fleet; others said it was brought from Candia; others from Cyprus. It mattered not from whence it came; but all agreed it was come into Holland again.
>
> Daniel Defoe, *Journal of the Plague Year* (1722)

In our times, reports of the earliest cases of COVID-19 came from China, where the regional newspapers (and later follow ups by health and science outlets) suggested that diagnoses in Hubei dated "back to at least November 17, 2019" (Lafee, 2021), a bit in advance of the Wuhan cluster of infections that were thought to be identified as the initiating event in late December of 2019 (Pekar et al., 2021). Subsequent reports, as the virus circulated worldwide, could be heard in the "ordinary discourse" of our present day. I, among my neighbors, colleagues, and collaborators in Scandinavia, Europe, and the USA, was updated endlessly about the Corona plague – unlike Defoe, whose contemporaries (in his words) "had no such thing as printed newspapers in those days to spread rumours and reports of things, and to improve them by the invention of men" (www.gutenberg.org/cache/epub/376/pg376-images.html). To *improve*, and additionally to *invent*: Defoe for his part held fast to a faith in our imaginative powers that might be communicated as much through literary fictions (like his own, *Robinson Crusoe*, published in 1719) as day-to-day journal entries, as much through narration as measured observation. His language keeps open the possibility of other, more ranging modes of human invention and imagination, as well as a sizable "spread of rumours." Without too much of a stretch, we may sense in this still-early Gutenberg era dispositions that are in line with both the technological, *transhumanist* orientation toward collaborative improvement and a literary *posthumanism* that situates itself, conceptually, on the periphery of our technical and linguistic enactments.

Defoe in the course of his journal recalls "a blazing star or comet" that "appeared for several months before the plague." And another, that appeared a year later, "a little before the fire":

> I saw both these stars, and, I must confess, had so much of the common notion of things in my head, that I was apt to look upon them as the forerunners and warnings of God's judgements; and especially when, after the plague had followed the first, I yet saw another of the like kind, but I could not but say God had not sufficiently scourged the city.

Defoe in the year of the plague was a child of five or six years. His awareness of "the common notion of things," which he almost apologetically sets out ("I must confess"), might alert us to the long tradition of a messianic disposition toward natural and technologically produced singularities – of a sort that we've encountered in transhumanist strains throughout this book's exposition. The "blazing star or comet" is said to have been heard by some – even if its "rushing, mighty noise, fierce and terrible" was "but just perceivable" at a distance. Defoe's star and comet, which are as much imagined as real, can be compared to the "screaming" of the V2 Rocket that "comes across the sky" (faster than the speed of sound) in Thomas Pynchon's *Gravity's Rainbow*, among other "forerunners and warnings of God's judgements." That's Defoe, deferring to the religion of his day – but we can recall Pynchon's similar affirmation: "It is a judgment from which there is no appeal" (*Gravity's Rainbow*, 4). The sciences were far enough advanced early in the eighteenth century for Defoe to know as well as Pynchon "that natural causes are assigned by the astronomers for such things, and that their motions and even their revolutions are calculated, or pretended to be calculated, so that they cannot be so perfectly called the forerunners or foretellers, much less the procurer, of such events as pestilence, war, fire, and the like" (*The Journal of the Plague Year*, www.gutenberg.org/cache/epub/376/pg376-images.html).

But of course, even as he dutifully expresses a consilience with astronomical knowledge, Defoe in the eighteenth century, like Pynchon in the twentieth, recognizes (and perhaps seeks in his writing to satisfy) the common reader who holds onto a messianic faith. And not just the common reader, but the transhumanist cohort that keeps the faith and circulates its predictions over a range of media, among a mass audience that is now orders of magnitude larger than the emerging audience for the printed journals and literary novels of Defoe's time.

The concern about what it means to both inhabit and collectively reflect on a shared (and admittedly unequal) vulnerability to a worldwide viral condition was very much felt in academic communities, and all the more so in the field of born-digital literary arts, which themselves have a "history," in the words of Aarhus University literary scholar Søren Pold, "of developing independent, purpose-specific platforms, since commercial platforms are often closed formats with largely rigid templates for 'content.' In this sense, forms of criticality are challenged by the fact that the platforms are typically owned, maintained, and often quickly updated (and sometimes made obsolete) by global corporations" (see text box).

ELO 2021 Conference and Festival: Platform (Post?) Pandemic

In May 2021, *ELO 2021 Conference and Festival: Platform [Post?] Pandemic* took place online, co-organized by the Digital Aesthetics Research Center (University of Aarhus, Denmark) and the Bergen Electronic Literature Research Group (University of Bergen, Norway) in collaboration with dra-ft site (India) and the Electronic Literature Lab (Washington State University Vancouver, USA). With over a year of experience with digital meetings, it was clear that the typical 20-minute conference presentations for a full week would simply be a battle of endurance rather than the generative space similar to the hustle and bustle of in-person conference. Instead, the organization chose a format of 5-minute presentations combined with extended time for engaged discussions. Most presenters also submitted written papers in advance, all of which were added to the conference documentation on elmcip.net as well as the conference website. This gathering [initiated in *electronicbookreview* 02 January 2022] makes up a small selection of the papers, revised from the original submission based on peer review comments and an author's own insights from their conference session. As such, we hope to allow for a generative process rather than product. The gathering will be published in three subsequent batches that correspond to the three parts of the conference theme: "platform," "[post?]," and "pandemic."

> Hannah Ackermans, gathering editor, *electronic book review* (https://electronicbookreview.com/gathering/platform-post-pandemic/)

Pold was speaking as a co-organizer, with Electronic Literature Organization–founding member Scott Rettberg, of a series of events and gallery exhibitions held in Bergen, Norway and the succeeding May ELO conference and exhibition in Aarhus, Denmark. As Rettberg himself noted, those of us who participated in the exhibition and conference organization witnessed, "in the course of barely a couple of months in 2020 ... the massive shift of transferring almost every aspect of our everyday life online" ("Covid E-Lit: Digital Art from the Pandemic, ELO 2021," www.eliterature.org/elo2021/covid/). Anastacia Salter, who hosted the previous year's ELOrlando,

Florida meeting at the very start of the COVID-19 disruptions, also recognized how the pandemic "prompted rethinking how to *organize* conferences to maximize their benefits to the community and mitigate their flaws." Salter recognizes that "social media communities can offer a sense of continuity beyond the conference dialogue," even as "the intensive event allows for a level of exchange that we have found vital for rekindling enthusiasm for our work." And even "as academia's resources grow scarcer, and the pressures of the day-to-day workload mount with the adjunctification of higher education, the need for connection, collaboration, and collective actions correspondingly grows" (Salter and Stanfill, "Pivot: Thoughts on Virtual Conferencing and ELOrlando").

Like Defoe, e-Lit authors such as Pold, Rettberg, Salter, Ackermans, and Tisselli bring to their work (and their readers' auditory and tactile senses) both essayistic and creative elements. All of them, in their curatorial statements, recognize chances for improvement in our suddenly extended (diversely assembled, but still locally controlled) media platforms and literary communities.

The March 2021 Society for Literature, Science, and the Arts (SLSAeu) conference in Bergen, Norway, and the May Electronic Literature Organization conference in Aarhus, Denmark, like most literary conferences that year, took place online. Although the papers were mostly reduced to five-minute in person presentations, all were readily accessible in full online and a selection has been further developed through peer review comments and insights that emerged with the conference discussions – a process that, for the gathering editor (and early career scholar) Hannah Ackermans, allows for a generative process rather than a product. (See text box "ELO 2021 Conference and Festival: Platform (Post?) Pandemic.") The glossary entries in the present volume, for example, derive mostly from the three-day-long SLSA conference, as both these entries and a selection of papers were further developed through peer review networks that the conference organizers also bring to the project, thus maintaining a post-conference, collegial interaction that continues over a period of several months, until the time of a work's publication. (After which, the work, like the scholars themselves, can find their niche.)

What is called for, in a time of globalized and corporately surveilled social media, is a more collaborative and curatorial interaction among scholarly and creative artists who are meeting in forums that both facilitate conversations and enable sustained peer review of selected works for recognized publishing venues. With this "processual" prospect (to again reference Hannah Ackermans's "generative process rather than product"), we might hold on today to a hope that is like Defoe's for the emergence – in and around many more media than print newspapers – of inventive, corrective, and sometimes disruptive in(ter)ventions. For Defoe, the appearance of newspapers and an increase in literacy had created a sizable audience for novelistic fictions (not least, *Robinson Crusoe*) as well as an emerging genre of literary journalism. For Søren Pold and his fellow researchers, artists, and curators, it should be possible today to re-enact literary procedures that maintain the "criticality" and "purpose-specific" character of the platforms being used.

One goal of an emergent, born-digital literature that we also find suggested in Defoe's journals and novelistic fictions could be to combine both the creative and scholarly approaches in the same work on the same platform. Pold himself participated, for example, with Scott Rettberg and ELO board member Anna Nacher, in a series of online interviews in the lead-up and follow-up to the conferences, with an emphasis specifically on how contemporary digital art and electronic literature were responding to the epidemic.

One of these interviews, with e-Lit author Ben Grosser, was gathered into a documentary film that premiered in June 2021 (a month after the Aarhus conference) at the Oslo Poesiefilm Festival. Grosser is one of the thirteen creators of displayed works who were interviewed for the project, and generously shared his thoughts on life and creative practice during the pandemic, along with the impact of platforms on digital culture, creativity, and platform culture in general. The questioning was started off by, but not limited to, Søren Pold:

> **Søren Pold** The first question is about your work in the exhibition. Can you describe it and also say what inspired you to produce it?
>
> **Ben Grosser** Sure, so the work is titled The Endless Doomscroller. (Web: endlessdoomscroller.com) It's a website that presents an endless stream of abstracted, generalized bad news headlines in a format that will feel familiar to a lot of people. It's a simplified social media feed kind of interface where it's just a headline in a box and another headline in a box and a headline in a box, etc. And you can scroll as long or as fast as you care to, but you will never get to the end. It just literally will keep feeding these bad news headlines to you, forever.
>
> The inspiration for this comes out of the early days of the pandemic and thinking about, well, my own experience of that time. But I think a lot of people had this experience and maybe to some degree still do, of especially, thinking in April 2020 for example, when I would be laying in bed late at night on my phone reading Reddit, the coronavirus subreddit, or looking at *The Washington Post* or *The New York Times* or just looking up news sources, kind of almost being stuck in a pattern of

continually scrolling and scanning, looking for, I guess, good news in the midst of all the bad, perhaps. And by about June or so, a term started to come into popular usage, which is doomscrolling. And it turns out that term had been around for a while, but maybe wasn't very well known.

In a formal paper, Grosser offers a more structured treatment of how, collectively

> the combination of algorithmic social media feeds, a populace largely stuck online, new gaps in the flow of time, heightened global anxiety, and an uncontrolled pandemic produced a perfect storm of excessive bad news reading. This storm often left users stuck in the scroll, "unable to disrupt [their] own behavior" (Lovink, 78). The activity became so pervasive that it gained a new term called "doomscrolling." (Grosser, 2021)

Along with Gert Lovink (2019), four more scholars are then named by Grosser, and their work cited: Mathew Fuller, Wendy Chun, Christian Ulrik Andersen, and Søren Pold. Only then, with this focused but continuing scholarly conversation in place and documented, are we presented with a discussion of Grosser's own

> net art / e-lit project, an alternative software interface called The Endless Doomscroller. Through its distilling of social media and news headlines down to their barest most generalized phrases and interface conventions, The Endless Doomscroller asks viewers to consider why social media users can't look away from the scroll, who most benefits from this new compulsive behavior, and what art can reveal about reading and being read in this digital and pandemic age. (Grosser, 2021)

We know how a plague that occurred during Defoe's childhood is described some decades later through the *Journal of the Plague Year* that circulates in the journalistic and print media of a given era. Our own plague years are being known likewise through media of our own, via softwares that are now omnipresent, endless, and (crucially) capable of themselves circulating virally.

There is nothing creative, or inventive about Grosser's literary project. The only creativity is in the compulsive continuation of the infinite spread and viral nature of social media and digital culture. What we've assembled for ourselves within social media and digital culture more broadly is an infinite frame for all experience. When that infinite frame intersects with an existential global crisis, we end up getting lost in endless doom.

The texts in Grosser's Doomscroller are all found and taken from "designed-to-be-addictive social media interfaces that know just what to

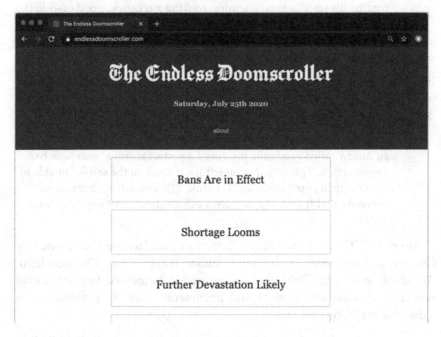

Figure 10.1 Ben Grosser, *The Endless Doomscroller*.

show us next in order to keep us engaged" (Grosser, "On Reading"). The only activity on the author's (Grosser's) part is to reduce the original, social media, and news headlines to their "most generalized phrases and interface conventions," none of them much longer, or more consequential than the three we have presented here, in Figure 10.1. (At least, none that this reader could catch, in my concentrated sessions skimming the seamlessly scrolling page.) The one difference we can observe, at this posthuman moment, is that language – what more than any capability constitutes our own humanity, as a species – is itself viral, in ways that are more than metaphorical.

Our conclusion linking language to a virus is neither original nor specific to born-digital literature. William S. Burroughs, in the early 1960s, was already moving in that direction, with remarks like this one:

> I have frequently spoken of word and image as viruses or as acting as viruses, and this is not an allegorical comparison. – William
> S. Burroughs (https://electronicbookreview.com/essay/language-has-a-virus-cyberliterary-inflections-in-pandemic-times/)

Language is viral insofar as it replicates, repeats, and inevitably takes on new forms over time as words and their sounds course through multiple minds and sensory fields. What the digital brings, in what we might term *new materialist* projects like Grosser's, is a materialization and capacity to see what it looks like, when the language that is ours, personally, pours through the images, sounds, and texts that are algorithmically watched and recorded. Working in the vein of Burroughs and other experimental authors of the postmodern era, such recurrent practices show that literary arts (and scholarship) have always been capable of extending to language, which itself can be regarded as an object. Its materialities on the page and in oral readings produce as much of a presence as its referential and linguistic enactments.

This, too, was a theme in a paper by Diogo Marques in the SLSA conference in Bergen (March 2021; https://electronicbookreview.com/essay/language-has-a-virus-cyberliterary-inflections-in-pandemic-times/), which can further extend our concluding viral thematic. "In the 1970s," Marques writes, "Burroughs was mainly thinking of the ways in which writing as a technology is an alien virus that goes undetected because it has a perfect symbiosis with its host (Burroughs 2005: 5). Yet, his mention of the 'word as a virus' goes back to his 1962 novel *The Ticket that Exploded*."

Citing Burroughs:

> The word is now a virus. The flu virus may once have been a healthy lung cell. It is now a parasitic organism that invades and damages the lungs. The word may once have been a healthy neural cell. It is now a parasitic organism that invades and damages the central nervous system. Modern man has lost the option of silence. Try halting your sub-vocal speech. Try to achieve even ten seconds of inner silence. You will encounter
> a resisting organism that forces you to talk. That organism is the word. In the beginning was the word. (Burroughs, 2010: 49; cited by Diogo Marques)

Here, again, we find it hard to avoid intersections with religious (in this case, biblical) texts and contexts. But these are no more original, and no less imaginary, than the connections that have been posited for many other singularities throughout the ages, like the blazing star or comet that turned up a year before Defoe's plague. We can also, with Diogo Marquez, go further back to the epic tradition for viral and plague antecedents. Here, for example, is the fifth-century Athenean historian and general Thucydides (1956: 355; with emphasis added):

> Such then was the calamity that had befallen them by which the Athenians were sore pressed, their people dying within the walls and

their land being ravaged without. And in their distress they recalled, as was natural, the following verse which their older men said had long ago been uttered: "A Dorian war shall come and *pestilence* with it." A dispute arose, however, among the people, some contending that the word used in the verse by the ancients was not λοιμός, "pestilence," but λιμός, "famine," and the view prevailed at the time that "pestilence" was the original word; and *quite naturally, for men's recollections conformed to their sufferings.*

After citing this passage, Marquez and Gago noted the persistence and multiplicity of viral strains, in a range of works:

From Sophocles' *King Oedipus* to Boccaccio's *Decameron*, Shakespeare's *King Lear* or Daniel Defoe's *A Journal of the Plague Year*, the experience of various pandemics by these and other authors seems to add other layers of meaning to William Burroughs' reflections on language as a virus, namely: in their variations, changes, ambiguities, errors, accidents, and/or mutations. If we are to recognize that language and viruses coexist with the experience and repercussion of every single pandemic, to what extent the concept of virality may suffer a new mutation by the influence of COVID-19, most particularly one that is specifically connected to digital media and the Internet? (https://electronicbookreview.com/essay/language-has-a-virus-cyberliterary-inflections-in-pandemic-times/)

Looking back, when I concluded this exploration of literary posthumanism at the start of the year 2022, the pandemic was in full force. With Defoe's precedent and Thucydides in mind, I would say, simply, that the pandemic has affected new media art just as much as the Athens Plague affected the writing and reception of Greek tragedies. The range and thought of post-humanist literature cannot be contained by terms like "poetry," "epos," or "novel," not any more than such terms could satisfy Bakhtin in the 1940s. Clearly, many more examples ranging from the epical to the essayistic will need to be presented, in multiple aesthetic forms, forums, and platforms that we ourselves, in our own professional spheres need to build and operate. And much more science needs to be cited if we wish to convey the many "variations, changes, ambiguities, errors, accidents, and/or mutations" (Marquez and Gago) that characterize both our ancient, and emerging, posthumanist literatures. What precise forms our future literatures might take can be no better predicted than the technological singularities that we hear about from time to time. But we can reasonably say that for us to *have* a literary post-humanism, these epical formations and viral perturbations from other times need to be carried forward into our present understanding. It's good that we can now hear one another and listen, in interviews, group meetings, and in response to the performative works that are being brought to our live exhibitions, and our websites. That is a multimedial performative space that conceivably can bring us closer to epic vocalizations and essayistic fictions than to conventional print publications. And instead of talking about novels and poems that will still be read for the most part, in solitude, we can make inroads into the otherness and timeliness of multivoiced, collaborative literary adventures.

A Collaborative Glossary of Terms (In Process)

> My subject is a barren one – the world of nature, or in other words life; and that subject in its least elevated department, and employing either rustic terms or foreign, many barbarian words that actually have to be introduced with an apology. Moreover, the path is not a beaten highway of authorship, nor one in which the mind is eager to range: there is not one of us who has made the same venture, nor yet one Greek who has tackled single-handed all departments of the subject.
>
> Pliny the Elder, *Naturalis Historia* (AD 77–79)

Glossaries, encyclopedias, maps, topical histories, and dictionaries: these were a formative presence at the start of the humanities, and together they enabled humanists to see how their own conceptual interests and vocabularies contributed to a long-term disciplinary project. With that deep history in mind, those of us wishing to establish a different, posthumanities praxis should not neglect the originating influence of precursors on the order of Samuel Johnson and M. H. Abrams, whose scholarly acumen imparted a new life to previously scripted disciplines. Published in 1755, Johnson's *Dictionary of the English Language* is not the first but, in the evaluation of modern lexicographer Robert Burchfield, "the *only* dictionary compiled by a writer of the first rank" (thoughtco.com/samuel-johnsons-dictionary-1692684). Abrams's *Glossary*, first published in 1957 (and developed in tandem with Geoffrey Galt Harpham from 2005 to Abrams's passing in 2015), is recognized as a primary reference in the literary humanities. Abrams's *Glossary* could not have been written without his foundational scholarship on "eighteenth- and nineteenth-century literature, literary theory and criticism, European Romanticism, and Western intellectual history" (*Glossary*, "About the authors"). Harpham is president and director of the National Humanities Center in North Carolina. The centuries running from Johnson's *Dictionary* to the Abrams/Harpham *Glossary* mark a sustained growth of the literary humanities. Each alphabetical listing (along with modern updates, additions, and reformulations of Pliny's model for encyclopedic entries) installed a basis for educational initiatives that could be carried across the generations. Such initiatives were grounded as much in a collective creation of terms, keywords, genres, structures, and institutions as they were joined with the production of new and (occasionally) newly canonized literary works, genres, and collectives.

The First English Dictionary

Many people mistakenly credit [Samuel] Johnson with writing the first English dictionary. That achievement belongs to a man named Cawdrey, who, 150 years before Johnson, published *A Table Aphabetical*. It was only 144 pages and defined some 2,500 difficult words; the rest people were just supposed to know. With its emphasis on boosting vocabulary, Cawdrey's book is a lot like modern-day titles that help you pump up your word arsenal before attacking the SAT or waging war in the corporate world.

    – Burchfeld, ThoughtCo.com: "What Is A Dictionary." www.thoughtco   .com/samuel-johnsons-dictionary-1692684.

With its "emphasis on boosting vocabulary," we might designate Cawdrey's dictionary as the original *transhumanist* foray. The 150-year adjustment also takes us back in our precursory humanities to the year 1605, not too far into the five-century-long duration of the Gutenberg parenthesis.

The literary glossary is well positioned to achieve a transformative posthumanist intervention – and not just to advance and redefine an established genre. It is time to rethink our institutional networks without necessarily holding onto humanist preferences and practices. The foregrounding (for example) of an individual author or long-term collaboration among coauthors within and among established disciplines: this is unlikely to be the default mode of our present posthumanities. A quite different model emerges, for example, from the 160 keywords and field-defining concepts compiled, contextualized, and carefully coedited by Rosi Braidotti and Maria Hlavajova in their *Posthuman Glossary*. Unlike Abrams, Harpham, and most other predecessors in the literary humanities, Braidotti and Hlavajova work collaboratively on the identification and description of keywords and concepts that are thought, *by others*, to be of relevance to the emerging posthumanist discipline. The invited authors, notably, are a mix of established and early career scholars who collectively make up an emerging literary field (and an alternative institutional framework). The multiauthored assemblage brought together by Braidotti and Hlavajova signals a departure from the humanities that Samuel Johnson initiated and Abrams and Harpham advanced. As Asker Bryld Staunæs and Mads Rosendahl Thomsen argue in their compelling review, in the assemblage initiated by Braidotti and Hlavajova (2018), "Posthumanism envisions institutionalization" (171).

Here's how:

> In continuation of Braidotti's long-held cartographic method, the *Posthuman Glossary* draws a conceptual assemblage that enables students and researchers to navigate in the field of posthumanist studies (the cover art by Natascha Unkart also signals the assemblage, where dried paint stains of light blue, salmon-pink, rust red, etc. intermesh as cracking layers of meaning). The assemblatic character of the work stays true to the rhizomatic philosophy of Gilles Deleuze and Felix Guattari by offering connections and relations among the entries without suggesting an overarching organization or hierarchy. This take on the glossary genre is avantgarde insofar as it, rather than representing what already is, situates itself in the frontline of what is to become. The reader is invited to follow its outlined trajectory, and if well-grounded one can pick the fruitful seeds from the critical posthumanist branch of the posthuman turn. ("The Posthuman in the Anthropocene," 172)

The eleven sample entries included here at the close of this volume can be regarded as another processual picking from the (still growing) "critical posthumanist" branch. Particularly, the assemblage was produced at a hybrid (in person and digital) conference I cohosted in March of 2021 at the University of Bergen in Norway. All who attended were invited to further develop keywords and terms on the theme of literary posthumanism into glossary entries for publication in Stephen Herbrechter's and Ivan Callus's *Genealogy of Critical Posthumanism*. (See text box, "A Critical Posthumanism.")

A selection of papers from the conference were also revised and published in the online journal *electronic book review*, with an introduction by Hannah Ackermans: https://electronicbookreview.com/gathering/platform-post-pandemic/.

And the eleven entries published here, in this selective sampling, will each be reproduced and, in some cases, expanded in archives and databases that we ourselves have under way. Like the conference presentations that were further developed for publication in the present volume, the circulation of these, and other entries will be part of a structured, collaborative enterprise: one that is appropriate for literary works and scholarship that emerge in both print and digital databases and venues.

A Critical Posthumanism

One of the key features of Ivan Callus's and Stefan Herbrechter's *Critical Posthumanism* website is that its material presentation accommodates precisely the transdisciplinary and multimodal discussion that too often goes missing in the literary humanities. Arguably, the organization of disciplines in both the university and industry do not match up with the promise of a posthumanist dialogue: one that embraces, as I have done in this volume, imaginative tendencies in the sciences along with informational databases in the literary humanities. What both literature and the sciences have in common is a shared *questioning* of the multiple ways that we make sense of the world. Recognizing the need to open discussions and debates across literature and the sciences, I have presented Glossary entries written by multiple scholars (both within and outside the humanities) on keywords and critical concepts. These can also be found at the online site: https://criticalposthumanism .net/critical-posthumanism/. And our continuing production of descriptive entries with a literary focus that can be both critical and creative are extensions of the 160 glossary entries, author bios, and Cumulative Bibliography gathered by Rosi Braidotti and Maria Hlavajova in their open-ended *Posthuman Glossary* (Bloomsbury, 2018). That corpus has since increased by another eighty entries in the second Bloomsbury volume, titled *More Posthuman Glossary* and presented by Braidotti, Emily Jones, and Goda Klumbyte in December 2022.

– Joseph Tabbi, (University of Bergen, Center for Digital Narrative)

Postdigital: Temporal, Economic, Aesthetic, Conceptual

Posthumanism is closely related to the notion of the *postdigital*. Indeed, posthumanism and the (post-)digital are – historically and continuously – thoroughly intertwined: As Laura Shackelford argues, the postdigital's "practice-based experimentation continues to pursue ... posthumanist inquiries and immanent engagements with technicity" (Shackelford, 2017, 349). In particular, these two "posts" share in their critical (re-)evaluation of the implicit logics to that which they are post: humanism and "the digital." However, none of them imply a simple periodization. None claim that the prefix means an end to the concept it clings onto, but a mutation, a negotiation. I here highlight central publications related to the concept from an e-literary and techno-cultural perspective and outline four central aspects that should make tangible the postdigital context in which most posthumanist inquiries and practices play out.

The term "postdigital" has become central to the field of electronic literature, as is exemplified in two recent anthologies edited by Joseph Tabbi. These are the 2017 *Bloomsbury Handbook of Electronic Literature*, in which there is a continuous engagement with the concept across multiple chapters, and the 2020 *Post-Digital: Dialogues and Debates from electronic book review*, in which the concept conspicuously serves as the title. As Tabbi observes in the introduction to the *Handbook*, "we are post-digital in the sense that the literary corpus is by now mostly already digitized but (just as important) nearly all new writing is now done digitally and is destined . . . to circulate in databases" ("Introduction," 5). Interestingly, the field of electronic literature has historically been involved in moving the creation, experience, and study of literary culture along the "upgrade path" of computation, but, as we have seen, that upgrade has itself been "normative" ("Introduction," 5). Accordingly, Tabbi argues that "[t]he post-digital is no place for avant-gardes" ("Introduction," 5). In other words, whereas electronic literature has previously been occupied with finding new and exciting ways of blending "the digital" with "the literary," the field now finds itself in a position where it is difficult to tease out and account for all the consequences of this blending. Instead of further upgrades, what we need is to engage with the contemporary actualities of our electronically literary culture.

In addition to these e-literary volumes, I want to highlight two other, slightly earlier, publications focusing more explicitly on the concept of the postdigital itself. In these discussions the prefix "post," and the accompanying debates over whether such a prefix even makes sense, are particularly articulate. The discussions appear in the 2014 special issue of *APRJA*, edited by Christian Ulrik Andersen, Geoff Cox, and Georgios Papadopoulos and focusing on *Post-digital Research*, and the 2015 anthology *Postdigital Aesthetics: Art, Computation and Design*, edited by David Berry and Michael Dieter.

The postdigital, in the words of Florian Cramer, is defined as "the messy state of media, arts, and design *after* their digitization" (Cramer, 2014: 17; original emphasis). An important part of the concept is the disappearance of often taken-for-granted distinctions between presumed "digital" and "analog" media. Within the postdigital, computational artifacts simply exist as part of a broader reality, not as a parallel or virtual reality that is cut-off from physical-analog contexts. Thus, the postdigital condition means that "digital technology holds less fascination . . . in and of itself" (Cascone, 2000: 12), and that artists increasingly "dismiss the notion of the computer as universal machine" (Cramer, 2014: 16). Rather than opting for a neo-Luddite rejection of all that is digital, postdigital practitioners "choose media for their own material aesthetic qualities . . . regardless of whether these are a result of analog material properties or of digital processing" (Cramer, 2014: 18).

From a more historical perspective, the concept of postdigital dates back to the year 2000, where musician Kim Cascone coined it to describe artistic practices and musical works emerging "from the 'failure' of digital technology" (13) – which is to say, from the decisive use of *glitch* in computer music. To Cascone, the postdigital could be seen as testimony that "the revolutionary period of the digital information age [had] surely passed" (12). As such, the postdigital was conceived as a direct artistic reaction to computational capitalism's "cranking out digital fluff by the gigabyte" (Cascone, 2000: 12). Or, in the words of Ian Andrews, who was among the first to take up and expand upon the concept, "post-digital refers to works that reject the hype of the so-called digital revolution" (www.ian-andrews .org/texts/postdig.pdf).

These early formulations from the dawn of the current millennium already point to multiple conceptual strands that coexist with the concept of the postdigital: a concept constructed as simultaneously (1) a temporal marker of the time after broad digitization ("the revolutionary period ... has surely passed"); (2) a general cultural condition that is marked by the economic ethos of computational capitalism (Cascone. "cranking out digital fluff ... "); and (3) a certain type of aesthetic artifact including associated practices (Andrews: "works that reject the hype ... "). These three strands coexist in the concept and are arguably all related to a fourth, namely: (4) a certain postdigital reflexivity – that is, a critical perspective on culturally shared notions of "the digital" that looks "back" at our present time while remaining situated in that same present. I have explicated an articulation of this fourth strand elsewhere (Erslev, 2021).

> – *Malthe Erslev (Aarhus University, Department of Communication and Culture)*

References

Andersen, Christian Ulrik, Geoff Cox, and Georgios Papadopoulos. *A Peer-Reviewed Journal About Digital Research, APRJA* 3.1: 2014. https://openresearch.lsbu.ac.uk/download/27822fb5812add5027f1347398e9c60efcec043607da6710b31abace8b6378ad/10447414/Prehistories%20of%20the%20Post-digital.pdf.

Andrews, Ian (2002) "Postdigital Aesthetics and the return to Modernism." *Ian-Andrews.org*. https://ian-andrews.org/texts/postdig.pdf.

Berry, David M., and Michael Dieter (ed.). *Postdigital Aesthetics: Art, Computation and Design*. Palgrave Macmillan, 2015.

Bridle, James. *Air Pollution Rots Our Brains. Is That Why We Don't Do Anything About It?* 24 September 2018. *Guardian*. www.theguardian.com/commentisfree/2018/sep/24/air-pollution-cognitive-improvement-environment.

Callus, Ivan, and Stefan Herbrechter (Fall 2003). "What's Wrong with Posthumanism?" *Rhizomes* 7. www.rhizomes.net/issue7/callus.htm.

Cascone, Kim. (2000) "The Aesthetics of Failure: 'Post-digital' Tendencies in Contemporary Computer Music." *Computer Music Journal* 24.4: 12–18.

Cohen, Anthony P. (1985). *The Symbolic Construction of Community*. Chichester: Ellis Horwood.

Cramer, Florian (2014) "What is 'Post-digital'?" *APRJA* 3.1, 2014: 10–24.

Erslev, Malthe Stavning (2021). "Contemporary Posterity: A Helpful Oxymoron." *electronic book review*. https://electronicbookreview.com/essay/contemporary-posterity-a-helpful-oxymoron/.

Shackleford, Laura. "Postmodern, Posthuman, Post-Digital." In *The Bloomsbury Handbook of Electronic Literature*, ed. Joseph Tabbi. London: Bloomsbury Publishing, 2017: 335–58.

Tabbi, Joseph (2020), ed. *Post-Digital: Dialogues and Debates from electronic book review*. Bloomsbury Publishing.

Tabbi, Joseph (2017), ed. *The Bloomsbury Handbook of Electronic Literature*. London: Bloomsbury Publishing.

Entanglement / Relational Poetics

The notion of entanglement seems to be *the* central trope in critical posthumanist thought. Without explicitly reflecting on its implications, almost all writing in this field – and increasingly also beyond – makes excessive use of it. Entanglement may well have displaced the ubiquitous network metaphor. Like the latter, it epitomizes the move away from human centrality, but it carries the subtext of organic messiness, of inextricable textures and unorderly weaves. Once unpacked and drawn out of a somewhat careless tropical usage, entanglement can become a productive figure. This figure may be especially useful when looking at the paradigms of the global and the planetary and their convergence in times of the climate emergency (Chakrabarty & Latour, 2020). Describing a form of connectivity that is fundamentally different from the network, entanglement also has other ethical implications. While a network-like connectedness entails links *between* elements that are ultimately thought of as distinct and distant, entanglement functions in the mode of an irreducible meshwork without containers. (See Ingold 2007 for an anthropological take on the meshwork/network distinction.)

Something that is entangled, then, is not just positioned within relationships to other objects and actors, but rather constituted by bundles of relationships. The mode of entanglement is not connectivity, but relationality; and in challenging the idea of boundaries, entanglement even questions the notion of connection itself. "To be entangled is not simply to be intertwined with another, as in the joining of separate entities," writes Karen Barad (2007, ix).

Barad is perhaps the only thinker to really work the term *entanglement* into her theory, making it productive within the framework of a relational, "agential realism" derived from the implications of quantum mechanics. Yet Barad notably does *not* use *entanglement* in the *strict* quantum physical sense – meaning two particles essentially behaving as one, in "a ghostly action at a distance," as Einstein said in the sense of a complex, multiple form of relationality. Drawing on the undecidability at the heart of quantum mechanics – where the agencies of observation cannot be separated from what is observed and a quantum entity can be both a wave and a particle (wildly simplifying) – Barad's notion of *entanglement* ultimately always works against binaries and logics of exclusion.

The prism of *entanglement* could also help to describe certain forms and narratives in current fiction, as well as to re-think the relationship between ethics and fiction more generally. A popular conception of literature understands literary texts as fictionalised versions of experience. Bringing ethics into the picture, then, is to think of literary texts as a kind of simulation for human actions and relationships – an arena in which we can begin to understand what it is like to be "in someone else's shoes." While this conception does have a point in some respects, it is a rather simplistic vision of literature, and more importantly, it falls short of more complex and non-anthropocentric texts that actively undermine Cartesian lines of separation; texts that operate through what I call a *relational poetics.* These texts often fold the itineraries of human and non-human agents (animals, molecules, plants. . .) into another, or even replace the modern novel's classically human protagonist with the latter, like in Richard Powers' *The Overstory* (2018). Powers' text is certainly *about* trees (deforestation, environmental activism, seed banks), but it also enfolds along the lifespan of trees, producing the kind of temporality that Australian philosopher Roman Knznaric calls for when he says we need a "cathedral thinking" beyond human scope (as opposed to the short-termism of capitalism and current politics; Knznaric (2020):

> The hottest year ever measured comes and goes. Then another. Then ten more ... The seas rise. The year's clock breaks. Twenty springs, and the last one starts two weeks earlier than the first. Species disappear. Patricia writes of them. .... We are not, as one of Adam's papers proves, wired to see slow, background change, when something bright and colourful is waving in our faces.

(Powers, 2018, 374)

In many ways, this is a novel that performs the paradoxical task of moving away from a human-centered perspective – its protagonist literally being the rhizomatic entanglement of vegetation – while, of course, subscribing to a necessarily human positionality that we cannot do away with.

To do justice to a relational poetics, we need to take the root of *poiesis* seriously, shifting away from aboutness: texts like *The Overstory* do not illustrate or describe, but rather *produce* an ethics that is no longer grounded in humanism and the human–human dialogic structure envisioned by (traditional) hermeneutics. As Barad offers in a reformulation of Levinas: "Responsibility – the ability to respond to the other – cannot be restricted to human-human encounters when the very boundaries and constitution of the human are continually being reconfigured. ... A humanist ethics won't suffice when the 'face' of the other that is 'looking' back at me is all eyes, or has no eyes, or is otherwise unrecognizable in human terms" (Barad, 2007, 392). Fiction can be thought of as a space of negotiation in which such a relational and nonanthropocentric ethics first comes into view. Relational poetics and the formation of a relational ethics are intertwined.

Of course, a certain understanding of entanglement spells a serious problem, as does a simplifed, holistic posthumanism in general. How exactly can we conceive of the preconditions for ethical accountability and political action if *everything* is in relation? Accountability, one could argue, needs a separable subject. With respect to the notion of an irreducible entanglement, it is worth keeping in mind the etymology of decision as *de-cisio*, cutting off. At the same time, the micrological close view of entanglement sometimes tends to erase anything that is distant in the sense of a human coordinate system, just like a Levinasian ethics fails to include not only nonhuman relations, but also human–human relations at a distance. It is crucial, though, to reintroduce the refractions of the global when thinking about relationality. How else, to pick just one example, could we account for the chain effect of our consumerist choices on unknown others? Or for the way everything we do in the digital realm is materially entangled with precarious labor, the mining of conflict materials, and their underlying colonial histories?

The work of Anna Lowenhaupt Tsing makes a productive effort in this respect: In *The Mushroom at the End of the World* (2015), the ethnographer investigates a fungal biosystem and its entanglement with human migration patterns and formal/informal economies, providing a micrological version of thinking the global and the planetary together while avoiding moralization – "life in the ruins of capitalism" (the book's subtitle) is, in the case of the matsutake mushroom, not only possible but a condition of existence (the mushroom thrives in deforested areas). Interestingly, parts of Tsing's book work in a narrative mode. The same goes for Donna Haraway's *Staying with the Trouble* (2016), in which Haraway presents her theory of kinship beyond genealogical filiation and interwoven with fictional stories of trans-species lives.

   This points to the way in which literature – not despite but precisely *because of* its fictionality – may play a key role in configuring a relational ethics, and in countering the separating effects of humanism while still working with the necessarily human-centered paradigms of connectivity that we simply cannot undo. Or do without.

   – *Dana Bönisch, Universität Bonn*

References

Barad, Karen (2007) *Meeting the Universe Halfway. Quantum Physics and the Entanglement of Matter and Meaning*, Durham: Duke University Press.
Chakrabarty, Dipesh and Latour, Bruno (2020) "Conflicts of Planetary Proportion – A Conversation." *Journal of the Philosophy of History* 14.3: 419–54.
Haraway, Donna (2016) *Staying with the Trouble: Making Kin in the Chthulucene*. Durham: Duke University Press.
Harman, Graham (2018) *Object-Oriented Ontology: A New Theory of Everything*. New York: Penguin.
Ingold, Tim (2007) *Lines: A Brief History*. London: Routledge.
Krznaric, Roman (2020) *The Good Ancestor: How to Think Long-Term in a Short-Term World*. London: Ebury Press.
Powers, Richard (2018) *The Overstory*. New York: Norton.
Tsing, Anna Lowenhaupt (2015) *The Mushroom at the End of the World: On the Possibility of Life in Capitalist Ruins*. New Jersey: Princeton University Press.

Neocybernetic Posthumanism: Transhumanism, Autopoiesis

Since its consolidation in the late 1940s, cybernetics has been the primary locus for defining the posthuman as a comingling of computational devices, cyborg amalgamations, and AI entities. That questioning, self-reflective process has endowed contemporary systems theory with a range of important differentiations. Foremost among these is the distinction between first-order and second-order cybernetics. First-order cybernetics maintains traditional scientificity in its stance of objective detachment toward the systems it designs and observes. Its classical focus is computation and communication for the command of control systems. Not surprisingly, first-order cybernetics remains the drug of choice for inducing the technovisions and unexplained singularities of transhumanism: what Ivan Callus and Stefan Herbrechter call "a particularly uncompromising expression of the posthuman" ("What's Wrong with Posthumanism?" 2003). Transhumanist discourses valorize evolutionary vectors and project them beyond the current state of human mind and embodiment. Such scenarios impose a detached mode of technological reason toward the self-overcoming of the physical or intellectual limits of the human being in its current form and capacities.

While holding on to an imaginary humanist exceptionalism, transhumanism also envisions a merger between the human body, with its organic nervous system, and "intelligent" informatic and computational mechanisms. The transhumanist branch of posthumanism tends to mute those non- or posttechnological affirmations in wider posthumanist theories that decenter the human technosphere and re-articulate its relations to ecological and systemic others – in particular, its Earthly milieu and coevolutionary planet mates.

I trace these organic posthumanist affirmations to the Biological Computer Lab at the University of Illinois at Urbana-Champaign. By the turn of the 1970s, its director, Heinz von Foerster, had formally generalized the concepts of computation and recursion for an epistemology of multiple cognitive systems. A series of philosophical reflections on the first cybernetics now programmatically include the scientific observer within the system to be observed, a move consistent with earlier introductions of the observer into the subatomic events observed in quantum mechanics (see the Introduction to this volume). Von Foerster terms this self-referential turn "the cybernetics of cybernetics," or, again, second-order cybernetics.

Working closely with von Foerster, neuroscientists Humberto Maturana and Francisco Varela (1980) bring to this nascent neocybernetics the concept of autopoiesis (self-production). In the living cell, cognitive self-reference and operational self-production are made possible by maintaining an organizational closure of the system. Autopoiesis, within the cell's operational sphere, is cognition. Social systems theorist Niklas Luhmann (1995) then lifts autopoiesis out of its biological instance for a general theory of self-referential, self-producing systems encompassing but also enclosing psychic and social levels of operation, the distinct and bounded events of consciousness as distinguished from disbursed and ephemeral events of communication.

In sum, neocybernetic systems theory (NST) is difference theoretical. This dialect of systems thinking observes operational distinctions as well as functional parallels among organic and computational, biotic and metabiotic systems and traces the differential environments they constitute due to these discrete operations. (Adapted from Clarke 2020).

> – *Bruce Clarke (Paul Whitfield Horn Distinguished Professor of Literature and Science, Texas Tech University)*

Readings

Bates, David and Nima Bassiri, eds. (2016) *Plasticity and Pathology: On the Formation of the Neural Subject*. New York: Fordham University Press.

Bich, Leonardo, and Arantza Etxeberria. (2013) "Autopoietic Systems." In Werner Dubitzky, Olaf Wolkenhauer, Kwang-Hyun Cho and Hiroki Yokota, eds., *Encyclopedia of Systems Biology*. New York: Springer-Verlag, 2110–13.

Clarke, Bruce (2009). "Heinz von Foerster's Demons: The Emergence of Second-Order Systems Theory." In Bruce Clarke and Mark B. N. Hansen, eds., *Emergence and Embodiment: New Essays in Second-Order Systems Theory*. Durham: Duke University Press, 34–61.

(2014) *Neocybernetics and Narrative*. Minneapolis: University of Minnesota Press.

(2020a) *Gaian Systems: Lynn Margulis, Neocybernetics, and the End of the Anthropocene*. Minneapolis: University of Minnesota Press.

(2020b) "Machines, AIs, Cyborgs, Systems." In Sherryl Vint, ed., *After the Human*. Cambridge: Cambridge University Press, 91–104.

(2021) "Worlding Systems Theory." In *Bloomsbury Handbook of World Theory*. Jeffrey diLeo and Christian Moraru, eds. Bloomsbury Academic, 445–56.

Clarke, Bruce, and Mark B. N. Hansen, eds. (2009). *Emergence and Embodiment: New Essays in Second-Order Systems Theory*. Durham: Duke University Press.

Clarke, Bruce, and Scott F. Gilbert. (2022) "Margulis, Autopoiesis, and Sympoiesis." In *Symbionts: Contemporary Artists and the Biosphere*, ed. Caroline A. Jones, Natalie Bell, and Selby Nimrod. Cambridge, MA: MIT Press, 63–77.

Froese, Tom. "From Second-order Cybernetics to Enactive Cognitive Science: Varela's Turn from Epistemology to Phenomenology." *Systems Research and Behavioral Science* (2011): 631–45.

Heylighen, Francis, and Cliff Joslyn. "Cybernetics and Second-Order Cybernetics." *Encyclopedia of Physical Science and Technology*, 3rd ed. San Diego: Academic Press, 2001.

Kauffman, Louis H. "Self-Reference and Recursive Forms." *Journal of Social and Biological Structure* 10 (1987): 53–72.

Luhmann, Niklas (1990) "The Autopoiesis of Social Systems." In *Essays on Self-Reference*. New York: Columbia University Press, 1–20.

(1995) *Social Systems*. Trans. John Bednarz, Jr. with Dirk Baecker. Stanford: Stanford University Press.

(2002) *Theories of Distinction: Redescribing the Descriptions of Modernity*, ed. William Rasch. Stanford: Stanford University Press.

Luisi, Pier Luigi (2016) "Autopoiesis – The Invariant Property." In *The Emergence of Life: From Chemical Origins to Synthetic Biology*, 2nd ed. Cambridge: Cambridge University Press, 119–56.

Maturana, Humberto and Francisco J. Varela. (1980) *Autopoiesis and Cognition: The Realization of the Living*. Boston: Riedel.

Thompson, Evan. (2009) "Life and Mind: From Autopoiesis to Neurophenomenology." In Bruce Clarke and Mark B. N. Hansen, eds.,

Emergence and Embodiment: New Essays in Second-Order Systems Theory. Durham: Duke University Press, 77–93.

Varela, Francisco J. (1979) *Principles of Biological Autonomy.* New York: Elsevier North Holland.

Varela, Francisco J., Humberto M. Maturana, and Ricardo Uribe (1974) "Autopoiesis: The Organization of Living Systems, Its Characterization and a Model." *BioSystems* 5: 187–96.

Varela, Francisco J., Evan Thompson, and Eleanor Rosch (2016) *The Embodied Mind: Cognitive Science and Human Experience.* Revised ed. Cambridge, MA and London: MIT Press.

von Foerster, Heinz (2003) *Understanding Understanding: Essays on Cybernetics and Cognition.* New York: Springer.

Cyborg

The term "cyborg" – a portmanteau of the words "cybernetic" and "organism" – was coined by Manfred Clynes and Nathan S. Kline in 1960 and was first used to describe an enhanced human being which, aided by technology, could endure the harsh conditions of outer space. Since then, this term has acquired different meanings, some of them conveyed by Diane Greco's *Cyborg: Engineering the Body Electric* (1989a). Published five years after Donna Haraway's seminal essay "A Cyborg Manifesto: Science, Technology, and Socialist-Feminism in the Late Twentieth Century" (1984), Greco's work continues several discussions raised by Haraway. Greco demonstrates that a cyborg is not only a hybrid creature inhabiting fictional worlds. Instead, a "cyborg" is presented as a metaphor of human existence in a technological world, where devices can be used to control, but also, empower citizens. As Greco claims, "[w]ith *hypertext*, as with any technology that transforms the relation of persons to machines, individual bodies can be possible sites either for domination or for transformation and resistance" (Greco 1996, 23).

According to Eastgate (1989; https://www.eastgate.com/catalog/Cyborg.html), Greco "explores the significance of the cyborg in 20th century writing, from Thomas Pynchon and William Gibson to Haraway and Derrida." Greco's work highlights the different shapes incarnated by this entity. As such, the "cyborg" mentioned in the title is able to mutate into a postmodern construction, a discursive experiment, a subversive entity that challenges boundaries and preconceptions, or a hybrid being made of cogs, data, and flesh.

Haraway demonstrated that the cyborg metaphor allows us to go beyond dichotomies "between mind and body, animal and human, organism and machine, public and private, nature and culture, men and women, primitive and civilized" (1984, 302). Due to its hybrid nature, the cyborg metaphor provides neutral ground on which feminism, as well as our relationship with technology, can be freely examined. As Greco claims: "[t]o imagine that a machine thinks, feels, and behaves like a human being is one way to get around the human/machine split. Using this interpretive scheme, we can avoid the temptation to segment the self – to classify the body as 'meat,' and to establish women as the inevitable consequence of this classification: meat puppets', prostitutes, objects" ("behaviorist approach," in Greco 1989a). The "body electric" mentioned in the title – an obvious reference to the Walt Whitman poem, "I sing the body electric" (2007[1855]) – refers both to the work's materiality and to the body's electrified state when traversing cyber highways. In his poem, which can be described as a celebration of the human body, men and women are said to share "The same [old] red-running blood" (96). The binary opposition men/women is thus dismantled and the reference to Whitman's "body electric" emerges in the poem's representation of a cyborg's androgyny.

Besides using the cyborg metaphor to address the Cartesian mind–body dualism, Greco's *Cyborg* also promotes what N. Katherine Hayles has described as "cyborg reading." While reading a digital text, the computer mediates all communication between reader and author/authors (Maduro 2012: 323). As Hayles explains, the symbiotic relationship with machines is foregrounded: "because electronic hypertexts are written and read in distributed cognitive environments, the reader is necessarily constructed as a cyborg, spliced into an integrated circuit with one or more intelligent machines" (Hayles 2004, 85). In Greco's work, as Hayles observes in her essay for the *electronic book review*, "Engineering Cyborg Ideology" (1995): "the cyborg body is the text, and the text is the cyborg body." Written in Storyspace, *Cyborg* can be regarded as part of the group of works which make use of hypertextual structure to represent the postmodern theme of shattered identity, as well as the postmodern deviation from literary conventions. Among those texts, we can find *Patchwork Girl* (1997), written by Shelley Jackson, in which the reader is invited to stitch the text's dispersed body parts together in order to keep reading. Once again, since *Patchwork Girl* invites the reader to collect the dispersed blocks of texts in a manner reminiscent of Victor Frankenstein, the reference to "body electric" in the title gathers a new meaning: the process of juxtaposing (or stitching together) the windows of *Cyborg* can be compared to the process of infusing life into the electric body of the text.

> – *Daniela Côrtes Maduro, Center for Portuguese Literature (Digital Mediation and Materialities of Literature research group), University of Coimbra.*[1]

[1] This entry results from a visit to the Electronic Literature Lab (Washington State University, Vancouver) and the research conducted under the project "Shapeshifting Texts: Keeping Track of Electronic Literature" (2015–2017) supported by the University of Bremen and the European Union FP7 Marie Skłodowska-Curie Actions.

References

Greco, Diane (1989a) *Cyborg: Engineering the Body Electric* [CD-ROM].
    Watertown: Eastgate Systems.
    (1989b) "*Getting Started with Cyborg: Engineering the Body Electric for Macintosh.*" Watertown: Eastgate Systems.

(1996) "Hypertext with Consequences: Recovering a Politics of Hypertext." *Seventh ACM Conference on Hypertext*, Washington DC, USA, March 16–20. https://cyberartsweb.org/cpace/ht/greco1.html.

Haraway, Donna (2001) *The Cybercultures Reader*, ed. David Bell and Barbara M. Kennedy. London: Routledge.

Hayles, N. Katherine (12–30–1995) "Engineering Cyborg Ideology," in *electronic book review*. https://electronicbookreview.com/essay/engineering-cyborg-ideology/.

(2004) "Print is Flat, Code Is Deep: The Importance of Media-Specific Analysis," in *Poetics Today* 25.1: 67–90.

Maduro, Daniela Côrtes (2012) "Cadáver Esquisito, Leitor Ciborgue E Inscrição Magnética: Três Visões Do Texto Eletrónico [Cadavre Exquis, Cyborg Reader and Magnetic Inscription: Three Perspectives On Electronic Text]," in *Revista de Estudos Literários*. Coimbra: Centro de Literatura Portuguesa.

Penley, Constance and Andrew Ross (1990) "Cyborgs at Large: Interview with Donna Haraway," *Social Text* 25.26, 8–23.

Whitman, Walt (2007) *Leaves of Grass. The Original*, 1855 ed. New York: Dover Thrift Editions, 92–7.

Fictionality in New Materialism

The spread of "New Materialism" (a topic that has already been analyzed on the *Critical Posthumanism* website) has confronted us with what appears to be a paradox: the return to materiality has entailed a return to fiction. Indeed, the very scholars united by a common interest in "getting real" (Barad 1998) in academic writings in and around the field of New Materialism consistently utilize a type of discourse defined precisely by not committing oneself to reality.

This tendency has been noted by critics such as Alaine Waime (2018), Helen Palmer (2019), and Sherryl Vint (2017), but Tobias Skiveren was the first specifically to set out "a proper fit between the fundamental nature of fictionality and the ontological claims of new materialism" ("Fictionality in New Materialism: (Re) Inventing *Matter*," 2020: 12). Therefore, we will rely on Skiveren's analysis to see how fictional discourse comes into play in new materialist essays and as a starting point for a posthumanist *literary realism*.

Skiveren distinguishes three distinct modes, all of them signaling invention: fictionalizing the non/human or inventing non/human entanglements, as in Jane Bennett's (2010) and Dominic Pettman's (2017) books; fictionalizing science or inventing scientific knowledge, as in Stacy Alaimo's (2010) and Astrida Neimanis's (2017); and fictionalizing the future or inventing future societies, as in Donna Haraway's (2016) and Rebekah Sheldon's (2016).

In all these cases, Skiveren notes, fictionality allows new materialist thinkers to "sidestep questions of falsehood and truthfulness, while at the same time proposing new postanthropocentric ontologies by imaginative and affective means" (5). The emotional-imaginative sphere is crucial here: the stories, Skriveren specifies, "are supposed to convince, not because they are true, but because they do not have to be" (5). Indeed, "fictionality differs from many other types of discourse . . . by not being committed to established versions of reality" (13).

As a result, Skiveren concludes, fictionality is not a mark of disqualification, but an epistemological and a speculative tool "that helps us abstain from anthropocentric regimes of truth while forwarding affective imagery of alternative worlds of lively, recalcitrant, spontaneous, agential, and unpredictable matterings" (13).

Skiveren's thesis can be reinforced and enriched by exploring some examples from the past. In Lucretius's *De rerum natura* and Ovid's *Metamorphoses* it is possible to identify many affinities with new materialist writings, including the use of fictionality: think, for example, of the description of the spiderwebs that envelop unsuspecting passers-by (in Lucretius) or the progressive transformation of Arachne into a spider (in Ovid). Such epic anticipations of our latter-day new materialism can be explained by the fact that both Lucretius and Ovid intended to focus on matter understood as a single common substance, claiming the essential parity between everything that exists, as opposed to any sort of hierarchy of powers or values.

Significantly, these examples are taken from the first of Italo Calvino's "Six Memos for the Next Millennium" (1988), the one centered on lightness. And both Skiveren's and Calvino's theses can be brought together by hypothesizing that the return of fictionality in new materialist writings can be traced back to a precise anthropological need: "the search for lightness as a reaction to the weight of living" (Calvino, 26).

It is worth noting that, for Skiveren, fictionality can embrace new, less anthropocentric perspectives on reality. Neither for him nor for Calvino is lightness to be confused with escapism. Quoting Calvino: "Whenever humanity seems condemned to heaviness, I think I should fly like Perseus into a different space. I don't mean escaping into dreams or into the irrational. I mean that I have to change my approach, look at the world from a different perspective, with a different logic and with fresh methods of cognition and verification" (7). And a little further on: "But if literature is not enough to assure me that I am not just chasing dreams, I look to science to nourish my visions in which all heaviness disappears" (8).

It should be emphasized that this turning to science also characterizes new materialist scholars. As Skiveren noted: "Although the field of new materialism shows an interest in fiction, it would be wrong to frame literature as its only source of inspiration. . . . the field of new materialism instead manifests a new turn toward the natural sciences within the humanities and social sciences. . . . physics, ecology, biology etc." (5–6).

Then every paradox melts away: science nourishes visions and lightness "goes with precision and determination, not with vagueness and the haphazard" (Calvino, 16).

The return of fictionality in New Materialism can thus be interpreted as a manifestation of the desire for lightness and consequently as a reaction to the weight of living, as it is precisely from gravity that lightness is born. (Calvino talks about the "lightness of thoughtfulness" [10].) Removing weight allows a radical change of perspective (flying high or descending deep) useful for detaching oneself from rationality and *feeling* even before rationally knowing the bonds which connect all material systems. And this is where the importance of writing (and fictionality) emerges. Quoting Calvino again: "the lightness is also something arising from the writing itself, from the poet's own linguistic power" (10). Writing makes it possible for authors of literary fictions "to distance themselves from their own drama" (19). Similarly, literature, intended as a search for knowledge, makes it possible to perpetuate that "anthropological device" (27) fueled by the tension between "the levitation desired and the privation actually suffered" (27).

> – *Roberta Iadevaia, independent journalist, researcher, and co-founder of Letteratura Elettronica Italia (LEI).*

References

Alaimo, Stacy (2010) *Bodily Natures. Science, Environment, and the Material Self*. Bloomington: Indiana University Press.

Barad, Karen (1998) "Getting Real: Technoscientific Practices and the Materialization of Reality." *Differences: A Journal of Feminist Cultural Studies* 10.2: 87–128.

Bennett, Jane (2010) *Vibrant Matter: A Political Ontology of Things*. Durham: Duke University Press.

Bergson, Henri (1998) *Creative Evolution*. Translated by Arthur Mitchell. New York: Dover.

Calvino, Italo (1988) *Six Memos for the Next Millennium*. Cambridge, MA: Harvard University Press.

Gjerlevsen, Simona Zetterberg and Nielsen, Henrik Skov (2020) "Distinguishing Fictionality." In Cindie A. Maagaard, Daniel Schäbler and Marianne Wolff Lundholt (eds.) *Exploring Fictionality: Conceptions, Test Cases, Discussions*. Odense: University Press of Southern Denmark, 19–40.

Haraway, Donna (2016) *Staying with the Trouble. Making Kin in the Chthulucene*. Durham: Duke University Press.

Neimanis, Astrida (2017) *Bodies of Water: Posthuman Feminist Phenomenology*. Bloomsbury Academic USA.

Palmer, Helen (2019) "A Field of Heteronyms and Homonyms: New Materialism, Speculative Fabulation, and Wor(l)ding." In Rudrum David ; Askin, Ridvan ; and Beckman, Frida (eds.) *New Directions in Literature and Philosophy*. Edinburgh: Edinburgh University Press.

Pettman, Dominic (2017) *Creaturely Love: How Desire Makes Us More and Less than Human*. Minneapolis: University of Minnesota Press.

Sanzo, Kameron (2018) "New Materialism(s)." In *Critical Posthumanism: Geneology of the Posthuman*. https://criticalposthumanism.net/new-materialisms.

Sheldon, Rebekah (2016) *The Child to Come: Life After the Human Catastrophe*. Minneapolis: University of Mennesota Press.
Skiveren, Tobias (2020) "Fictionality in New Materialism: (Re)Inventing Matter." *Theory, Culture & Society* 39.3.
Vint, Sherryl (2017) "Science Fiction." In Stacy Alaimo (ed.), *Gender: Matter*. New York: Macmillan Reference USA. https://dokumen.pub/gender-matter-9780028663203.html.
Waime, Alaine (2018) "Deleuze and Haraway on Fabulating the Earth." *Deleuze and Guattari Studies* 13.4: 525–40.

Metainterface

With the term "metainterface" (Andersen and Pold 2018), scholars Christian Ulrik Andersen and Søren Bro Pold refer to interfaces that deliberately reduce friction so as to induce a repetitive behavior in the user. Friction is understood as the effort, first of all cognitive, necessary to make a conscious choice.

According to Andersen and Pold (2018, 71–2), a metainterface hides the layers of computation going on in cloud computing infrastructures behind its immediate, minimalist user-interface: "Such distancing blurs the interdependence of user-directed consumption and use (e.g., reading posts on a social network feed) with system-directed consumption and use (e.g., the social network's reading of user behavior and preference through surveillance-based data analysis of that user's every action)."

The type of interaction encouraged by the metainterface is close to pure *labor* insofar as it is based on habitual and unreflective behavior: on the automatism of repeated gestures, on "being acted upon by necessity" (Lorusso 2020). The goal of the metainterface is to limit the user's action; that is, the possibility of the user to make meaningful choices capable of "interrupting, or better, rupturing, their behaviour" (Lorusso 2020) or, quoting Hannah Arendt, breaking the "fateful automatism of sheer happening" (Arendt 59; https://monoskop.org/images/b/bf/Arendt_Hannah_On_Revolution_1990.pdf).

In *The User Condition: Computer Agency and Behavior* (2021), Silvio Lorusso synthesized the transition from interface to metainterface through the "click-scroll-pause" formula, associating each component with a specific phase of the industrial rationalization, or modernization.

A computer "click" is "characteristic of pre-industrial society," that of the advent of mass computing and Web 1.0. At that stage some tasks were "just unrelated to one another (hyperlinks and pagination)" (Lorusso 2021), but the choice of the fruition path was still made manually by the user precisely through the "click." (Infinite) "Scroll" was the typical mode of industrial society, whose tasks were organized to require manual and mechanical labor, becoming semiautomated. Here "the mindful action of going through pages is turned into a homogeneous, seamless behavior" (Lorusso 2021). However, "it's an automatism that hasn't been yet automated. This automatism doesn't produce an event (such as clicking on a link) but modulates a rhythm: it's analog instead of digital" (Lorusso 2021).

"Pause" is the typical mode of the post-industrial society of web 2.0, in which the fruition process becomes fully automated and only requires supervision (think of YouTube playlists which are reproduced automatically, or Instagram stories, where "the behavior is reversed: the user doesn't power the engine, but instead stops it from time to time)" (Lorusso 2021).

This progressive reduction of the user's agency goes hand in hand with the progressive reduction of nonlinearity (or multilinearity). As Lorusso noted, if the era of the "click" represented the apex of the breakdown of linearity (think of Hypertext Fiction), that of "pause" represents the quintessence of a kind of hyperlinearity – namely: "the networked linearization of disparate content, sources, and activities into list form – which can take the form of personal photos, articles, discussions, polls, adverts, etc." (Lorusso 2021). The user's navigation fades into the background and any attempt to click their way out "feels more like sedentary zapping than an active exploration of networked space" (Lorusso 2021).

Metainterfaces exploit three main strategies: addictive techniques, societal pressures, and minimalist hiding. As Lorusso noted, "it's hard to block the dopamine-induced automatism of scrolling, and maybe it's even harder to delete your account when all your friends and colleagues assume you have one" (Lorusso 2021). Metainterfaces tend to hide their ways of working behind a minimalism, that, as Andersen and Pold (2021) note, not only rules "the visual appearance of the interface (the template that is easy to decode and avoids information overload), but also the functionality of the interface" (automatic suggestions vs manual configuration). As Ben Grosser summarized, metainterfaces "hide user datafication that structures user action."

French philosopher Bernard Stiegler, for his part, named this process "proletarianisation," as the metainterface expropriates the user of the fullness of their gestures (their know-how) and puts them at its service, reconfiguring these gestures to fit the system's logic before making them completely useless.

Proletarianization has led to what Andersen and Pold call a "new metainterface spectacle," one that is based precisely on "instrumentalist hiding of the production of the mass perspective" (Andersen and Pold 2021). Paraphrasing Lorusso (2021), this type of spectacle produces heteronomous convenience, or misconvenience, as the knowledge necessary to take the decision is made opaque by algorithmic display criteria, becoming neither accessible nor modifiable.

Lorusso defined this new context as "impersonal computing" as the user's preferences, behavior and know-how are first registered by the system (personalized), and then made alien to the user themselves (impersonal). As a result, "users' desires weren't expressed by them within the computer medium. Instead, they were defined a priori within the controlled setting of interaction design" (2021).

While Lorusso minimizes the link between metainterface and surveillance capitalism, interpreting hyperlinearity and techno-proletarianization as the mere result of modernization, Grosser emphasizes the link, stressing that both metainterface and surveillance capitalism rely on "double-sided reading," the process whereby "social media platforms read us while we read them," for the sole purpose of increasing user engagement by predicting "what content we are most likely to consume next." Both Lorusso and Grosser denounce the risks of the expropriation of users' action determined by metainterfaces, the former citing psychologist and computer scientist J. C. R. Licklider, who noticed "how often automation meant that people would be there to help the machine rather than be helped by it." Grosser (2021), for his part, noted how metainterfaces are "transforming users into machines that iterate on lists of doom in never-ending loops."

To quote Lorusso (2021): "Nowadays, we long for the good ol' web, the bulky desktop computer, the screeching 56 k modem. We live in a time of netstalgia."

Rather than closing oneself in netstalgia, scholars such as Lorusso and Grosser have suggested several counterstrategies to challenge metainterfaces: asserting non-user rights (boycott, resist, do not use certain platforms); using platforms not designed as metainterfaces; and, following the example of net artists and electronic literature authors (whose work is cited by Lorusso 2021 and Grosser 2021), contrasting minimalist hiding with "minimalist revealing" (Grosser) – that is, using abstraction (reduction) to deconstruct metainterfaces, thus illuminating the structures that underlie the cultural effects of software.

A longer-term strategy, which requires a greater effort, consists in changing our approach to computation, moving away from the dominant models based on "speedrun" and "busyness" (Lorusso 2021), and from the personal/impersonal computing dichotomy, to arrive at what Lorusso in *The User Condition* defines as "communal computation" – that is, computation understood not as device, but as a phygital, collaborative, open (also in the sense of general purpose) environment encouraging full read-write literacy.

> – *Roberta Iadevaia, independent journalist, researcher, and co-founder of Letteratura Elettronica Italia (LEI).*

References

Andersen, Christian Ulrik and Søren Bro Pold (2018) *The Metainterface: The Art of Platforms, Cities, and Clouds*. London: MIT Press.
    (2021) *The Metainterface Spectacle*. 15th SLSAeu Conference, Bergen, Norway, March 4–5.
Arendt, Hannah (2018 [1958]) *The Human Condition*. Chicago: The University of Chicago Press.
Grosser, Ben (2021) "On Reading and Being Read in the Pandemic: Software, Interface, and The Endless Doomscroller." Electronic Literature Organization Conference 2021: Platform (Post?) Pandemic. Bergen Norway, May. Published in *electronic book review*. https://electronicbookreview.com/essay/on-reading-and-being-read-in-the-pandemic-software-interface-and-the-endless-doomscroller/.
Licklider, J. C. R. (1960) "Man-Computer Symbiosis." *IRE Transactions on Human Factors in Electronics HFE-1*, March 4–11.
Lorusso, Silvio (2020) Angry Birds vs Flappy Bird: On Action and Behaviour. https://silviolorusso.com/about/.
Stiegler, Bernard (2016) *Automatic Society. Volume 1: The Future of Work*. Cambridge: Polity.

Overmediation

When considering the nature of mediation, Bolter and Grusin argued that the difference between the digital and previous media is that, through the manipulation of symbols, computational systems digitally encode and *r*epresent information. Remediation, or "the representation of one medium in another," is thus "a defining characteristic" (1999: 45) of digital media. From this perspective, contemporary computational techniques such as machine learning could be understood as just another form of remediation. Yet, machine learning systems are not simply tools, like a pencil or a typewriter, nor do they merely represent previous tools, like software does: they don't simply mediate, nor do they remediate. They overmediate. I propose the term "overmediation" to refer to an increase of complexity in mediation processes: the prefix "over" signals an augmentation, as in going beyond previous modalities of mediation. From pen to typewriter to word processor and to automated systems, there is an exponential increase in the gap between subject and medium. "Over" also points to the sense of one thing over another, as in "meta." As a medium, machine learning is overloaded with meta-writing, which translates into abysses of intricate, recursive computation. I also want to propose that three characteristics of machine learning systems, here understood as "overmedia," demonstrate how overmediation differs from remediation: opacity, overfitting, and scale.

Opacity

While in conventional programming logic is programmed, run on the input data, and outputted, in machine learning logic is inferred from the input and the expected output. Procedural rules authored by humans are grounded on human reason, but machine learning runs on algorithmic predictions. The core of machine learning is artificial neural networks. A neural network is a mathematical structure that reads sets of data from which it abstracts a model through the inference of probabilities of distribution in a computational space. Neural networks were first proposed in a 1943 paper by Warren McCulloch and Walter Pitts, but only today, with enough data and computing power, have they become widespread in the automation of tasks based on statistical association and pattern recognition. A neural network has three types of layers: input, output, and, in between, the hidden layers. If a network has more than three layers, it is considered a deep learning algorithm. The adjective stands for the depth of the multiple layers, which may be unbound and heterogeneous. From the first layer to the next, information flows in arborescent networks through which it is recursively and progressively filtered into higher forms of abstraction. Because of the multiple hidden layers, algorithmic processes of inference remain largely inaccessible.

Despite its opacity, machine learning does leave some room for human intervention, through the selection and labeling of the training data, correction of errors, or classification of the output. Most of today's machine learning applications do indeed rely on human supervision, or what has come to be known as "human-in-the-loop" (https://info.cloudfactory.com/humans-in-the-loop?). But contrarily to contexts where the code is explicitly and integrally manipulated by the programmer, this intervention is reduced to a supervising function. There is a lessening of the writer's space for interpretation and inscription, as layers of code remain inaccessible and their inner correlations illegible. The notion of "punctuated agency," proposed by Katherine Hayles, fits well in describing human supervision in machine learning: "punctuated agency operates within regimes of uneven activity, longer periods when human agency is crucial, and shorter intervals when the systems are set in motion and proceed on their own without direct human intervention" (Hayles, 2017: 32). Autonomous systems are thus intrinsically dependent on human cognitive work not only at the level of conception and design but also at the level of procedure. Linda Kronman, who writes about human agency and decision-making automated systems, highlights the manual labor that is implicit in machine learning: although this "is mostly hidden labour, it is nevertheless often required in order to achieve shorter intervals of machine autonomy" (Kronman: 61; https://bora.uib.no/bora-xmlui/bitstream/handle/11250/2756810/document-1.pdf). Opacity not only characterizes algorithmic processes in machine learning, it also veils the human effort that enables them, be it at the individual level, or the sum of collective knowledge that machine learning is intended to reproduce. The human may be "in-the-loop," but as a function of the apparatus. Vilém Flusser has argued that, unlike the artisan (constant) and the tool (variable), or the industrial worker (variable) and the machine (constant), those who work or play with opaque technical apparatuses act "as a function of the apparatus" (Flusser, 2000 [1983]: 83), being neither variable nor constant, not separated from the device but intermingled within it. This kind of inter-absorption of subject and apparatus is indeed verifiable in machine learning, in its entanglement of human and technical cognition, where the programmer doesn't know exactly what the program is doing at any given moment nor what it will do next.

Overfitting
The metaphor of intelligence misrepresents the core of machine learning – pattern recognition – if we consider intelligence to be the discovery and the creation of new forms and relations. One direct consequence of automating pattern recognition is that, if training data shows bias, a network will amplify and distort such bias instead of revealing new correlations. Similarly, machine learning algorithms generate patterns against noisy backgrounds, "seeing" objects where there are none. This tendency is known as "overfitting." In statistics, overfitting is the process by which a mathematical model fits too closely to a particular set of data, thus failing to reliably fit to additional data. It happens when a model extracts noise from the data, interpreting such noise as constitutive of the model's structure. Overfitting shows the inability to accurately process data outside of known categories. The problem with categorical thinking is how easily it leads to mistakes: namely, underestimating how different two facts are when they fall on the same category; overestimating

how different two facts are when they fall on different categories; and the difficulty to see the big picture when focusing on boundaries.

Neuroendocrinologist Robert Sapolski dedicated the opening lecture of his course on Human Behavioral Biology (Stanford University, March 29, 2010) to categorical thinking. Interestingly enough, what contemporary machine learning techniques are automating is what human critical reasoning tries to avoid. (Lecture available online: www.youtube.com/watch?v=NNnIGh9g6fA.)

Human reasoning, particularly the discovery of relations of cause and effect, is replaced by data-driven correlation. As stated by Vladan Joler and Matteo Pasquinelli, who write about the archaeology of algorithmic culture, "machine learning obsessed with 'curve fitting' imposes a *statistical culture* and replaces the traditional episteme of causation (and political accountability) with one of correlations blindly driven by the automation of decision making" (Joler & Pasquinelli, 2020). As the distortions generated by algorithmic interpretations of complexity spill onto the social field, they reinforce the prejudices and exclusions already written in the corpora of digitized culture. Wendy Chun stresses how human prejudice is embedded not only in datasets, but also at the level of procedure: "machine learning programs are not only trained on selected, discriminatory, and often 'dirty' data; they are also verified as true only if they reproduce these data" (2021: 243). As Chun explains, "predictive algorithms, which tolerate higher bias and lower variance to avoid 'overfitting,' are verified as correct if they predict the past correctly" (46). Able to "see" only what they have already seen, these programs end up reinforcing normativity and confirming structural disequilibria.

Scale
The recursive crossed processing on a deep layered architecture depends on an extraordinarily high computing power that goes beyond the affordances of common hardware. The computing power necessary to run machine learning algorithms reflects the modality of computation at stake in these systems and highlights the differences between wetware and software's modes of operation: "living intelligence learns a great deal from very little ... Machine 'learning' derives very little – and merely in terms of pattern and abstraction rather than as actionable judgement – from vast amounts of data at the expense of vast amounts of energy-burning, heat-producing computation" (Charles R. Galistell, in Cayley, 2019: 146). Machine learning works on massive scales, but the complexity and extension of the consumed input produces comparatively simple results, as data is compressed and statistically represented. Waste is thus a feature of these systems. Overmedia is in tune with a globalized economic model where everything seems to be over the top, excessive, and disproportionate: large-scale processing, large-scale logistics, large-scale production and consumption of information, the social field being a gigantic, generative database. Overmedia might be said to fall in line with what Lewis Mumford called, in 1964, "authoritarian," not "democratic technics" – the first system-centered, the latter human-centered. Rather than fitting the human scale, mediation is increasingly system-oriented. There is a close relation between the

automation of production and the autonomization of technics: the more autonomous a technical system is, the less it is subjected to unpredictability, noise, and inefficiency. What determines the efficiency of authoritarian technical media is thus their autonomy, their separation from the social context.

Overmediation expresses how machine learning evades human reading, distorts representation, and exceeds the human scale. From tool to machine to meta-machine, mediation processes evolve toward growing abstraction. Yet, as procedural complexity and opacity increase, human decision making is further deferred to unaccountable technical proxies. As Katherine Hayles writes, "the higher nonconscious cognition rises in importance and visibility, the lower consciousness declines as the arbiter of human decision making and the dominant human cognitive capability" (2020: 4). Or, as Alfred North Whitehead said more than a century ago, "civilization advances by extending the number of important operations which we can perform without thinking of them" (1948 [1911]: 42). The externalization of interpretation into statistical meta-machines is but a symptom of such "advances."

– Ana Marques, Center for Portuguese Literature, University of Coimbra

References

Bolter, Jay David and Richard Grusin (1999) *Remediation: Understanding New Media*. London: MIT Press.

Flusser, Vilém (2000[1983]) *Towards a Philosophy of Photography*. London: Reaktion Books, 2000.

McCulloch, Warren, and Walter Pitts (1943) "A Logical Calculus of the Ideas Immanent in Nervous Activity," *Bulletin of Mathematical Biophysics*, Volume 5. https://link.springer.com/article/10.1007/BF02478259.

McLuhan, Marshal (1964) *Understanding Media*. Cambridge, MA: MIT Press.

Mumford, Lewis (Winter 1964) "Authoritarian and Democratic Technics," *Technology and Culture* 5.I. www.mom.arq.ufmg.br/mom/02_babel/textos/mumford_authoritarian.pdf.

Crip Technoscience

The notion of embodiment saturates posthumanism. Unlike transhumanism, which aims to transcend the human, posthumanism embraces varying embodiments of humans as "situated knowledges" (Haraway, 1988). Posthuman embodiment is thematized in relation to the formal innovation and technological experimentation of (electronic) literature, but often in implicit reference to the abled bodymind, dangerously close to "the human" that posthumanism tries to move beyond. This can cause a gap in the potential of posthumanist approaches, as scholars in posthuman disability studies argue: "disability necessarily demands and affirms *interdependent* connections with other humans, technologies, non-human entities, communication streams and people and non-peopled networks" (Goodley et al., 2014, 348). The concept of crip technoscience illuminates the ways that (dis)abled people and practices can affirm and contest normative technologies. I highlight the concept here because it entangles with the posthumanist imperative to name "the embodiment and embeddedness of the human being in not just its biological but also its technological world" (Wolfe, 2010, vx). I will first introduce the critical concept of crip technoscience and then illustrate its application to artistic practice as relevant to literary posthumanism.

Crip technoscience takes apart normative notions of embodiment and innovation by focusing on disabled bodyminds and practices. In their *Crip Technoscience Manifesto*, Aimi Hamraie and Kelly Fritsch (2019) argue for "the powerful, messy, non-innocent, contradictory, and nevertheless crucial work of crip technoscience: practices of critique, alteration, and reinvention of our material-discursive world" (2). Although the manifesto itself does not mention posthumanism, it decenters the abled human experience in a parallel manner. They explain that:

> In contrast to dominant forms of knowing-making for disability, we invoke crip technoscience to describe politicized practices of non-compliant knowing-making: world-building and world-dismantling practices by and with disabled people and communities that respond to intersectional systems of power, privilege, and oppression by working within and around them. (4–5)

As such, crip technoscience, although focused on technological extensions, is not transhumanist in its approach: "Haraway's approach to the cyborg takes for granted that disabled people easily meld into technological circuits, an assumption shaped by imperatives for rehabilitation, cure, independence, and productivity" (Hamraie and Fritsch 13). Rather than transcending human limitations, Hamraie and Fritsch's *Manifesto* positions disabilities as situated and politicized knowing-making that refuse to assimilate.

Hamraie and Fritsch posit their approach in critical opposition to mainstream accessibility rights that focus on compliance, explaining that: "emerging out of historical fights for disability rights, the terms accessibility and access are usually taken to mean disabled inclusion and assimilation into normative able-bodied relations and built environments" (10). Instead, "by endorsing accessible futures, we refuse to treat access as an issue of technical compliance or rehabilitation, as a simple technological fix, or a checklist. Instead, we define access as collective, messy, experimental, frictional, and generative. Accessible futures require our interdependence" (22). This is an entry point to conversation between electronic literature and crip technoscience. Electronic literature and crip technoscience share a distrust of access(ibility) compliance as a threat of seamless or frictionless design. In her insightful response to my first article to call for more accessible electronic literature, Deena Larsen replies: "I contend that experimental journeying into possibilities inherent in mixing text and imagery and sound is worthwhile in and of itself – without a defined audience and purpose – and without reaching the breadths of accessibility that Ackermans passionately envisions" (n.p.). I consider this shared distrust as a productive overlap for critical engagement with literary posthumanism because in disability approaches, the notion of the posthuman means moving beyond the normative notion of the human as an idealized abled bodymind: "disability complicates the myopic perspective and non-representative nature offered by humanism. . . . Posthuman and critical disability studies share an antithetical attitude toward the taken-for-granted, ideological and normative under-girdings of what it means to be a valued citizen of society" (Goodley et al., 2014, 348). Crip technoscience rejects compliance to a humanistic ideal of "the human," to embrace the friction provided by the plethora of posthuman technological practices.

Crip technoscience covers a variety of practical uses of technology, but also manifests as an artistic practice. Jenny Chamarette, for example, analyzes filmmaker Stephen Dwoskin's films as digital activism, bringing forth the practices and knowledge called for in the *Manifesto*: "In the case of Dwoskin, the issue is not any absence or lack of data, but rather pertains to a new methodology: how to reveal the productive specificities of Dwoskin's creative activity as active tactics of technological adaptation and crip technoscience?" (17). Chamararette, in her own words, "backdates" crip technoscience in her analysis. A well-known deliberate application of crip technoscience to art production is the art exhibition *Recoding CripTech*, curated by Lindsey D. Felt and Vanessa Chang for the SOMArts Cultural Center (San Francisco, USA) from January 24 to February 25, 2020. To exemplify the contestatory designs of crip technoscience, I will describe three works from the *Recoding CripTech* exhibition in relation to wider creative experimentation with technology.

In the installation *Ancestral Songs*, Darrin Martin explores technologically mediated experiences that are both individual and generational. In a space with "large video projections of expansive pastoral scenes" (artist's description), the audience is invited to put on stereoscopes that show interior spaces, in which "hands enter the frame holding hearing aids left by the artist's deceased relatives, which are cupped to initiate audible feedback" (artist's description). The work conveys the sounds in a multimodal way, with the "silent large projections closed captioned to describe all the environmental sounds the images once contained. Meanwhile, audio emanates from the stereoscopic viewers and bleeds throughout the installation" (artist's description). Audible feedback from hearing aids, although still present in some hearing aids for severe hearing loss, was more common before current digital hearing aids which are designed to minimize feedback. *Ancestral Songs*, then, uses the unwanted side effect of older technology as an artistic product: a conversation with human ancestors and the environment. In Martin's words: "the work activates an inversion of assistive listening devices as they are used to derive sound in defiance of the ways in which those with deafness can become silent participants in a hearing world" (artist's description). Subverting the technology's use pushes against the stigma that disability is something to be erased by access, transforming the unintended effect of technology into an intended, deliberate practice. More broadly, this subversion of technology resonates in electronic literature through glitch poetics. An iconic anecdote is Deena Larsen's exploitation of a bug in StorySpace as a narrative strategy, which led to a confrontation when the bug was fixed and therefore broke Larsen's work (recounted by Bly in Grigar and Moulthrop 2015). Likewise, Lonneke van Kampen uses the concept of the glitch and glitch art to consider a disabled perspective on the environmental crises, invoking both posthumanism and crip technoscience in her reading of the "crip Anthropocene."

And these creative practices do not stop at older technologies. AI has been heralded and forewarned as the future of technology and society, often in reference to Big Tech and governments. M. Eifler's *Prosthetic Memory* (https://ars.electronica.art/starts-prize/en/prosthetic-memory/), on the other hand, was created in their home without use of the cloud, asking the question "do our assumptions, fears, and uses for AI change when data and machine learning models are created by individuals and families at personal, instead of corporate, scale?" (artist's description). *Prosthetic Memory* is a multimodal work of self-augmentation of the author's long-term memory, which is damaged due to brain injury. As such, Eifler subverts the AI ideology of scale and transcendence above the personal in their uncharacteristically intimate work. At the same time, this leads to new posthuman approaches to sensory experience: "when memories are external, mediated, and public what is the difference between how they are experienced by their creator and an audience?" (artist's description). This question brings out the intimacy of technology, which is thematized in many digital artworks. Whereas a work like Kate Pullinger's *Breathe* becomes uncanny due to its access to the reader's world, *Prosthetic Memory* does the opposite, by giving an uncanny insight into the author's experience that is not only a curated representation of the author's memory, but a direct algorithmic generation. Compagna and Şahinol (2022) connect discussions of posthuman studies to crip technoscience in their consideration of assistive technologies, stating that "the cyborg body becoming a habit would eventually lead to the loss of meaning of current normality and favor human enhancement" (16). The intimacy of Eifler's work, then, explores the wider concept of the influence of technology on people's "identities and perceptions" (artist's description).

The final work I highlight here from *Recoding CripTech* is Sara Hendren's *Infrastructure Song* (2020). Instead of legacy and emerging technologies, Hendren explores the omnipresence of assistive technologies in urban environments: "Crosswalk signals are both infrastructure and culture. They sound like beeps, chirps or drums, or other sounds, depending on the city or town. They are everyday wayfinding infrastructure and unusual bits of the hyperlocal soundscape" (artist's description). In other words, they are a posthuman reminder that our everyday (inter)actions are guided by technology. *Infrastructure Song* remixes audible crosswalk signals from around the world along with other motorway sounds like tires and sirens and finally human voices – "all forms of infrastructure that color the aural cityscape" (artist's description) – into song, which placed in the exhibition space displaces their omnipresence in infrastructure. As such, the sound installation foregrounds the background which many people filter out of their conscious experience while for others it is their main connection to the infrastructure of the city.

Each of these examples points to the posthumanist acknowledgment of "the prosthetic coevolution of the human animal with the technicity of tools and external archival mechanisms" (Wolfe, 2010, xv), drawing attention to our embodied and situated knowledges of our physical and digital encounters with the world. Goodley et al. (2014) conclude that "disabled people will continue to fight to be recognized as humans (in the humanist sense and register of humanism) but equally (and simultaneously) are already enacting forms of activism, art and relationality that push us all to think imaginatively and critically about a new epoch that we might term the posthuman" (358). Crip technoscience, then, needs to be recognized as a critical tool to understand the diversity of Wolfe's "coevolution" to reveal the political potential of literary posthumanism.

– Hannah Ackermans, University of Bergen

References

Chamarette, J. (2022) "Backdating the Crip Technoscience Manifesto: Stephen Dwoskin's Digital Activism." *Film Quarterly, 76*(2), 16–24.

Compagna, D., & Şahinol, M. (2022) "Enhancement Technologies and the Politics of Life." *NanoEthics, 16*(1), 15–20.

Eifler, M. (2020) *Prosthetics Memory. Exhibited in Recoding CripTech* (San Francisco: SOMArts Cultural Center), curated by L. D. Felt and V. Chang, 2020.

Goodley, D., Lawthom, R., & Runswick Cole, K. (2014) "Posthuman Disability Studies." *Subjectivity*, 7, 342–61.

Hamraie, A., & Fritsch, K. (2019) "Crip Technoscience Manifesto." *Catalyst: Feminism, Theory, Technoscience, 5*(1), 1–33.

Haraway, D. (1988) "Situated Knowledges: The Science Question in Feminism and the Privilege of Partial Perspective." *Feminist Studies, 14*(3), 575–99.

Hendren, S. (2020) *Infrastructure Song. Exhibited in Recoding CripTech* (San Francisco: SOMArts Cultural Center), curated by L. D. Felt and V. Chang, 2020.

Kampen, L. van (2021) "Employing Glitchspeak: Glitch Theories for a Crip Anthropocene." *Posthuman Futures: Art and Literature*. Netherlands Research School for Literary Studies & Netherlands Institute for Cultural Analysis Symposium. https://feministsagainstableism.nl/wp-content/uploads/2021/11/PaperCC2L_vKampen.pdf.

Larsen, Deena (2021) "Better with the Purpose in: or, the Focus of Writing to Reach All of Your Audience." *electronic book review*.

Martin, D. (2020) *Ancestral Songs: Exhibited in Recoding CripTech* (San Francisco: SOMArts Cultural Center), curated by L. D. Felt and V. Chang, 2020.

Grigar, D. M., & Moulthrop, S. A. (2015) *Pathfinders: Documenting the Experience of Early Digital Literature.* Nouspace Publications.

Wolfe, C. (2010) *What is Posthumanism?* Minneapolis: University of Minnesota Press.

Morphological Freedom

The thought of enhancing the human body and thus transgressing physical boundaries has been deeply rooted in ancient history, such as the example of Daedalus and Icarus in Greek mythology. Daedalus, an exceptional inventor, wanted to flee the island of Crete. However, King Minos blocked the sea path, so Daedalus became inventive and decided to fly to freedom. He built wings for himself and his son, Icarus, by using feathers and wax. He also warned Icarus not to fly too close to the sun since the heat would melt the wax. Icarus, who became adventurous and careless, did not listen and thus fell into the sea and drowned. This myth, ending with Icarus' death, not only serves as a powerful allegory for human hubris and pride but also focuses on Daedalus' technological achievement. Hence, attached enhancements to improve or even transgress the limits of the human body have always been part of history. This notion is called "morphological freedom," a term that first appeared in transhumanist Max More's article "Technological Self-Transformation: Expanding Personal Extropy" (1993).

Here, the adjective "morphological" derives from "human morphology," which describes a form or structure of the human body in terms of its development and vital activity in a medical field. Posthuman thought, specifically the transhumanist branch of it, not only involves medical progress and enhancements of the body, but also involves human rights claims (Sandberg) such as the right of self-ownership, but also the right of modifying one's own body on their own terms. This includes consensual interventions in the human body because of medical, therapeutic, or aesthetic reasons.

As a result, *Body Morphology* becomes highly embodied in a socio-cultural and political global discourse. The argument of self-determination is a human right to be emphasized, not only as part of "a future democratic society" (Moore), but also in the field of transgender transitioning and gender inclusivity. McElvaney et al. (2021) provide information on how facial information and body morphology can unfairly bias the perception and cultural interpretation of human beings. This is significant for issues such as discrimination and exclusion of minorities (cf. *internalization of society's appearance*; Matz et al., 2002).

The idea of uploading one's mind and entering a bodily-free state of being is one of the ultimate goals of transhumanist thought. "Mind Uploading," which Häggström (2021) defines as "the transferring of our minds to computer hardware using whole-brain emulation" (3), is the positive outcome of full *Morphological Freedom*. Emulation here refers to the opposite of simulation: to the precise replica of the mind. In a bodiless state of existence, human prejudices about other bodies would simply be annulled. Humankind can simply transgress issues such as racism and discrimination. However, this bears both a financial and an ecological danger: Equality is needed, but who is, in fact, financially able to become a virtual posthuman being? And what toll does it take on electricity production and hardware maintenance for the rest of us on our only Earth? Does bodily freedom coincide with freedom under the maxim of inalienable rights within Human Rights? Do hybrids, posthumans, and cyborgs fall under the same category? Defining what is human and what is not might be the greatest challenge for legal and political thought.

Another striking factor in this discussion is the dilemma of body and consciousness as a unit or as two separate entities. The two clashing theories about philosophical and medical/psychological positions in the field of Morphological Freedom are identified by Cappuccio as The "Mind-Upload" hypothesis (MU) vs. the Embodied Mind theory (EM). The "Mind-Upload" hypothesis is in favor of transferring the whole human mind to a digital device (and thus transhumanist thought). An uploaded mind would possess the advantage of fast travelling (much like the transfer of computer files); it would no longer be framed by a body and not face physical diseases. Copies of "selves" could offer humankind a possibility to live several lives at once and become immortal by doing so. Furthermore, an uploaded mind can be manipulated, and certain bad experiences or traumatic memories can be erased. Thus, MU offers a possibility for shaping memory and more easily overcoming obstacles in life. Yet, ironically, MU is still bound to the new (digital) matter it would exist in.

The Embodied Mind theory, by contrast, states that in order for a mind to exist it needs to be embodied. The latter also implies that a mind's individual identity is directly intertwined with its physical body (cf. *Phenomenology and Physical Embodiment*, Martin Heidegger (1975), Edmund Husserl (1929), and Maurice Merleau-Ponty (1962) who all highlight the significance of the influence between body and consciousness). Embodied Mind theory is therefore also more in line with ecological and new materialist frameworks in the humanities, stressing the recursive ongoing processes, entanglements, and its interactivity, as well as making matter *matter* (cf. Karen Barad [2007]). By taking away certain matter and replacing it with other matter, is it still a human mind? Or is the human mind a unique entanglement of specific, yet malleable, matter? Embodied Mind theory would respond in favor of the latter.

Both theories, however, try to grasp the essence of human beings and discuss whether or not a bodily frame is needed for our existence. Both also address *Morphological Freedom* and what that means for human *bodily* enhancement. *Body Morphology* could pave a way toward a more tolerant and "post-exclusive" society (a term coined by Ferrando [2014]); whether it is the chosen tool, and what is possible to do with this as a tool, to overcome racism, sexism, and discrimination against minorities, remains highly debatable.

– Jessica Wädt, MA student of English, University of Stuttgart

References

More, Max (1993) "Technological Self-Transformation. Expanding Personal Extropy." *Extropy* 4.2, 15–24.

Cappuccio, Massimilliano L. (2017) "Mind-upload. The ultimate challenge to the embodied mind theory." *Phenomenology and the Cognitive Sciences* 16, 425–48.

Ferrando, Francesca (2014) *POSTHUMANISM, TRANSHUMANISM, ANTIHUMANISM, METAHUMANISM, AND NEW MATERIALISMS:*

DIFFERENCES AND RELATIONS. "Existenz," Published by The Karl Jaspers Society of North America.

McElvaney, T. J., Osman, M., & Mareschal, I. (2021) "Perceiving threat in others: The role of body morphology." *PLoS ONE,* 16.4.

Matz, P. E., Foster, G. D., Faith, M. S., and Wadden, T. A. (2002) Correlates of body image dissatisfaction among overweight women seeking weight loss. *Journal of Consulting and Clinical Psychology* 70, 4: 1040–4.

Häggström Olle (2021) "Aspects of Mind Uploading." In Hofkirchner, W. and Kreowski, HJ. (eds.) *Transhumanism: The Proper Guide to a Posthuman Condition or a Dangerous Idea?* Cognitive Technologies (series): Cham: Springer.

Sandberg, Anders (2013) "Morphological Freedom – Why We Not Just Want It, but Need It." In M. More and Natasha Vita More (eds.), *The Transhumanist Reader.* Hoboken, New Jersey: Wiley-Blackwell.

Further Reading

BBC News. *The immortalist: Uploading the mind to a computer.* www.bbc.com/news/magazine-35786771.

United Nations on "Gender Inclusive Language." www.un.org/en/gender-inclusive-language/#:~:text=Using%20gender%2Dinclusive%20language%20means,does%20not%20perpetuate%20gender%20stereotypes.

Francesca Ferrando (2014) "The Body," in Robert Ranisch & Stefan Lorenz Sorgner (eds.), *Post- and Transhumanism: An Introduction.* Frankfurt: S.L. Peter Lang, 213–26.

Winterson, Jeanette (2019) *Frankissstein: A Love Story.* London: Vintage.

Braidotti, Rosi (2013) *The Posthuman.* Cambridge: Polity Press.

Plasticity and Posthumanism

The term "plasticity" is closely associated with the work of the contemporary philosopher Catherine Malabou. Plasticity is a critical concept through which Malabou revisits and reinterprets key writers in and around the continental philosophical tradition from Kant to Derrida, including Hegel, Heidegger, Freud, Bergson, Levinas, amongst others.

Best thought of as a philosopher of metamorphosis, a part of Malabou's aim has always been to locate metamorphic concepts and logics in the works of predecessors for the sake of constituting a modern tradition of plastic philosophy that has always been there, though it has also been difficult to see due to long-standing philosophical prejudices, as exemplified in the fetishization of monolithic identity. When Malabou writes in *The Future of Hegel* (2005) that self-determination is "the originary operation of plasticity" (12), she writes against the grain of a predominant post-Hegelian tradition, including Martin Heidegger, Alexandre Kojève, and Alexandre Koyré, that construes the dialectic as an absolutely totalizing process of identity formation, where "everything that occurs can only be the indication of what has already come to pass" (3). (See *The Heidegger Change* [2011] for Malabou's subsequent reinterpretation, or plasticization, of Heideggerian ontology.) Similarly, when Malabou writes in her book on Kant that "[t]he problem of the origin of the agreement between categories and objects is necessarily compounded by . . . the question of the structure of auto-affection through which the subject receives its own spontaneity" (*Before Tomorrow*, 2016, 91), she does so in contradistinction to the conventional notion of the transcendental as programmed invariance, or as predisposition. Malabou's interpretation of Kant pivots on her adoption of an epigenetic rather than a genetic approach to philosophy, biology, neuroscience, and psychology. Her work participates in a broad cultural and epistemological shift from the integral to the ecological, from monadism to collectivism, and from the humanities to the posthumanities.

Though we may be prejudiced against the word "plastic" for culturally specific reasons ("plastic" as vulgar, infinitely malleable, without soul), Malabou uses the word partly to draw attention to the significance of form, and, thereby, materiality, for any philosophy which would seek, as hers does, to move beyond discursivity and communicate with the world of substance and science. This is an aspect of her work which lends itself powerfully to any posthumanist critical-theoretical orientation looking beyond metaphysics. Malabou's philosophy addresses itself not just to thinking, but to the form, and the materiality, of thought. Plasticity is not only Malabou's central philosophical motif; it is also the most salient formal/material feature of thinking itself. The plasticity of the neuron synapse is not only a model for thought, it is how thinking operates.

In books such as *What Should We Do with Our Brain?* (2008), *The New Wounded* (2012), and *Ontology of the Accident* (2012), Malabou appropriates the image of synaptic plasticity from neuroscience, synthesizes it with insights from continental philosophy, and articulates a new form of plasticity: destructive plasticity. Unlike the scientifically sanctioned forms of plasticity (developmental, modulational, and reparative), destructive plasticity is a neuro-philosophical hybrid concept, designed, in a sense, to crystalize Malabou's critique of metaphysical subjectivity. Unlike in mythological metamorphoses, where a human may be turned into a tree but otherwise keep her former soul or identity (see the story of Daphne in Ovid's *Metamorphoses*), destructive plasticity insists on the possibility of "a real and total deviation of being" (*Ontology*, 7) due to the inextricable connection between form and substance, or materiality and thought. Writing of Kafka's *Metamorphosis*, Malabou suggests that we must "imagine a Gregor perfectly indifferent to his transformation, unconcerned by it" (*Ontology*, 18), in order to understand the stakes of a nonmetaphysical approach to identity.

Such ruminations about *another* Gregor Samsa's automaticity and soullessness are provocative, but they also risk the danger of promoting the notion that plasticity is a singular feature of the human brain, or the human condition. In *Morphing*

Intelligence, Malabou flatly dispels this prejudice by arguing that neuronal plasticity is always a kind of automaticity: "intelligence is always already artificial" (99). This harder turn to a more distinctively, and conventionally, posthumanist logic and rhetoric of the dissolving boundary between human and artificial intelligence is, I would argue, a foreseeable outcome, given, for example, Malabou's keen attention in her very first book to Hegel's analysis of the role of habit in the constitution of selfhood. In *The Future of Hegel*, habit is an automaticity that sutures together the corporeal and the spiritual. In *Morphing Intelligence*, human intelligence is always part automatism, because one cannot function without the other: "automatism and spontaneity appear as two sides of a single energy reality" (99).

   Beyond philosophy, the motif of plasticity informs recent scholarship on pathology, politics, social theory, law, ecology, and literature. Recent essay collections on plasticity include *Plastic Materialities: Politics, Legality, and Metamorphosis in the Work of Catherine Malabou* (2015), and *Plasticity and Pathology: On the Formation of the Neural Subject* (2016). In literary studies, see Heather H. Yeung's *On Literary Plasticity: Readings with Kafka in Ecology, Voice, and Object-Life* (2020). Also see S. Pearl Brilmyer's essay "Plasticity, Form, and the Matter of Character in *Middlemarch*" (2015); Stephen Dougherty's "Plasticity and the Event of Literature: Reading Catherine Malabou with Anne Carson" (2022); and Matthew Scully's "Plasticity at the Violet Hour: Tiresias, 'The Waste Land,' and Poetic Form" (2018).

> *– Stephen Dougherty, Professor of American Literature, University of Agder, Norway*

References and Further Reading

Bates, David and Nima Bassiri, eds. (2016) *Plasticity and Pathology: On the Formation of the Neural Subject*. New York: Fordham University Press.

Bhandar, Brenna and Jonathan Goldberg-Hiller, eds. (2015) *Plastic Materialities: Politics, Legality, and Metamorphosis in the Work of Catherine Malabou*. Durham: Duke University Press.

Brilmyer, S. Pearl (2015) "Plasticity, Form, and the Matter of Character in *Middlemarch*." *Representations* 130.1 (Spring): 60–83.

Dougherty, Stephen (2022) "Plasticity and the Event of Literature: Reading Catherine Malabou with Anne Carson." In *Literature and Event: Twenty-First Century Reformulations*. Ed. Mantra Mukim and Derek Attridge. New York: Routledge, 27–41.

Dougherty, Stephen (2023) "'At the Crossroads . . . ': Essence and Accidents in Catherine Malabou's Philosophy of Plasticity." In *Contingency and Plasticity in Everyday Technologies*. Ed. Natasha Lushetich, Iain Campbell and Dominic Smith. London: Rowman & Littlefield, 219–34.

Malabou, Catherine (2016) *Before Tomorrow: Epigenesis and Rationality*. Translated by Carolyn Shread. Cambridge: Polity Press.

   (2005) *The Future of Hegel: Plasticity, Temporality, and Dialectic*. Translated by Lisabeth During. London: Routledge.

(2011) *The Heidegger Change: On the Fantastic in Philosophy*. Translated by Peter Skafish. Albany: State University of New York Press.

(2019) *Morphing Intelligence: From IQ Measurement to Artificial Brains*. Translated by Carolyn Shread. New York: Columbia University Press.

(2012) *The New Wounded: From Neurosis to Brain Damage*. Translated by Steven Miller. New York: Fordham University Press.

(2012) *Ontology of the Accident: An Essay on Destructive Plasticity*. Translated by Carolyn Shread. Cambridge: Polity Press.

(2008) *What Should We Do With Our Brain?* Translated by Sebastian Rand. New York: Fordham University Press.

Scully, Matthew (2018) "Plasticity at the Violet Hour: Tiresias, 'The Waste Land,' and Poetic Form." *Journal of Modern Literature* 41.3 (2018): 166–82.

Yeung, Heather H. (2020) *On Literary Plasticity: Readings with Kafka in Ecology, Voice, and Object-Life*. (Springer Nature Switzerland). Cham: Palgrave Macmillan.

Phage Literature

As with bacteriophages – viruses that parasitize a bacterium by infecting it and reproducing inside it – language is permeated by a series of virulent inf(l)ections. Moving away from the printed page, or being even more deeply impregnated in its textures, these viral processes can either offer a truly literal meaning to the expression "language is a virus," or simply emphasize its metaphoric sense, just as they can be analyzed simultaneously in vivo by means of laboratorial practices and scrutinized by digital algorithms.

By exposing the ways in which literature gains new possible readings by means of its disruptive interconnections with different fields of knowledge, phage literature is an example of the boom in transdisciplinary studies and posthuman poetics potentiated by digital technologies.

An early example of these interconnections and material transformations would be Eduardo Kac's innovative biopoems from the 1980s (www.ekac.org/), a manifestation of bioart combining literature and biotechnology, and making use of technoscientific developments such as video, holography, programming, and the web as a way of exploring new poetic languages beyond its print manifestation. Acting as and with living organisms, Kac's poems in vivo, through mutation of molecules, can imply either the continuity and preservation of life through the creation of new living organisms, or its destruction. In "Bacterial Poetics," for instance, Kac associates the idea of two different poems encoded in a plasmid of two identical colonies of bacteria. As the colonies compete for resources or share their genetic material, they can either outlive the other or open a place for the emergence of new bacteria.

While most of the examples described by Kac imply some sort of manipulation of genes and germs, hence giving to his artistic practice the status of a laboratory experience, none of his biopoems specifically mention viruses. Nonetheless, Kac's appropriation and disruption of terminology and tropes associated with the invasion and multiplication of life within life already operates as a viral process in itself (toward poetry as an institution, toward compartmented knowledge and other stagnated environments). In the same way as viruses, Kac's words act as parasites – that is, living in or on an organism of another species (its host) and benefiting by deriving nutrients. Just as parasites require living cells or tissue in which to grow, Kac's biopoems need to invade a foreign field of knowledge (often biotechnology) and use their components to grow and multiply. Along the way, it can be said that some of these experiences might even "kill" host cells as part of their life cycle, as is the case of his Transgenic poetry, implying (1) the synthesitization of DNA in order to perform writing through combinations of nucleotides, (2) the incorporation of this writing into a living organism's genome, (3) the combination of words belonging to different organisms, through their offspring. One of these results put into practice is the transgenic biopoem Cypher (2003; www.ekac.org/cypher.html), a hybrid between sculpture, an artist book (a poem-object), and a DIY transgenic kit. Built out of stainless steel, the kit opens like a book. It's a minilab containing laboratory material, including synthetic DNA with a poem by Kac encoded in its genetic sequence. In order to activate the poem, the reader needs to follow a specific set of instructions that will give "literal and poetic" life to the artwork – namely, by manually integrating the synthetic DNA into the bacteria.

Another example of a transgenic poem is "Genesis," first exhibited in 1999 at Ars Electronica. It all starts with the creation of an artist's gene, as Kac called it, a synthetic gene nonexistent in Nature. To do this, Kac translated a portion of the Old Testament into Morse code and then passed the Morse code into DNA. Later, the gene was introduced into bacteria arranged in Petri dishes, and, at the installation, the dishes were placed on a box of ultraviolet light, remotely controlled by participants via the web. In this way, actual and virtual participants could cause a mutation in the genetic code and thus alter the initial text. In Eduardo Kac's biopoetry, poem and code reach a symbiotic stage of interpretation in which the language and code of the poem intertwine with the language and code of the gene. Reminiscent of the two strands coiled around each other to form a double helix in each molecule of DNA, in order to read the full genetic/poetic information of Kac's biopoems, the reader must have in mind the double nature of art and science, biological and artificial, word and molecule.

Another well-known example of phage literature working with the hybridization of words and molecules is Canadian transdisciplinary poet Christian Bök (pronounced Book, as in the Book of Books). Author of experimental literature books *Eunoia* (2001; www.engadget.com/2015-12-30-christian-bok-the-xenotext-bacteria-poetry.html) and *Crystallography* (1994; www.poetryfoundation.org/harriet-books/2011/04/the-xenotext-works), Bök is perhaps best known for his project "The Xenotext," for which he was interviewed by "Nature" (the first poet ever to feature in a journal of science). THE XENOTEXT is a project that officially started around 2007, when Christian Bök came up with the idea of crossing poetry, cryptography, and bioengineering as a way of making literal

William S. Burroughs's aphorism "the word is now a virus." More specifically: the creation of a DNA-encrypted micropoem with a view to replicating it in a given organism until the end of time – that is, one assumes, until the Sun explodes.

THE XENOTEXT consists of a single sonnet called "Orpheus," translated into a gene and integrated into a cell, causing the cell to read the poem, and interpreting it as an instruction to build a protein whose sequence of amino acids encode another sonnet titled "Eurydice." In this way, not only was Bök able to archive a poem in a cell, he was also able to use this cell-archive as a writing machine. After a successful experiment with an E. coli bacterium, the next step consisted in repeating the experiment, but this time with what is known as the most resistant and hypothetically indestructible bacteria: Dienococcus radiodurans. Although this bacterium did transcribe RNA from the inserted DNA, Bök has not yet been able to produce the proteins necessary for the propagation of his poem. (Precisely stated: in the process of bacterial transcription, a segment of bacterial DNA has been copied into a newly synthesized strand of messenger RNA [mRNA] with use of the enzyme RNA polymerase.)

Apart from the controversy around the questions and implications that his work poses and instigates, Bök's work should be analyzed, understood, and experienced by what it represents in terms of literature – namely, an expanded notion of literature working as a continuum between tradition and innovation, and thus opening avenues for future transdisciplinary research in art, science, and technology, without losing its foundational poetic and aesthetic grounds.

From Kac's biopoems and Bök's first experiments with transgenetic literature to nowadays, a wide range of practices have emerged in which biotechnology intermingles with arts, causing the roles of scientist and artist to be practically indistinguishable. Consisting of Cesar Baio (Brazil) and Lucy HG Solomon (USA), the "Cesar & Lois artist collective" merges social, technological, and biological systems, often through bio-inspired computing such as microbiological mappings and bio-AI architectures. Breaking boundaries between culture and nature, in their transdisciplinary series of installations titled "Degenerative Cultures," Cesar & Lois take advantage of bio-inspired computing to explore the hybridism between the logic inherent in microbiological organisms and environments, human knowledge, and AIs.

One of those installations is "The Bhiobrid Logic of Degenerative Cultures," from 2019, in which the artists place a plasmodial slime mold, Physarum polycephalum, over a book on the human impulse to control nature. As this acellular slime mold grows over the text, erasing the book's initial layer like a palimpsest, it feeds an AI through an algorithm capable of reading the new text-organism and tweeting what it reads. Cesar & Lois's choice for this multi-brain organism has essentially to do with a "decentralized logic" that, according to them, enables a shift in this species from traditional conceptions of AI as individual brains with a unilateral logic of control to a paradigm ruled by an ecosystemic dynamics. In Bhiobrid Logic, connected to human knowledge and the AI, the polychephalum becomes a potential model for the creation of an ecosystemic connection.

An important detail in this entire process is what Cesar & Lois call Digital Fungi, since with each new installation, always in different places around the world from

Belo Horizonte to Porto and Singapore, AI is directed to find online texts that relate to human interventions in the field of climate change. This is done in the same geographic regions where the exhibition takes place, allowing the authors to later compile and consume these same texts. In this way, a potential model for the creation of a truly ecosystemic connection is obtained, one that also includes the holding of workshops with local communities. Moreover, Baio and Solomon's extension of their idea of sociotechnical systems deriving from learning with microbes amplifies even further the meaning of the expression *viral behavior* – as much as the term "amplification" itself in (for example) medical scientific terminology, a process considered responsible for the formation of new genes, as well as for the appearance of mutations that may or may not be favorable to evolution, and therefore, playing an important role in heavy words like cancer (for example) when a tumor cell copies DNA segments.

Thinking of the microbiological AI created and developed by Cesar & Lois, the self-reflective nature of Bhiobrid Logic evinces a potential model of knowledge that amplifies the ways in which we see ourselves – in this case, through books and, consequently, words formed into sentences that are capable of defining and redefining. However, as soon as sentences start to be erased by another organism, other textual layers begin to unveil. In a first layer, a potential poem deriving from a technique of erasure not necessarily intentional; on the following layers, a linguistic model that is the result of the aforementioned connection between biological, artificial, and (ultimately) both intelligences.

Taking into account Bök's xenotext and Cesar and Lois' degenerative cultures, at first sight both projects make us think of a certain continuity with ancient alchemists in search of the Philosopher's Stone, aka immortality. But, on closer inspection, they work as diametrical opposites. Whereas in The Xenotext project the objective is to preserve a human poetic form through a bacterium, in keeping the essential information that allows us today to configure it and reconfigure it as a poem, in the work of Cesar and Lois, human knowledge, allegedly immortalized in the pages of a book, is destroyed to make room for another form of knowledge, that is, the annulment of poetics or literature as we know it (with Kac operating somewhere in the middle). Ultimately, Cesar & Lois' degenerative cultures can be seen as a truly antidisciplinary model of knowledge. One that is made of natural losses and gains; one that needs to destroy the nature of a text (a field of knowledge, a compartment, a paradigm), perhaps even the nature of a poem, definitely the nature of viruses as we humans understand them, in order to create a universal, or, better said, ecosystemic language.

> – Diogo Marques, a founding member of Portuguese artist collective, www.wreading-digits.com

Works Cited

Alaimo, Stacy (2020) "New Materialisms." In Sherryl Vint, ed., *After the Human: Culture, Theory, and Criticism in the 21st Century*. Cambridge: Cambridge University Press, 177–91.

Alaimo, Stacy and Susan Hekman, eds. (2008) *Material Feminisms*. Bloomington: Indiana University Press.

Amin, Osama S. M. (2016, April 7). "Flood Tablet of the Epic of Gilgamesh." *World History Encyclopedia*. www.worldhistory.org/image/4821/flood-tablet-of-the-epic-of-gilgamesh/. See also Wikemedia, File: The Newly Discovered Tablet V of the Epic of Gilgamesh, The Sulaymaniyah Museum, Iraq: https://commons.wikimedia.org/wiki/user: Neuroforever.

Anderson, Benedict (1983) *Imagined Communities: Reflections on the Origin and Spread of Nationalism*. London: Verso.

Anderson, Christian Ulrich and Søren Bro Pold (2018) *The Metainterface: The Art of Platforms, Cities, and Clouds*. Cambridge, MA: MIT Press.

Arlett, Robert (1996) *Epic Voices: Inner and Global Impulse in the Contemporary American and British Novel*. Selingsgrove: Susquehanna University Press.

Badmington, Neil (2000) *Posthumanism*. Houndmills: Palgrave.

   (2011) "Posthumanism." In Bruce Clarke and Manuela Rossini, eds., *The Routledge Companion to Literature and Science*. London: Routledge, 374–84.

Bakhtin, M. M. (1981) *The Dialogic Imagination: Four Essays by M. M. Bakhtin*, ed. Michael Holquist, trans. Caryl Emerson and Michael Holquist. Austin: University of Texas Press.

Barad, Karen (Spring 2003) "Posthumanist Performativity: Toward an Understanding of How Matter Comes to Matter." *Signs: Journal of Women in Culture and Society* 28.3: 801–31.

   (2007) *Meeting the Universe Halfway: Quantum Physics and the Entanglement of Matter and Meaning*. Durham: Duke University Press.

Barthes, Roland (1977) "Death of the Author," *Image, Music, Text*. Trans. S. Heath. London: Fontana, 142–8.

Baum, Frank (2010) Prologue to The Patchwork Girl of Oz. www.gutenberg.org/files/32094/32094-h/32094-h.htm.

Bennett, Claire-Louise (2015a) "On Writing Pond." *The Irish Times*, May 26. www.irishtimes.com/culture/books/claire-louise-bennett-on-writing-pond-1.2226535.

(2015b) *Pond*. Ireland: The Stinging-Fly Press.

Bennett, Jane (2010) *Vibrant Matter: A Political Ecology of Things*. Durham: Duke University Press.

(2012) "Systems and Things: A Response to Graham Harman and Timothy Morton." *New Literary History* 43.2: 225–33.

Bergthaller, Hannes (2017) "Climate Change and Un-Narratability." *Metaphora: Journal for Literature Theory and Media. EV 2: Climate Change, Complexity, Representation*. https://metaphorajournal.univie.ac.at/climate-change/volume2_bergthaller.pdf.

(2018) "Beyond Ecological Crisis: Niklas Luhmann's Theory of Social Systems." *electronic book review*. https://electronicbookreview.com/essay/beyond-ecological-crisis-niklas-luhmanns-theory-of-social-systems-2/.

Bergthaller, Hannes, and Carsten Schinko (2011) *Addressing Modernity*. Amsterdam: Rodopi.

Bergson, Henri (1998) *Creative Evolution*. Trans. Arthur Mitchell. New York: Dover.

Berner, Justin (2020, September 6) "Unhelpful Tools: Reexamining the Digital Humanities through Eugenio Tisselli's *degenerative and regenerative*." *electronic book review*. https://electronicbookreview.com/essay/unhelpful-tools-reexamining-the-digital-humanities-through-eugenio-tissellis-degenerative-and-regenerative/.

Berry, Ralph, and Jeffrey DiLeo (2007) *Fiction's Present: Situating Contemporary Narrative Innovation*. Albany: SUNY Press.

Bloom, Harold, ed. (2006) *Frankenstein (Bloom's Modern Critical Interpretations)*. New York: Chelsea House Publications.

Bloom, Harold (2007) *Mary Shelley's Frankenstein / Edited and with an Introduction by Harold Bloom. Updated edition*. New York: Chelsea House.

Bogost, Ian (n.d.) "What is Object-Oriented Ontology?" https://bogost.com/writing/blog/what_is_objectoriented_ontolog/.

Boldizsár Simon, Zoltán (2019) "Two Cultures of the Posthuman Future." *History and Theory* 58.2: 171–84.

Bostrom, Nick (2005a) "A History of Transhumanist Thought." *Journal of Evolution and Technology* 14.1: 1–25.

(2005b) "Transhumanist Values," in Frederick Adams, ed., *Ethical Issues for the 21st Century*. Charlottesville: Philosophy Documentation Center.

(2014) *Superintelligence: Paths, Dangers, Strategies*. Oxford: Oxford University Press.

Bouchardon, Serge and Victor Petit (2019) "Digital Writing: Philosophical and Pedagogical Issues." *electronic book review*. http://electronicbookreview.com/essay/digital-writing-philosophical-and-pedagogical-issues/.

Boxall, Peter (2006) *Don DeLillo: The Possibility of Fiction*. New York: Routledge.
    (2013) *Twenty-First-Century Fiction: A Critical Introduction*. Cambridge:
        Cambridge University Press.
    (2015) "Science, Technology, and the Posthuman," in David James, ed., *The
        Cambridge Companion to British Fiction Since 1945*. Cambridge:
        Cambridge University Press, 127–42.
Braidotti, Rosi (1994) Nomadic Subjects: Embodiment and Sexual Difference in
        Contemporary Feminist Theory. New York: Columbia University Press.
    (2002) *Metamorphoses: Towards a Materialist Theory of Becoming*.
        Cambridge: Polity Press.
    (2006a) "Affirming the Affirmative: On Nomadic Affectivity." *Rhizomes*
        11.12.
    (2006b) "Posthuman, All too Human: Towards a New Process Ontology."
        Theory, Culture and Society 23.7–8: 197–208.
    (2006c) *Transpositions: On Nomadic Ethics*. Cambridge: Polity.
    (2013) *The Posthuman*. Cambridge: Polity Press.
    (2019) "A Theoretical Framework for the Critical Posthumanities." *Theory,
        Culture & Society* 36.6: 31–61.
Braidotti, Rosi and Maria Hlavajova, eds. (2018) *Posthuman Glossary*. London:
        Bloomsbury Academic.
Braidotti, Rosi, Emily Jones and Goda Klumbyte, eds. (2022) *More Posthuman
        Glossary*. London: Bloomsbury Academic.
Brown, Bill (2001) "Thing Theory." *Critical Inquiry* 28.1: 1–22.
Buell, Lawrence (1995) *The Environmental Imagination: Thoreau, Nature
        Writing, and the Formation of American Culture*. Cambridge, MA:
        Harvard University Press.
Burchfield, Robert. "The Features, Functions, and Limitations of Dictionaries."
        Thought.Co.
Burdick, Anne (2021) "Researching Writing Technologies through the
        Speculative Prototype Design of *Trina*." *electronic book review*. https://
        electronicbookreview.com/essay/speculative-trina/.
Burdick, Anne, Johanna Drucker, Peter Lunenfeld, Todd Presner, and
        Jeffrey Schnap (2012) *Digital Humanities* Boston: MIT. https://mitpress
        .mit.edu/9780262528863/digital_humanities/.
Burroughs, William S. (2010) *The Ticket That Exploded*. New York: Harper
        Collins.
Cage, John (1961) "Lecture on Nothing," In *Silence: Lectures and Writings*.
        Middletown: Wesleyan University Press, 109–27.
Callus, Ivan (2022) "Literature and Posthumanism." In S. Herbrechter, I. Callus,
        M. Rossini, et al. (eds), *Palgrave Handbook of Critical Posthumanism*.
        Cham: Palgrave Macmillan. https://doi.org/10.1007/978-3-031-
        04958-3_21.
Callus, Ivan, and Stefan Herbrechter (2003) "What's Wrong with
        Posthumanism?" *Rhizomes* 7, www.rhizomes.net/issue7/callus.htm.

Callus, Ivan, Stefan Herbrechter, and Manuela Rossini (2014) "Introduction: Dis/Locating Posthumanism in European Literary and Critical Traditions." *European Journal of English Studies* 18.2: 103–20.

Carpenter, J. R. *The Gathering Cloud.* http://luckysoap.com. Commissioned in 2016 by NEoN Digital Arts Festival. Published in print by Uniformbooks, 2017. www.uniformbooks.co.uk/thegatheringcloud.php.

Carrington, Damian (2018, 21 May), "Humans Just 0.01% of All Life But Have Destroyed 83% of Wild Mammals – Study." *Guardian.* www.theguardian.com/environment/2018/may/21/human-race-just-001-of-all-life-but-has-destroyed-over-80-of-wild-mammals-study.

Casanova, Pascale (2004) *The World Republic of Letters.* Cambridge, MA. Harvard University Press.

Cavell, Stanley (2003) "Finding as Founding: Taking Steps in Emerson's 'Experience,'" in *Emerson's Transcendental Etudes*, ed. David Justin Hodge, Stanford University Press, 111, **79.**

Chaplin, Joyce E. (2017) "Can the Nonhuman Speak? Breaking the Chain of Being in the Anthropocene," *Journal of the History of Ideas* 78.4: 509–29.

Childs, Jason (2021) "Assaying the Novel," in *The Essay at the Limits: Poetics, Politics, and Form*, ed. Mario Aquilina. London: Bloomsbury Academic.

Clarke, Bruce (2020) "Machines, AIs, Cyborgs, Systems," in *After the Human: Culture, Theory, and Criticism in the 21st Century*, ed. Sherryl Vint. Cambridge: Cambridge University Press.
    (2014) *Neocybernetics and Narrative.* Minneapolis: University of Minnesota Press.
    (2008) *Posthuman Metamorphosis: Narrative and Systems.* New York: Fordham University Press.

Clarke, Bruce and Manuela Rossini, eds. (2011) *The Routledge Companion to Literature and Science.* London: Routledge.
    (2017) *The Cambridge Companion to Literature and the Posthuman.* Cambridge: Cambridge University Press.

Collado-Rodriquez, Francisco (2018) "On Human Consciousness and Posthuman Slavery: Representations of the Living Dead in T. S. Eliot, Thomas Pynchon and William Gibson," in *A Critical Gaze from the Old World.* Ed. Isabel Duran, Rebeca Gualberto, Eusebio De Lorenzo. Carmen M. Mendez-Garcia, & Eduardo Valls. Bern: Peter Lang.
    When Immortality Becomes a Burden: Transhuman Vulnerability and Self-Consciousness in William Gibson's Neuromancer (1984). London: Routledge.

Crogan, Patrick (2006) "Essential Viewing." *Film Philosophy* 10.2: 39–54.

Crawford, T. Hugh (2015) "Bruno Latour: From the Non-Modern to the Posthuman." In M. Hauskeller, T. D. Philbeck, and C. D. Carbonell (eds.) *The Palgrave Handbook of Posthumanism in Film and Television.* London: Palgrave Macmillan. https://doi.org/10.1057/9781137430328_5.

Coover, Robert (2018) "The End of Literature," *American Scholar*, 4 September, https://theamericanscholar.org/the-end-of-literature/.

Culler, Jonathan (1997) *Literary Theory: A Very Short Introduction*. Oxford: Oxford University Press.

Damrosch, David (2003) *What Is World Literature*. Princeton: Princeton University Press.

Deleuze, Gilles (1997) "Bartleby; or, The Formula." *OnCurating* 40. www.on-curating.org/issue-40-reader/bartleby-or-the-formula.html.

Derrida, Jacques (1995) *The Gift of Death*, transl. David Wills. Chgicago: University of Chicago Press.

Davies, Tony (1997) *Humanism: The New Critical Idiom*. London: Routledge.

Domanska, Ewa (2015) "Ecological Humanities," *Teksty Drugie*, special issue – English edition, 186–210. https://depot.ceon.pl/bitstream/handle/123456789/10911/12_doma%C5%84ska_ecological.pdf?sequence=1&isAllowed=y.

Economides, Louise and Laura Shackelford, eds (2021) *Surreal Entanglements: Essays on Jeff VanderMeer's Fictions*. London: Routledge.

Edelman, Lee (2013) "Occupy Wall Street: 'Bartleby' Against the Humanities." *History of the Present* 3.1: 99–118. Springfield: University of Illinois Press. https://doi.org/10.5406/historypresent.3.1.0099.

Elias, Amy J. (2001) *Emerson's Prose and Poetry*, selected and edited by Joel Porte and Saundra Morris. New York: Norton.

(2015a) "Cyberpunk, Steampunk,Teslapunk, Dieselpunk, Salvagepunk: Metahistorical Romance and/vs the Technological Sublime." In *Metahistorical Narratives and Scientific Metafictions: A Critical Insight into the Twentieth-Century Poetics*. Ed. Giuseppe Episcopo. Napoli: Edizioni Cronopio, 201–20.

(2015b) "The Futureless Future." *American Book Review*, July/August 12–13.

(2015c) "Pynchon, *Gravity's Rainbow*, and OOO, that Mysterious Rag." Short Paper delivered at "NARRATIVE: An International Conference" Roundtable "Reading Rainbow: Pynchon's Narrative Poetics Revisited," with Brian McHale, Kathryn Hume, Luc Herman, John Hellman. Chicago, IL, March.

Emmett, Robert S. and David E. Nye (2017) *The Environmental Humanities: A Critical Introduction*. Boston: MIT.

Esposito, Elena "Artificial Communication? The Production of Contingency by Algorithms," *Zeitschrift für Soziologie* 46:4 (2017): 251.

Ercolino, Stefano (2014) *The Maximalist Novel: From Thomas Pynchon's Gravity's Rainbow to Roberto Bolaño's 2666*. London: Bloomsbury.

Erkan, Ekin (2019) review of Bernard Stiegler's "The Age of Disruption: Technology and Madness in Computational Capitalism," in *Rhizomes: Cultural Studies in Emerging Knowledge*, Issue 35. https://link.springer.com/article/10.1007/s42438-019-00093-4.

Ferrando, Francisca (2019) *Philosophical Posthumanism*. London: Bloomsbury.

Ferrari, Emiliano (2016) "'A Knowledge Broken': Essay Writing and Human Science in Montaigne and Bacon." *Montagne Studies* 28: 211–21.

Gallix, Andrew (2015) Pond by Claire-Louise Bennett: Review. *The Guardian*, November 18, 2015.

Gibson, William (1984) *Neuromancer*. New York: Ace.

Glavanakova-Yaneva, Alexandra (2003) "Body Webs: Re/constructing Boundaries in Shelley Jackson's Patchwork Girl." *Journal of American Studies of Turkey* 18 (2003): 65–79.

Grosser, Ben (2021) "On Reading and Being Read in the Pandemic: Software, Interface, and The Endless Doomscroller." Electronic Literature Organization Conference 2021: Platform (Post?) Pandemic, Bergen Norway, May. Published in *electronic book review*, 03–06–2022. https:// conferences.au.dk/fileadmin/conferences/2021/ELO2021/Full_papers/ Ben_Grosser_On_Reading_and_Being_Read_in_the_Pandemic__ Software__Interface__and_The_Endless_Doomscroller__217.pdf.

Grusin, Richard, ed. (2015) *The Nonhuman Turn*. Minneapolis: University of Minnesota Press.

Hacking, Ian (1983) *Representing and Intervening*. Cambridge: Cambridge University Press.

Hainsworth, J. B. (1991) *The Idea of EPIC*. Berkely: The University of California Press.

Halpern, Mark (2020) "No ghost in the machine: Artificial intelligence isn't as intelligent as you think." *The American Scholar*. https:// theamericanscholar.org/no-ghost-in-the-machine/.

Haraway, Donna (1985) "A Cyborg Manifesto: Science, Technology, and Socialist-Feminism in the Late Twentieth Century." In *Simians, Cyborgs and Women: The Reinvention of Nature*. New York: Routledge, 1991.

(1988) "Situated Knowledges: The Science Question in Feminism and the Privilege of Partial Perspective." *Feminist Studies* 14.3 (Autumn): 575–99.

(1997) *Modest_Witness@Second_Millennium. FemaleMan©_ Meets_OncomouseTM*. London: Routledge.

(2003) *The Companion Species Manifesto: Dogs, People and Significant Otherness*. Chicago: Prickly Paradigm Press.

(2008) *When Species Meet*. Minneapolis: University of Minnesota Press.

(2016a) Manifestly Haraway: "A Cyborg Manifesto," "The Companion Species Manifesto." In *Companions in Conversation (With Cary Wolfe)*. Minneapolis: University of Minnesota Press.

(2016b) *Staying with the Trouble: Making Kin in the Chthulucene*. Durham: Duke University Press.

(2018) "Capitalocene and Chthulucene," in Rosi Braidotti and Maria Hlavajova (eds.), *Posthuman Glossary*, London: Bloomsbury Academic, 79–83.

Hardt, Michael, and Antonio Negri (2000) *Empire*. Boston: Harvard University Press.

Harman, Graham (2010) *Towards Speculative Realism: Essays and Lectures.* Zero Books.
    (2011) "Realism without Materialism." *SubStance* 40.2: 52–72.
    (2012) "The Well-Wrought Broken Hammer." *New Literary History* 43.2: 205–24.
    (2013) "An Outline of Object-Oriented Philosophy." *Science Progress* 96.2: 187–99.
Hassan, Ihab. 1977. "Prometheus as Performer: Towards a Posthumanist Culture." *Georgia Review* 31, 4: 830–80.
Hayden, Patrick (1997) "Gilles Deleuze and Naturalism: A Convergence with Ecological theory and Politics." *Environmental Ethics* 19.2: 185–204.
Hayles, N. Katherine (1984) *The Cosmic Web: Scientific Field Models and Literary Strategies in the Twentieth Century.* Ithaca: Cornell University Press.
    (1995, December 30) Engineering Cyborg Ideology. *electronic book review.* https://electronicbookreview.com/essay/engineering-cyborg-ideology/.
    (1999) *How We Became Posthuman: Virtual Bodies in Cybernetics, Literature and Informatics.* Chicago: The University of Chicago Press.
    (2000) "The Invention of Copyright and the Birth of Monsters: Flickering Connectivities in Shelley Jackson's *Patchwork Girl.*" *Journal of Postmodern Culture* 10.2. www.semanticscholar.org/paper/Flickering-Connectivities-in-Shelley-Jackson's-Girl-Hayles/7c04adb8feecba58d6aad9edd561123a6e1dec19.
    (2007) "Hyper and Deep Attention: The Generational Divide in Cognitive Modes," *Profession* 13: 187–99.
    (2012) *How We Think: Digital Media and Contemporary Technogenesis.* Chicago: The University of Chicago Press.
    (2017) *Unthought: The Power of the Cognitive Nonconscious.* Chicago: The University of Chicago Press.
    (2019) "Literary Texts as Cognitive Assemblages: The Case of Electronic Literature." *electronic book review.* August 5. https://electronicbookreview.com/essay/literary-texts-as-cognitive-assemblages-the-case-of-electronic-literature/.
Heims, S. J. (1991) *The Cybernetics Group.* Cambridge, MA: MIT Press.
Heise, Ursula (2010) "Afterword: Postcolonial Ecocriticism and the Question of Literature." In *Postcolonial Green: Environmental Politics and World Narratives,* ed. Bonnie Roos & Alex Hunt. Charlottesville: University of Virginia Press.
    (2016) *Imagining Extinction: The Cultural Meaning of Endangered Species.* Chicago: University of Chicago Press.
Herbrechter, Stefan (2012) "Posthumanism, Subjectivity, Autobiography." *Subjectivity* 5.3: 327–47.
    (2016) *Posthumanism: A Critical Analysis.* London: Bloomsbury.
    (2020) "Posthuman/ist Literature? Don DeLillo's Point Omega and Zero K." *Open Library of Humanities* 6.2: 18.

Herman, Luc and Steven Weisenburger (2013) *Gravity's Rainbow, Domination, and Freedom*. Athens: University of Georgia Press.

Hollinger, Veronica (2020) "Historicizing Posthumanism," in *After the Human: Culture, Theory, and Criticism in the 21st Century*, ed. Sherryl Vint. Cambridge: Cambridge University Press, 15–31.

Huhtamo, Erkki (2013) *Illusions in Motion: Media Archaeology of the Moving Panorama and Related Spectacles*. Cambridge, MA: The MIT Press.

Huxley, Julian (1957) New Bottles For New Wine. *Internet Archive*. https:// archive.org/details/NewBottlesForNewWine.

Iyer, Lars (2011) "Nude in Your Hot Tub, Facing the Abyss (Manifesto after the End of Literature and Manifestos)." *The White Review*, www .thewhitereview.org/feature/nude-in-your-hot-tub-facing-the-abyss-a-literary-manifesto-after-the-end-of-literature-and-manifestos/.

Jackson, Shelley (1997) *Stitch Bitch: the patchwork girl. Transformations of the Book* conference held at MIT on October 24–5, 1996. https://web.mit .edu/m-i-t/articles/jackson.html.

Johnson, David Jhave (2019) "UpSift: on Johanna Dricker's *DownDrift*." *electronic book review*. https://electronicbookreview.com/essay/upsift-on-johanna-druckers-downdrift/.

Johnston, John (1997) "Mediality in Vineland and Neuromancer." In Joseph Tabbi and Michael Wutz (eds.) *Reading Matters: Narrative in the New Media Ecology*. Ithaca: Cornell University Press, 173–92.

(1998) *Information Multiplicity: American Fiction in the Age of Media Saturation*. Baltimore: Johns Hopkins University Press.

Jung, C. G. (1973) *Synchronicity: An Acausal Connecting Principle*. Translated by R. F. C. Hull, Bollingen Series Volume 20. The Princeton University Press.

Kittler, Friedrich (1986) *Gramophone, Film, Typewriter*. Berlin: Brinkman and Bose. Translated by Geoffrey Winthrop-Young and Michael Wutz. Stanford: Stanford University Press, 1999.

(1997a) "Media and Drugs in Pynchon's Second World War," in Joseph Tabbi and Michael Wutz (eds.) *Reading Matters*. Ithaca: Cornell University Press.

(1997b) "There Is No Software," in *Literature, Media, Information Systems: Essays*. Ed. John Johnston (Amsterdam: G + B Arts International): 147–55.

Krevel, Mojca (2021) "The Monstrous Cosmos of Jeanette Winterson's Frankissstein." *ELOPE* 18.2: 85–100.

Kurzweil, Ray (1999) *The Age of Spiritual Machines: When Computers Exceed Human Intelligence*. New York: Viking.

(2006) *The Singularity is Near: When Humans Transcend Biology*. New York: Penguin.

LaFee, Scott (2021, March 18) "Novel Coronavirus Circulated Undetected Months before First COVID-19 Cases in Wuhan, China," UC San Diego Health Newsroom.

Latour, Bruno (1993) *We Have Never Been Modern*. Translated by
    Catherine Porter. Cambridge, MA: Harvard University Press.
    (1996) "On actor–network theory: A few clarifications and more than a few
    complications." *Soziale Welt*, 47. Jahrg., H. 4: 369–81. www
    .semanticscholar.org/paper/On-actor-network-theory-%3A-A-few-
    clarifications-Latour/a0b6048ae60ca88c38c9db0450228a9a250a7c92.
    (2008) "Powers of the Facsimile: A Turing Test on Science and Literature," in
    Intersections: Essays on Richard Powers., ed. Stephen J. Burn and
    Peter Dempsey. Champaign: Dalkey Archive Press.
    (2010) "An Attempt at a Compositionist Manifesto," *New Literary History* 41:
    471–90.
    (2014) "Agency at the Time of the Anthropocene." *New Literary History*
    45.1: 1–18.
Latour, Bruno and Vincent Antonin Lepinay (2009) *The Science of Passionate
    Interests: An Introduction to Gabriel Tarde's Economic Anthropology*.
    Chicago: Prickly Paradigm Press.
LeClair, Tom (1987) *In the Loop: Don DeLillo and the Systems Novel*. Urbana:
    University of Illinois Press.
    (1989) *The Art of Excess: Mastery in Contemporary American Fiction.*
    Urbana: University of Illinois Press.
Lemmens, Pieter (2015) Robert Ranisch and Stefan Lorenz Sorgner: *Post- and
    Transhumanism: An Introduction*: Peter Lang, Frankfurt am Main, 2014,
    313 pp, Human Studies 38.3: 431–8.
Longinus, Cassius (1st Century C.E.) "On the Sublime." Translator: H. L. Havell.
    Project Gutenberg. www.gutenberg.org/files/17957/17957-h/17957-
    h.htm.
Lovelock, James with Brian Appleyard (2019) *Novacene: The Coming Age of
    Hyperintelligence*. Cambridge, MA: MIT Press.
Lovink, Geert (2019) *Sad By Design*. London: Pluto Press.
Luers, Will (2020) "Having Your Story and Eating it Too: Affect and Narrative in
    Recombinant Fiction." In *Electronic Literature as Digital Humanities:
    Contexts, Forms, and Practices*, ed. Dene Grigar and James O' Sullivan.
    London: Bloomsbury, 226–33.
Luhmann, Niklas (1986) "The Autopoiesis of Social Systems." In *Sociocybernetic
    Paradoxes: Observation, Control and Evolution of Self-Steering Systems*,
    ed. Felix Geyer and Johannes van der Zouwen. London: Sage: 172–92.
    (1995) *Social Systems*. Translated by J. Bednarz, Jr. with D. Baecker. Stanford:
    Stanford University Press.
    (1997) "Globalization or World Society? How to Conceive of Modern
    Society." *International Review of Sociology* 7.1. www.generation-online
    .org/p/fpluhmann2.htm.
Lyotard, Jean-François (1983) *The Differend: Phrases in Dispute*. Minneapolis:
    University of Minnesota Press.
    (1984) "Answering the Question: What is Postmodernism?" *The Postmodern
    Condition: A Report on Knowledge*. Translated by Re´gis Durand,

Geoff Bennington, and Brian Massumi. Minneapolis: University of Minnesota Press, 71–82.

McCaffery, Larry (ed.) (1992) *Storming the Reality Studio: A Casebook of Cyberpunk and Postmodern Science Fiction.* Durham: Duke University Press.

McCarthy, Tom (2005) *Remainder.* Reprinted by Alma Books in 2015 and 2016. Surrey: Alma Modern Classics, with a Preface by McKenzie Wark.

(2008, 23 Nov.) "What's Left Behind: An Interview with Tom McCarthy." Conducted by Roger Orwell. *Static 7.* www.jstor.org/stable/24735046.

(2014) "'Ulysses' and Its Wake," *London Review of Books* (36.12, 19 June).

(2015) "The death of writing – if James Joyce were alive today he'd be working for Google." *The Guardian*, March 7.

McHale, Brian (2015) *The Cambridge Introduction to Postmodernism.* Cambridge: Cambridge University Press.

McHale, Brian and Randall Stevenson (2006) *The Edinburgh Companion to Twentieth-Century Literatures in English.* Edinburgh: Edinburgh University Press.

MacCormack, Patricia (2012) *Posthuman Ethics: Embodiment and Cultural Theory.* Surrey: Ashgate Publishing Limited.

(2013) Daily Nexus, University of California. "Patricia MacCormack Talks About Ahuman Theory, Importance of Non-Speciecist Ways." November 6. https://dailynexus.com/2013-11-06/patricia-maccormack-talks-about-ahuman-theory-importance-of-non-speciecist-ways/.

(2020a) *The Ahuman Manifesto: Activism for the End of the Anthropocene.* London: Bloomsbury.

(2020b, 27 January) Talk presented at Konstfact University of Arts, Crafts, and Design. Vimeo.

MacInnes, Paul (2019) "Adam Curtis and Vice Director Adam McKay on how Dick Cheney masterminded a rightwing revolution." *The Guardian*, January 18.

Madoff, Steven Henry and Brian Kuan Wood (n.d.) "We Would Prefer Not To." *On Curating, Issue* 40. www.on-curating.org/issue-40-reader/we-would-prefer-not-to.html.

Mailer, Norman. "Norman Mailer Insults Your Favorite Writers." *Electric Lit.* https://electricliterature.com/norman-mailer-insults-your-favorite-writers/.

Manovich, Lev. (2002) *The Language of New Media.* Cambridge, MA: MIT Press.

Mark, Joshua J. (2018, 10 April) "The Eternal Life of Gilgamesh." *World History Encyclopedia.* www.worldhistory.org/article/192/the-eternal-life-of-gilgamesh/.

Maturana, Humberto M. and Francisco J. Varela (1980) *Autopoiesis and Cognition: The Realization of the Living.* Dordrecht: D. Reidel.

Melville, Herman (1975) "Bartleby." In *Billy Budd, Sailor and Other Stories*, ed. Harold Beaver. Penguin.

Mendelson, Edward (1976) "Encyclopedic Narrative: From Dante to Pynchon." *MLN* 91.6: 1267–75.

Miller, Sydney (2015) "Intentional Fallacies: (Re)enacting the Accidental in Tom McCarthy's Remainder." *Contemporary Literature*, University of Wisconsin Press 56.4: 634–59.

Montaigne, Michel de (1957) *The Complete Essays of Montaigne*. Translated by Donald M. Frame. Stanford: Stanford University Press.

Montfort, Nick and Stephanie Strickland (2010) "Sea and Spar Between." www.stephaniestrickland.com/sea.

Moore, Steven (2010) *The Novel: An Alternative History: Beginnings to 1600*. London: Bloomsbury.

Morton, Timothy (2018) *Being Ecological*. Cambridge, MA: MIT Press.

Moretti, Franco (1996) *Modern Epic: The World System from Goethe to Garcia Marquez*. London: Verso.

Murray, Simone (2019) *The Digital Literary Sphere*. Minneapolis: University of Minnesota Press.

Musil, Robert (1930–43) *The Man Without Qualities*. Translated by Sophie Wilkins (1996). New York: Vintage International.

Nayar, Promod K. (2014) *Posthumanism (Themes in 20th and 21st Century Literature)*. Cambridge: Polity Press.

Nordcrist, Richard (2019) "Ah Introduction to Dr. Johnson's 'Dictionary of the English Language.'" www.whichenglish.com/Johnsons-Dictionary/index.html.

Odin, Jaishree K. (1998) "The Performative and Processual: A Study of Hypertext/Postcolonial Aesthetic." www.postcolonialweb.org/poldiscourse/odin/odin18.html.

Parikka, Jussi (2012) *Media Archeology as a Transatlantic Bridge*. Cambridge: Polity Press.

(2014) *The Anthrobscene*. Minneapolis: University of Minnesota Press.

Paulson, William (1992) *Noise of Culture: Literary Texts in a World of Information*. Ithaca: Cornell University Press.

(2001) *Literary Culture in a World Transformed: A Future for the Humanities*. Ithaca: Cornell University Press.

(1997) "The Literary Canon in the Age of its Technological Obsolescence," In Joseph Tabbi and Michael Wutz (eds.) *Reading Matters: Narrative in the New Media Ecology*. Ithaca: Cornell University Press, 227–49.

Pekar, J., Worobey, M., Moshiri, N., Scheffler, K., & Wertheim, J. O. (2020) Timing the SARS-CoV-2 Index Case in Hubei Province. *SCIENCE* 372.6540: 412–17.

Popper, Karl (1935) *Logik der Forschung*, published in 2002 by Routledge Classics: The Logic of Scientific Discovery. London: Routledge.

Postman, Neil (1985) *Amusing Ourselves to Death: Public Discourse in the Age of Show Business*, London: Penguin, 2005.

Powers, Richard (2000) "Being and Seeming: The Technology of Representation." *Context* 3: 15–17.

Priyanka, Anne Jacob (2021) "Surfaces and Signs: On the Pond in Claire-Louise Bennett's *Pond*." In *Thing Theory in Literary Studies*, a colloquy for Arcade: A Digital Salon, curated by Sarah Wasserman and Patrick Moran.

Pynchon, Thomas (1973) *Gravity's Rainbow*. New York: Viking.
(1963) *V.* New York: J. B. Lippencott & Co.

Ranisch, Robert & Stefan Lorenz Sorgner, eds. (2014) *Post- and Transhumanism: An Introduction*. Frankfurt am Main: Peter Lang.

Rasmussen, Eric Dean (2016) "Narrative and Affect in William Gillespie's *Keyhole Factory* and Morpheus: *Biblionaut*, or, Post-Digital Fiction for the Programming Era." *CounterText* 2.2, 140–71.

Retallack, Joan (2003) *The Poethical Wager*. Berkeley: University of California Press.

Rettberg, Scott, Joseph Tabbi, Nathan Jones, Chris Ingraham, Kjersti Aarstein. (2018, 7 April) "Our Struggle: Reading Karl Ove Knausgaard's Min Kamp" in *electronic book review*. https://electronicbookreview.com/essay/our-struggle-reading-karl-ove-knausgards-min-kamp/.

Rettbert, Jill Walker (2013) *Machine Vision: How Algorithms are Changing the Way we See the World*. Cambridge: Polity Press.

Richardson, Robert D. (1995) *Emerson: The Mind on Fire*. Berkeley: University of California Press.

Rockoff, Marcus (2014) "Literature," in Robert Ranisch, & Stefan Lorenz Sorgner, eds. *Post- and Transhumanism: An Introduction*. Frankfurt am Main: Peter Lang, 251–70.

Roden, David (2014) "A Defence of Pre-Critical Posthumanism," in *Posthuman Life: Philosophy at the Edge of the Human*. London: Routledge. www.semanticscholar.org/paper/Posthuman-Life%3A-Philosophy-at-the-Edge-of-the-Human-Roden/67c988f4d16eb15b5f0b0bd442f85024646a872a.

Rossini, Manuela (2005, April) "Figurations of Posthumanity in Contemporary Science/Fiction – all too Human(ist)?" Published in "Literature and Science," *Revista canaria de estudios ingleses* (No.50).
(2016) "Submarine Experiments with Human Lives by Christoph Ransmayr – A Waterman Narrates Narrating Life." In Stefan Herbrechter and Elisabeth Friis (eds.), *Experiments with Human and Animal Bodies in Literature, Science and Art*. Brill, 135–46.

Rouyan, Anahita (2017) "Singing Gravity's Rainbow: The Interface of Song, Narrative and Sonic Performance in Thomas Pynchon's 1974 Novel." *Partial Answers* 15.1: 117–33. https://muse.jhu.edu/article/646677.

Salter, Anastasia and Mel Stanfill (2020) "Pivot! Thoughts on Virtual Conferencing and ELOrlando 2020," *electronic book review*, June 6, 2021.

Sandars, N. K. (1960) *The Epic of Gilgamesh*. London: Penguin.

Schwarzbach. F. S. (1978) "A Matter of Gravity," in *Pynchon: A Collection of Critical Essays*, ed. Edward Mendelson. Engelwood Cliffs: Prentice Hall.

Sebald, W. G. (2001) *Austerlitz*. Translated by Anthea Bell. New York: Random House.

Self, Will (2014) "The novel is dead (this time it's for real)." *The Guardian*. May 2. www.theguardian.com/books/2014/may/02/will-self-novel-dead-literary-fiction.

Shackelford, Laura (2014) *Tactics of the Human: Experimental Technics in American Literature*. Ann Arbor, Michigan: University of Michigan Press.

Shelley, Mary (1818) *Frankenstein*, the 1818 Text, Contexts, Criticism. Ed. J. Paul Hunter. New York: Norton.

   (1932) "Note on Prometheus Unbound, by Mrs. Shelley." *John Keats and Percy Bysshe Shelley: Complete Poetical Works*, Vol. 2, Modern Library, 1932, 293–8.

Shelley, Percy Bysshe (written 1821, published 1840) "A Defence of Poetry." *Poetry Foundation*. www.poetryfoundation.org/articles/69388/a-defence-of-poetry.

Simon, Zoltán Boldizsár (June 2019) "Two Cultures of the Posthuman Future." *History and Theory* 58.2: 171–84. Wesleyan University. https://onlinelibrary.wiley.com/doi/10.1111/hith.12108.

Simons, Massimiliano (2017) "The Parliament of Things and the Anthropocene: How to Listen to 'Quasi-Objects.'" *Techné: Research in Philosophy and Technology* 21, 2/3: 1–25.

Smith, Zadie (2008, November 20) "Two Paths for the Novel," Review of *Netherland* by Joseph O'Neill and *Remainder* by Tom McCarthy. *The New Yorker*.

Snow, C. P. (1961) *The Two Cultures and the Scientific Revolution*. The Rede Lecture. New York: Cambridge University Press.

Spinosa, Dani (2018) *Anarchists in the Academy: Machines and Free Writers in Experimental Poetry*. Edmonton: University of Alberta Press.

Sterling, Bruce (1986) *Mirrorshades; The Cyberpunk Anthology*. New York: Ace Books.

Stiegler, Bernard (1998) *Technics and Time 1: The Fault of Epimetheus*. Stanford: Stanford University Press.

   (2015) *Lo que hace que la vida merezca ser vivida*. Madrid: Avarigani.

   (2016) *The Automatic Society. Volume 1: The Future of Work*. Translated by Daniel Ross. New York: Wiley.

   (2019) *The Age of Disruption: Technology and Madness in Computational Capitalism*. Cambridge: Polity Press.

Strawson, Galen (2004) "Against Narrativity." *Ratio* (new series) XVII.

Swanstrom, Lisa (2019, December 15) "The Effulgence of the North: An Introduction to the Natural Media Gathering," *electronic book review*. https://electronicbookreview.com/essay/an-introduction-to-the-natural-media-gathering/.

Tabbi, Joseph (1995) *Postmodern Sublime: Technology and American Writing from Mailer to Cyberpunk*. Ithaca: Cornell University Press.

(2002) *Cognitive Fictions*. Ithaca: Cornell University Press.

(2006) "1991: The Web, Network Fictions." In Brian McHale and Randall Stevenson *The Edinburgh Companion to Twentieth-Century Literatures in English*. Edinburgh: Edinburgh University Press, 240–51.

(2008) "Afterthoughts on The Echo Maker," in *Intersections: Essays on Richard Powers*. Ed. Stephen Burn and Peter Dempsey. Champaign: Dalkey Archive Press (219–29).

(2010) "Electronic Literature as World Literature," Special issue on Constrained Writing, ed. Jan Baetens and Jean-Jacques Poucel, *Poetics Today* 31.1: 17–50.

(2020) *Post-Digital: Dialogues and Debates from electronic book review* (2 volumes). London: Bloomsbury Press.

(2021) "Is Writing All Over, or Just Dispersed? Digital Essayism in Trina: a Design Fiction." *The Essay at the Limits: Poetics, Politics, and Form*, ed. Mario Aquilina. Bloomsbury Academic.

Tabbi, Joseph, and Michael Wutz, eds. (1997) *Reading Matters: Narrative in the New Media Ecology*. Ithaca: Cornell University Press.

Thiher, Alan (2001) *Fiction Rivals Science: The French Novel from Balzac to Proust*. Columbia: University of Missouri Press.

(2005) *Fiction Refracts Science: Modernist Writers from Proust to Borges*. Columbia: University of Missouri Press.

Thucydides (1956) *History of the Peloponnesian War*. Translated by Charles Forster Smith. Loeb Classical Library. Cambridge, MA: Harvard University Press. www.loebclassics.com/view/LCL108/1919/volume.xm.

Tisselli, Eugenio (2011) "Why I have stopped creating E-Lit." November 25. Netartery: http://netartery.vispo.com/?p=1211.

(2018) "The Heaviness of Light." *MATLIT: Materialidades da Literatura* 6.2, https://impactum-journals.uc.pt/matlit/article/download/2182-8830_6-2_1/4687.

(2020) "The gate: A game-essay on coexistence and spectrality in the Anthropocene." *The Digital Review*, June 7. https://thedigitalreview .com/issue00/the-gate/index.html.

Torres, Rui and Eugenio Tisselli (2020) "In Defense of the Difficult," *electronic book review*, May 3. https://doi.org/10.7273/y2vs-1949.

Trexler, Adam (2015) *Anthropocene Fictions. The Novel in a Time of Climate Change*. Charlottesville: University of Virginia Press.

Trotter, David (2020, 17 December) "Head in an Iron Safe." Review of *The Artful Dickens: Tricks and Ploys of the Great Novelist* by John Mullan. *London Review of Books*.

Turner, Jenny (2017, 1 June) "Life with Ms Cayenne Pepper." Review of *Manifestly Haraway* and *Staying with the Trouble: London Review of Books*. www.lrb.co.uk/the-paper/v39/n11/jenny-turner/life-with-ms-cayenne-pepper.

Turner, Mark (1994) *The Study of English in the Age of Cognitive Science*. Princeton: Princeton University Press.

VanderMeer, Jeff (2019) *Dead Astronauts*. New York: Farrar, Strause, and Giroux.

Vermeulen, Pieter (2014) "Posthuman Affect." *European Journal of English Studies*, 18.2: 121–34.

Vinge, Vernor (1993) "The Coming Technological Singularity: How to Survive in the Post-Human Era," in *Vision-21: Interdisciplinary Science and Engineering in the Era of Cyberspace*, proceedings of a symposium cosponsored by the NASA Lewis Research Center and the Ohio Aerospace Institute, Westlake, Ohio, March 30–1, 1993.

Waldby, Catherine (2000) *The Visible Human Project: Informatic Bodies and Posthuman Medicine*. London: Routledge.

Wamberg, Jacob and Mads Rosendahl Thomsen (2016) "The Posthuman in the Anthropocene: A Look through the Aesthetic Field." *European Review*. October 10. www.cambridge.org/core/journals/european-review/article/abs/posthuman-in-the-anthropocene-a-look-through-the-aesthetic-field/6FE87B2673985E5BFE59CD155D85C543.

Weisenburger, Steven and Luc Herman (2013) *Gravity's Rainbow, Domination, and Freedom*. Athens: University of Georgia Press.

White, Curtis (2006) *The Spirit of Disobedience: Resisting the Charms of Fake Politics, Mindless Consumption, and the Culture of Total Work*. London: Routledge.

Whitehead, Colson (1999) *The Intuitionist*. Anchor Books.

Whitman, Walt (1855) "Preface 1855," in *Leaves of Grass and Other Writings*, ed. Michael Moon. New York: Norton, 2002.

Whyte, Jessica (2009) "'I Would Prefer Not To': Giorgio Agamben, Bartleby and the potentiality of the law." *Law and Critique* 20.3: 309–24.

Wilkie, Brian (1965) *Romantic Poets and the Epic Tradition*. Madison: University of Wisconsin Press.

Wills, David (2008) *Dorsality: Thinking Back through Technology and Politics*. Minneapolis: University of Minnesota Press.

Winterson, Jeanette (2019) *Frankissstein: A Love Story*. London: Vintage.

Wolfe, Cary (2018) "POSTHUMANISM," *glossary entry in Braidotti and Hlavajova, Posthuman Glossary*, 356–60. London: Bloomsbury Academic.

(2010) *What is Posthumanism?* Minneapolis: University of Minnesota Press.

Wood, James (2000) "Human, All Too Inhuman: On the formation of a new genre: hysterical realism." *The New Republic* (July 24). https://newrepublic.com/article/61361/human-inhuman.

Worster, Donald (2018) "What is it about this 'Anthropocene.'" In conversation with Agnes Kneitz. *Weber: The Contemporary West* 35.1: 8–23.

Index

Cambridge Introductions to . . .

Authors

Margaret Atwood Heidi Macpherson

Jane Austen (second edition) Janet Todd

Mikhail Bakhtin Ken Hirschkop

Samuel Beckett Ronan McDonald

Walter Benjamin David Ferris

Lord Byron Richard Lansdown

Chaucer Alastair Minnis

Chekhov James N. Loehlin

J. M. Coetzee Dominic Head

Samuel Taylor Coleridge John Worthen

Joseph Conrad John Peters

Jacques Derrida Leslie Hill

Charles Dickens Jon Mee

Emily Dickinson Wendy Martin

George Eliot Nancy Henry

T. S. Eliot John Xiros Cooper

William Faulkner Theresa M. Towner

F. Scott Fitzgerald Kirk Curnutt

Michel Foucault Lisa Downing

Robert Frost Robert Faggen

Gabriel Garcia Marquez Gerald Martin

Nathaniel Hawthorne Leland S. Person

Zora Neale Hurston Lovalerie King

James Joyce Eric Bulson

Kafka Carolin Duttlinger

Thomas Mann Todd Kontje

Christopher Marlowe Tom Rutter

Herman Melville Kevin J. Hayes

Milton Stephen B. Dobranski

George Orwell John Rodden and John Rossi

Sylvia Plath Jo Gill

Edgar Allan Poe Benjamin F. Fisher

Ezra Pound Ira Nadel

Marcel Proust Adam Watt

Jean Rhys Elaine Savory

Edward Said Conor McCarthy

Shakespeare Emma Smith

Shakespeare's Comedies Penny Gay

Shakespeare's History Plays Warren Chernaik

Shakespeare's Poetry Michael Schoenfeldt

Shakespeare's Tragedies Janette Dillon

Tom Stoppard William W. Demastes

Harriet Beecher Stowe Sarah Robbins

Mark Twain Peter Messent

Edith Wharton Pamela Knights

Walt Whitman M. Jimmie Killingsworth

Virginia Woolf Jane Goldman

William Wordsworth Emma Mason

W. B. Yeats David Holdeman

Topics

American Literary Realism Phillip Barrish

American Poetry Since 1945 Andrew Epstein

The American Short Story Martin Scofield

Anglo-Saxon Literature Hugh Magennis

Printed in the United States
by Baker & Taylor Publisher Services